FROM SHAME TO PEACE

From Shame to Peace

TEO VAN DER WEELE

MONARCH
Crowborough

British Library Cataloguing Data
A catalogue record for this book is available
from the British Library.

ISBN 1 85424 261 X

Produced by Bookprint Creative Services
P.O. Box 827, BN21 3YJ, England for
MONARCH PUBLICATIONS
Broadway House, The Broadway,
Crowborough, E. Sussex, TN6 1HQ
Printed in Great Britain.

Dedicated to those
for whom the church had
no eyes to see nor ears to hear
or if they did lacked the courage
to act

CONTENTS

FOREWORD

I have known Teo van der Weele for many years. He is a man of compassion for the hurting, and possesses tremendous insight for their healing.

When Teo first began to speak out about the issue of abuse and molestation, he was overwhelmed by the response. His openness and concern gave people the courage to confront and share painful experiences from their past.

For some of us, incest is inconceivable. Unfortunately, it is a nightmarish reality. Unless this subject is dealt with forthrightly, sensitively and in balance, many of God's children will remain prisoners to their fears and false guilt.

It is also important to recognize that sometimes the most complex problems have very simple solutions. Notice, I did not say simplistic solutions. Nor did I say easy solutions.

Forgiveness, honesty, and openness with others has brought hope and healing to thousands of people. The peace of God is released as we confess our sins—and the sins committed against us—if we do it God's way.

The Scripture says, 'If we walk in the light, as he is in the light, we have fellowship with one another, and the blood of Jesus his Son cleanses us from all sin.'

The Scriptures also say in Galatians 6 that we are to bear one another's burdens and so fulfil the law of Christ. There is no sin committed by us or against us that God cannot forgive. And there is no burden that he will not carry.

I commend to you my friend Teo van der Weele, and trust

that this book will be helpful in opening a door to heal hidden memories and horrible hurts. May the peace of God rule in your heart as you read this book.

Floyd McClung Jr

ACKNOWLEDGEMENTS

This book would have been impossible without the hundreds of abuse survivors who sought help. You will read about them in real-life stories, sufficiently altered to protect their identity.

Many people have influenced my life and ministry. I think of Paul Davis, an outstandingly effective veteran missionary with the Christian Missionary Alliance in Ubon province in Thailand. A son of a very gifted missionary pioneer in China himself, Paul helped me to understand other cultures. He was very affirming when I sought new ways to share the gospel. Paul Hiebert, professor in missiology in Fuller Theological Seminary, challenged me to think deeper and harder and left a lasting impression, long after his memorable lectures were past. Also in Fuller I met John Wimber, whose example of frankness, laughter, creativity, and humility gave a whole new perspective to the practice of pastoral ministry. His insight helped me to focus on the expectation of a manifestation of the presence of Jesus.

Wil and I have again and again been encouraged by Sally and Floyd McClung Jr. who, when they served with Youth With A Mission in the Netherlands, contributed vital impulses for our personal life and ministry over a prolonged period.

To the many who have kept urging me to sit down and write, my sincere thanks, even though I have often groaned, wondering why I agreed to it in the first place.

Above all, my warmest appreciation to my life companion, Wil, who has spurred me on to move beyond the practical issues of ministry and to keep looking for more insights and growth. Her faith helped me to enter graduate and post-graduate studies as a late starter—and took the consequences, mostly with a smile.

We have been blessed in the Netherlands with many books in English. The bibliography will show my own debt to English language authors. I am grateful for the opportunity to share some of what I digested in my studies and return it. *From Shame to Peace* was originally written for use in Denmark, and because of translation needs, directly written in English. It took several dedicated people to get it in the final form as we have it now, among them Linda Smit and Cheryl Gagliasso. To Jane Collins of Monarch Publications, thank you for the courage to work on my 'Dutch accent' and make this manuscript ready for publication.

INTRODUCTION

Never before in history have so many people witnessed waves
of violence, while it happens. Most of us see it through 45-
second segments of TV newscasts, but the experience of watching live TV images pales beside the experience of being there.
When I see refugee children staring into nothingness or see their
subtitled stories of brutalities, an unseen hand turns back my
clock to the carnage of World War II. It is not the masses which
suffer, but millions of frightened individuals. Who will hold the
hand of a child trembling because of the nightmares following
the genocide in Rwanda? How many trauma therapists should
we send to the former Yugoslavia? Where can people squashed
by dictatorial systems turn? Who will put courage into a child's
heart in the jungles of the inner-cities of the West, where
weapons now enter into American gradeschools?

Eclipsed by all this visible violence, there is a further hidden
world: children who suffer from mental, emotional and physical
violence by family members or carers. At its darkest this
evolves into the worst violence of all: sexual traumatisation
while the personality still is being formed: early–childhood
sexual abuse.

Over the past years, scores of new books have been published
about helping survivors of sexual abuse and incest. As John
Briere (1992) shows, suffering early childhood trauma and lack
of positive caring can deeply twist or fragment one's personality, resulting in a variety of psychiatric labels. Several dangers
arise for those who suffered 'abuse of power': they may live in

denial; become the captive of a specialist-helper; or be so focused on the traumatising events that they become locked into an unchangeable past. Two thousand years ago Nicodemus realised that he was in trouble. In one of the rare private talks which Jesus had, he came 'into the light' and was willing to stop denial. He realised that the past can't be undone: it is impossible to return to your mother's womb. Jesus' answer is still valid for today: only an infusion of life 'from Above', as an ongoing process, opens a door to the future.

Through coaching people how to help themselves, I have seen how such an infusion of life can empower survivors of abuse to choose a new destiny. In this book I try to explain how pastoral volunteers, as coaches, can encourage this process in those who suffered child sexual abuse or any other debilitating trauma. While individual western psychotherapy can be effective, it is only available for the affluent. A pastoral approach opens up possibilities which psychotherapy cannot afford: team-work by volunteers and healing communities. Also, this approach does not depend on digging into the past or the need to do much talking. This makes the training of pastoral volunteers more feasible too.

My own understanding about trauma treatment grew as a missionary in Asia, where I had to learn to help people who came with deeply-felt personal needs, but were unable to talk about it. The intense sense of shame would make disclosure of deep personal needs perhaps more painful than the abuse itself. It is there that I realised that the gospel can set people free from a life ruled by shame, and bring them to the inner tranquillity of the peace of God, even if they have no words to express their thoughts and feelings.

Back in the Netherlands I discovered a 'hidden people group' whose life was shaped by a culture of sexual abuse. My missionary experience provided keys to enter their world. While they taught me their language and thoughtworld, an approach developed which I call 'Powerful Peace'—a divine enabling for both helpers and seekers to face reality, supported by an inner sense of security, through the presence of Jesus. In this approach the starting point is not the traumas, but the possibility of an experience of Shalom; the grace and peace of God which became the cornerstone of the ministry of the apostle Paul. Empowered by that presence, painful realities can be faced, if they come to the surface. This can happen alone before God, together with other believers, or in the counselling room. On the other hand there is grace in nature as well, by his personal intervention, that some memories do not surface at all. This empowerment seems to speed up the healing process in comparison to more traditional methods.

As a male counsellor, I have been very grateful that where men were the abusers, other men can be used to bring healing. As a pastoral counsellor it is gratifying to see that the church, which was unable—or unwilling—to see what went on among its own, is waking up as well. The extent of the problem is, I believe, not yet fully known, because denial and silence still very much keep a grip on people's lives. I anticipate an upsurge in the known cases of male survivors, as men cease their denials of early sexual abuse. It is also more and more evident that abuse is not done just by male offenders. Men and women are coming forward who have been abused by females, both inside the immediate family as well as those in the rôle of guardian, kindergarten workers, hospital nurses, baby sitters, etc.

Up till nine years ago, I had only met two incest survivors who asked for pastoral help. Now there have been several hundred. I believe the difference is because:

- Secular literature opened my eyes to what was happening.
- I found that my pastoral approach was in harmony with caring principles which I found in existing research on child sexual abuse. I could benefit from the many insights others developed, and this encouraged me to continue.
- The growth of pastoral counselling has enabled hidden survivors to 'come out' and seek pastoral help. The idea of going to a professional counsellor is too great a step.
- As an itinerant teacher in lay counselling, I have discovered that people find it easier to open their hearts to a trusted outsider—a kind of travelling garbage-can. I have also encouraged cross-church counselling, in which abused people of one

church obtain help from pastoral workers of another church. In this way they can return to their own church, without the past still hanging around them. This resulted in many invitations of pastors to deal with hurting people in their church, without the need for the pastor to know details.

This last aspect has been insufficiently understood in Protestant circles, where the anonymity of the confessional booth has been lost. There are issues that church members will never talk about, unless it is to a respected stranger. Therefore the demand for non-local church-based Christian counselling is soaring.

The church is a latecomer in the abuse counselling field. In one way I am glad that secular studies provided us with many facts, figures and insights before we opened our mouths on the subject. Too often the church tends to give answers before we even hear the questions people are asking.

The aim of this book is to reassure abuse survivors that they are not crazy; that their lifestyle and value system, the 'culture of abuse', is common; that there are ways 'to help oneself'; and that an infusion of life from Above can work effectively in everyday life.

I hope that baffled spouses of abuse survivors find some insight into the confusing world of their partner. For most of them, they have already had an heroic struggle to cope and they deserve a medal! In a similar way to co-dependents of alcoholics, they often develop a lifestyle which helps them adjust to the special needs and demands of their partner. Tensions building up, in a similar way to a pending earthquake, can send minor shocks as warning signals or suddenly explode, tearing families apart. Also, the effect of this adjusted lifestyle often goes on from generation to generation.

Then I hope that pastors and church leaders will be encouraged to seek ways to equip believers for effective ministry in a violent world. As we live in a complex society where caring sciences have developed rapidly, I also hope that they can discover ways in which church workers and pastoral volunteers can work together in harmony with secular helpers.

The fact that I encourage volunteers to do what they are best at, encouraging empowerment of abuse survivors, does not mean that specialist helpers are not needed. The opposite is true. The question is, how do we utilise specialists when there are so many who need help? Training, supporting and supervising volunteers appears to me to be one vital answer. Therefore I hope that this book will give some understanding to secular helpers about questions faced by abuse survivors with a Christian background. A major cross-cultural counselling principle—understanding and respect for different value-systems—is vital for a helpful co-operation between pastoral counsellors and mental health professionals. In this way I have seen positive outcomes from referrals of clients to secular helpers who were able to accept Christian values as parameters for the helping process. More attention to this could eradicate unnecessary barriers which Christians often experience as they face psychological needs without Christian professional health workers to help, and are unwilling to go to secular helpers.

The church has a moral, and in some countries also a legal responsibility, to take measures to prevent child sexual abuse. Who is working with our children and young teens? Look for attitudes which show servanthood and respect, rather than manipulation and authority. This book will provide some suggestions as to how this can be done.

There are many more abusers than we know. Those who contacted me shared their fear of exposure and rejection. If you once were involved or still battle with this, don't give up hope either. Knowing intellectually that something is wrong is insufficient; one needs to feel the pain. As Alice Miller has shown, to discover one's own pain is often the first step towards healing. I hope that some of what I write about 'God who comes in our pain' will point a way to a new future.

In Chapter One I introduce one of the toughest problems of abuse survivors: how to deal with the recurring nightmares, the flashbacks, and how memory can become our enemy. I propose the idea of 'Powerful Peace' and how just being there as helpers can be a great help in itself. How to be a good listener is stressed in Chapter Two which invites you to walk along with some of those who shared their story, including some parts of my own traumatic past. Again there is a focus on hope and how churches can start to become healing centres. In Chapter Three definitions and concepts about child sexual abuse and incest are presented. Chapter Four gives attention to major trends which we can observe in the culture of sexual abuse. Variations of responses between male and female victims, as well as the introvert/ extrovert differences also receive attention. With more insight into the culture of the sexually abused, Chapter Five explains how one can cross cultural barriers to understand and counsel abuse survivors.

A rather personal excursion into the question of 'Where is God when people suffer?' can be found in Chapter Six. It would be presumptuous to say that this is a definitive statement. It is more a testimony of how common sense and faith in a God who still suffers himself have helped me not to turn a deaf ear to those who feel that God deserted them and the church betrayed them. Chapter Seven shows how culture, once designed to help people to survive and thrive, can become an agent of oppression. When a person is stuck in a cultural jail, there is still the possibility of inner freedom, whatever the social conditions are. After centuries of historic failures of the church (as well as secular caring systems) there is now a better understanding of the plight of survivors of abuse, but are people in leadership willing to consider that they might be part of an abusive system? In Chapter Eight I affirm the priesthood of all believers and the right as well as the duty of believers to stand next to those who hurt. As pastoral volunteers often stand closer to seekers of help, they can form a bridge to professional workers.

Based on the insights developed in the previous chapters the last chapters are devoted to practical issues. Chapter Nine focuses on the power of symbolism, including the power of our self-image. Victims, or survivors who learn to thrive, which will it be? In Chapter Ten I take you along to Thailand where we learned to minister in situations where shame would prevent people from speaking out. The expectancy of the presence of God and the possibility of having an inner dialogue with him, where we could not touch, became a foundation stone of our ministry. The power of 'prayers of blessing' and the effect which the peace of God can have is the topic of Chapter Eleven. It is here that pastoral practice takes some novel routes to see how the impact of the peace of God on spirit, soul and body counteracts the pervasive shame. In Chapter Twelve the place of the church as a focus of ministry is affirmed. At the same time I work out the idea that feelings of shame often will keep people away from pastoral workers whom they know and will continue to meet. In Chapter Thirteen the practical problems of preventing and responding to sexual abuse within the church are discussed. Chapter Fourteen has as its title the prayer of many a concerned parent: 'Please God, not my child'. How does one respond when child sexual abuse is suspected or did occur? In a closing reflection I appeal for biblical realism, but within a framework of hope. Where sin abounds, so is God's grace available to counter sin. While the church has been silent for centuries in an abusive society, it can make choices to evaluate the way in which we deal with each other. In a spirit of servanthood, we can affect the abusive systems around us, in our own homes, in schools and in the workplace, in the refugee camps and slums of this world, or in any other place where violence abounds.

My approach to ministry has been greatly influenced by the books of that eminent 'doctor of the soul' Dr Paul Tournier. I just happened to pick up a book by him in the fifties and his gracious approach became instrumental in slowly peeling away the layers of legalism of my strict Calvinistic upbringing. In one of his last books *The Violence Within*, he accurately forecast the increase of violence which we face today. His observation was that when people increase in power, the inner moral voice is stifled. Thus abuse of power grows, at times rising to the level of unthinkable atrocities. These are sobering words for those who seek 'empowerment' for ministry, especially in view of the endless reports of abusive pastoral care, including sexual abuse! Tournier's medicine, a spirit of servanthood, echoes the antidote to power abuse which Jesus gave. I hope that this book will somehow continue this echo.

Summer 1994, Harderwijk, The Netherlands

ADVICE TO READERS

My experience with readers of my books in Dutch and Danish teaches me that people come to a book like this from different angles, and I would encourage you to skip the parts which initially seem less relevant to your situation. The summary on pages 17–19 should help you here.

- *Survivors of sexual violence should focus first on the practical chapters on how 'powerful peace' can encourage restoration.*
- *Trained counsellors may focus on the theoretical parts, which survivors will turn to later, when they begin to help others.*
- *If you want to know whether someone with little or no psychological training can help, you will need first to understand how a 'culture of sexual violence' influences those who live in it, and later turn to the practical application of 'powerful peace'.*

CHAPTER ONE

THE MEMORY PROBLEM

Snapshots

Elizabeth once made a vow: 'I will never let a man touch me'. She had been persistent and successful in her endeavour. At the age of forty she was still single. There had been some fast job changes when some of her bosses became unpleasant and 'touchy'.

Vera could not get enough of men. She was always surrounded by them, made sure they paid for all her drinks and meals, and she went flirting through life. She loved the way she could wind men around her little finger.

Alice wondered about her attraction to women. A young woman of classic Nordic beauty, she was pursued by many male friends for a date, but was totally non-responsive.

Edgar knew he had homosexual inclinations. He had chosen a life of celibacy. A homosexual lifestyle did not fit into his Christian value-system.

Living with troublesome memories

All four had one common root problem, hidden among other pressing needs: an early sexual trauma. Elizabeth never forgot how she once woke up as a hand played softly over her young developing body. Frozen stiff, she acted as if she were still asleep. She heard her father whisper over and over again 'You are so beautiful . . .' When his hands became more probing, she could stand it no longer. Then she gasped in convulsions, as waves of emotion engulfed her body. The shadow beside her bed looked into her shocked face. He fled. They never talked about it, and it never happened again . . . except in recurring nightmares. Only much later, as an adult woman, did she dare to open up and speak about it.

Vera is much more extrovert. She still remembers the exciting games she played with the new boy neighbour. He always knew more than she did. He was also eight years older. She realises now how he slowly seduced her, waking her up sexually, stimulating her, creating their own secret world. Vera knew instinctively that her mother would not approve. Her father had left when she was a baby. The neighbour's son was the only friendly young man this vivacious nine-year-old girl knew, and he was much more fun than some of the girls in the area. Then, one day, her mother discovered what was going on. The boy was taken away by the police. Vera had no friends left at all. She was shunned in the village, until they moved. As she grew up, she could never feel attached enough to anyone to get married.

Alice sat opposite me, shocked. Her mother had finally told her why, twelve years ago, the nice school teacher who lived with them had had to leave so suddenly. Alice had been very close to her and had often crawled into her bed. Then the woman would caress her and say nice things. Until one day her mother came home unexpectedly and found out that the caressing was happening while both were nude and saw how Alice was sexually aroused. Alice had forgotten all about it; it was so long ago and she was only seven at the time. Now, totally out of the blue, her mother had started to talk about it. Alice's first question was 'Am I lesbian, Teo? I hardly sleep any more. Waves of feelings and memories just surge through my body. I hate it, but can't stop it.'

Edgar related how he was slowly seduced by his own, single-parent mother. He could not recall exactly when it all started, nor when it finished. It had just come back to him and that's when he sought help. He had already recognised that he had homosexual inclinations. Now he had started thinking about that. 'Perhaps I never had a chance to develop into the person I really am. Perhaps I just can't stand women that close because of my own mother.'

When Edgar shared his story, I was rather shocked. Do women do this too? It forced me to face a need *I* had, as a counsellor, to be more realistic about sin. If fathers can do it, why not mothers, sisters, aunts, school teachers, youth workers? Abuse apparently does not acknowledge gender.

Living with flash-backs

Sleep was a problem for Elizabeth. It often took hours before she finally fell into a light sleep. Any sound would wake her up with a shock and she would look for the shadow next to her. She knew people could see how tired she often was. Whenever Vera got close to a man, she would become restless and keep seeing the mischievous grin on the face of her neighbour friend. That would be enough for her to back off. Alice's work in school suffered dramatically. According to her teachers, she would often just sit and stare into space. Edgar had not had problems with what had happened because he had honestly forgotten about it—until the flash-backs came and he was shattered by their implications.

Will flash-backs stop?

'Will there ever be an end to all this?' Many survivors of serious trauma struggle with this question as they are haunted by yet another unexpected flash-back. It is as if an unseen hand turns on an old video, causing a recurring nightmare, even in the daytime.

Memory, that precious gift of creation, can turn into a fierce enemy, chasing us to final destruction. The natural response is to resist these flashes. For many people this works partially, at least for a time. But there are those who lose this battle with the shadows of the past. Once again they are victims. A cruel hand puts back the clock. An eternity passes before they recover.

Bystanders hardly notice the seconds of panic and the accompanying paralysis. The sense of dread and helplessness linger on long after the ugly pictures fade away.

From the many stories I have heard, there is no guarantee that flash-backs will cease. It is possible, though, to learn to face them, neutralise them and even to give them new meaning. For me, the monthly testing of the civil air-raid siren has bothered me for decades. I finally decided to make it my call to prayer for peace. The sound of the siren has gradually acquired a new meaning: my first response is now no longer the reliving of the sounds of the planes and the subsequent change of tone as the bombs were released, but a plea to the God of Peace! Others have also told me how their 'old story' changed from a video on the *inside* to a video on a large screen *outside*. They could walk away from it, stand at a greater distance and watch as the shocking images shrank and faded out. Then there are those who, in the middle of a flash-back, learn to superimpose another experience: Jesus, who knows what suffering is, becomes the focus. As his presence fades in, ugly memories fade out.

The lonely memories of an abuse survivor

A person who suffered in concentration camp or—more common today—has been the victim of a series of robberies, or a rape, can still expect some sympathy. But a survivor of sexual abuse often has to hide in shame, unable to talk. Some of them even decide to take their secret along with them in a premature death. Incest survivors face not only the burden of one major trauma, but they also carry the effects of living in an environment which has caused them many other kinds of traumas.

People usually don't suffer only one trauma. There tends to be a kind of 'roof-tile construction', where one trauma covers the others. This tile construction of traumas is one reason why the most deeply-felt trauma of all—incest—often remains hidden from those trying to help. Both secular mental health workers and church workers have often missed the signals of sexual abuse, as we either didn't know about it, or we didn't know how to ask the right questions. Often we were not ready to hear what was being said and switched topics to other traumas which we could handle better.

Without the help they need, victims find their own ways to survive. I never cease to marvel at the insight and creativity which has gone into some of their escape mechanisms and survival strategies, as they learn to deal with these flash-backs in a variety of ways. Some slip into a fantasy trip, others into prayer and many just slip into a dark, moody silence. A constant alertness to avoid any memories of the past is another survival skill. This steely thought-control also influences the way they respond to other things. This can range from rigid personal habits to clowning around, just as long as they are in control of what happens, wherever they are. For all of them, one thing is sure: whatever happened then still actively influences behaviour today.

But should we remember again?

If dealing with the flash-backs is so tough, shouldn't those who can't remember be thankful? Why did Alice's mother decide to revive those old memories? Edgar told me that the memories started to return only after he had received inner peace, because of a heightened awareness of the presence of God.

In a TV programme on psychotherapeutic approaches in Israel some fundamental questions were asked about the validity of 'waking-up past horrors'. Is there not a time to let the past sleep? Should we talk so much about the past, especially with older survivors? Would it not be better to keep the door to the skeleton cupboard tightly locked?

That same question is valid as more and more people come forward with their stories of an incestuous past. Some talk because they have known it all along. Others, because of probing by counsellors and therapists, have woken up to hitherto hidden parts of reality. This question is even more pertinent for lay pastoral counsellors, particularly as there are now many books about 'emotional healing' as part of the ministry of the church. Are we providing something like the equivalent of a do-it-yourself kit for open heart surgery to lay counsellors? I have met people who have been subjected to unskilled painful probing of their past by such enthusiastic volunteers. They needed healing from emotional healing processes!

The need for memories

Memories are important. More than that: the ability to remember is one of the most precious gifts of creation. There would be no history without it. No legacies of the past would remain; we would all have to make new original moves, unable to use what others had learned. Our motivation is also fuelled by a desire to be remembered. We see this vividly in the beauty of the arts, the architecture of buildings, or the claims of discoveries in research publications.

But in order not to drown in all the information, we also have another gift of nature: the ability to forget. One tool in selecting what to remember and what to forget is our set of emotions. The more intense our experiences, the more we remember. The smell of mothballs always makes me smile. It brings back some very fond memories of my grandmother! However, I am sure that this association between grandmother and mothballs would soon be broken if we still used mothballs today. As I only rarely encounter that smell, the signal stands out loud and clear. But when certain experiences happen regularly, they become 'common' and we do not retain them so easily. This happens for instance with smokers. Many people who have stopped smoking have concluded after a time that they did not realise how strong the odour of smoke is.

Yet another mechanism which nature has given to us to remember or to forget involves our will. We can choose to remember or to turn a deaf ear. As countless police investigations have shown, we can see things we hoped to see, or hear things we feared would be said. The powers of denial, expectation and imagination shape our lives! But this is also a survival tool for when life is tough. Denial of painful realities can create some sort of inner peace. The choice to live today, rather than fret about the past, is one element of a contented life in tough situations.

The importance of memory is most evident in our need to survive. Memory helps us to adjust to new situations: we learn, because we remember; we live, because we remember. Without memory, we only vegetate. One can say, 'I remember, therefore I am.' The power of that statement is easily affirmed when one looks into the empty eyes of an Alzheimer patient.

Memory as enemy

The creation gift of life, which is to be found in a cell, can turn into a deadly enemy when life turns against itself and becomes destructive, cancerous. Memory too, as beautiful as it is, can turn from friend to enemy, forcing us to remember constantly for memory's sake. Not the memory which helps us learn to adjust to new situations, but an endless replay of past horrors, like a never-ending super-video with taste, touch, sound and smell capacities. Such memories bind a person to past actions, and drain them of the energy needed to live today.

Yet the spark of life is incredibly strong. Just think how many refugees survive under the worst circumstances. This spark can also be turned into a survival mechanism in the body to deal with destructive life forms. Thus cancer cells in healthy people are destroyed. In a similar way, we can counter destructive memory-videos in a healthy way. We can deal with them, make choices, and above all learn from them.

Deformed memories

Traumas work like lenses, which deform what we observe. This results in a very private and twisted view of the world around us.

I know about such deforming effects of traumas through first-hand experience. Even now, 50 years later, I and those close to me are still aware of some of the crippling effects of World War II. The events are ingrained, as it were, in black mental marble.

This deformation of memory is also a reason why so many eye-witnesses give conflicting reports. There will be situations in which we will never be able to tell how accurate a story of abuse actually is. However, as I will show later, great accuracy is not of primary importance as we assist and empower a survivor in a healing process.

The accuracy of a child's memory, in particular, could be questioned. It is often challenged in courtcases involving sexual abuse.[1] I discovered that mine was painfully accurate. After several decades I finally visited the medieval castle of Haamstede, in the south-western part of the Netherlands, which was at one time a children's home. I had been placed there due to the internment of my parents in different concentration camps. For a long time I had both longed for and dreaded this real encounter with my past. A strange dream prepared me for this visit. In that dream I walked around the place and left laughing. When I walked into the building in reality, I was shaken by the accuracy of my childhood memories. I had hoped that the encounter with this place would bring clarity between fantasy and reality. There I stood in the dining room in the basement where, when my stomach could not take what was served up, they made me eat my own vomit. The children's playroom with the huge windows gave me another jolt. There it was; nothing but the furniture had changed. In that room I had discovered, among the toys for toddlers, a wooden car sent to me by my father from jail. My name was on it, but they had never given it to me. As I clutched at my discovered treasure, they took it away. It is still not pleasant to recall the floods of violence which arose at that time and how a small boy turned into a vicious tiger.

Now I know that these memories blocked my quest for freedom and the urge to discover my identity. As I could not find that outside, I turned inside, into a world of my own. It took many years before I found a way back out again.

The need to deny reality

One lady, who had spent several years in a psychiatric institution, improved enough to go home for a weekend. It was then that she heard about a seminar I was giving on sexual abuse and she made sure she attended it. Through a personal encounter with God, she felt sufficiently strengthened after the seminar to go back to her therapist, to open up and talk about things she had persistently pushed down until then. Denial of what had happened had been her survival mechanism. As the abuse had touched so many areas of her life, the denial system grew deeper and deeper and affected her normal functioning, until she ended up in the psychiatric institution. The seminar gave her hope; it empowered her to start breaking the denial. There was such a change that pretty soon she was able to return home permanently. As I talked with her it became clear to me that years of careful psychiatric help had taught her some coping skills which had enabled her to attend my seminar and face new layers of trauma. This in turn speeded up the therapy, which made it possible for the professionals to proceed.[2]

Until recently it seemed that girls were usually the victims of sexual abuse, the offenders being male. But there are now more and more reports indicating a different picture.[3] A comparison between the incidental and fast-changing contacts of paedophiles and the number of boys asking for help at a later age[4] warrants the question of whether male survivors have a stronger need (and capacity) to suppress these ugly realities and go on with life anyhow. Too often now I have met men like Edgar, who for a long time had no idea what happened earlier. Many onion layers of other traumas had covered the sexual-abuse experiences and relegated them to the dim and distant past.

Variations of denial

Not all people respond in the same way to the violence which engulfed them. For example, many Dutch people have been able to suppress, deny or walk away from their war past. In weaker moments, often at a later age, some start to show cracks in their defence systems. Others stoically take their untold stories with them to the grave. For myself, the traumatic events of the war time described above, plus many others, were emotionally crippling. Even now, as I write this, I know that I am still handicapped. I have learned to cope; I am confident that I can say (in the past tense), 'I was a victim.' I am not haunted any longer by the images of the past. Those who have stood with me in the healing process affirm that there have been essential changes. Now I am living in the present. However, those consequences of the past still hinder my way of relating to others and my ability to communicate, or lack of it.

Churches and the denial of abuse

Some time ago, when I visited a small church in southern Portugal, I saw a statue of Mary with six swords piercing her heart. In the past I have felt uneasy with these 'suffering images'. Now I realise that this suffering look on the face of Mary must have appealed to countless women who also faced suffering in those 'good old days'—mothers who lost their children through disease, hunger and war.

For many generations, the church has tried to speak words of compassion and comfort to those whose lives are shattered by grief. This is done by pointing to a suffering Jesus, who knows how life can hurt, through the lives of others who followed in his footsteps and especially through the word of God. Sharing hope, giving new perspectives, becoming a new person, receiving a new identity; these are all themes which the church has used in the past for those who were suffering.

Personal suffering has resulted in some outraged cries hurled in the face of God, like Job, or Bunyan's eloquent cry of the heart in *Pilgrim's Progress*. Another gem, written by the Icelander Hallgrimur Petursson and first published in 1666, shows how sorrows can be woven into poetry of such powerful beauty that it has even survived translation into English.[5]

While the church has ministered to a suffering world, in one respect it has failed with miserable consistency. The reality of early sexual abuse, among its own and even by its own leaders, was denied. However, it was not alone in this. The secular world also refused to acknowledge this reality, even when the Enlightenment led to a reappraisal of the value of a child's life. Humanists can perhaps be forgiven for their optimism, for their naivety or for being too involved in suppressing the pain of their own sexual abuse.[6] The church, however, should have been more aware of the extent of human depravity. After all, the Bible is a very honest history book. Its message can equip us to face the pain of the past.

Dealing with unresolved memories

Understanding trauma processes has helped me to accept myself more readily for who I am. I don't feel so guilty about some traits. Nor have I resigned myself to the present condition. This, I admit, causes painful tensions at times, both within as well as with others. Yet I know I am more alive and enjoy life so much better than before. I also have found that I can stand with others who are struggling in their own healing process. Helping incest survivors is not just dealing with the sexual abuse, but with many other forms of abuse as well. It includes the need to help them face the long-term results: a wrecked marriage, the inability to form lasting relationships, or trouble holding down a job.

Elizabeth, whom we met at the beginning of this chapter, was obviously deeply hurt. Could that be the result of a once-only abusive experience with her father? I meet this frequently in persons who, like Elizabeth, are raised in a strict moral environment. The inconsistency of her father's behaviour, the icy silence that followed, the power of the words 'You are so beautiful,' coupled with a feeling of guilt: 'I made him do this'—all effected a deep emotional trauma. It was kept alive by the revulsion she developed for that one sentence. When anyone said it with the right intentions, it still backfired, as it recalled the old bad memory. But she was never able to tell anyone about it, not even when probed by a counsellor. Only through a new encounter with God did she find the strength to open up.

Vera became dissatisfied with her inability to maintain deep relationships. Through pastoral counselling she discovered a need for an emotional 'fast', to stop being a butterfly, restlessly moving from person to person. She needed to find an inner peace, peace with creation and the Creator. After that, she could cope emotionally with what she had previously known intellectually about the devastating impact of the gradual and cunningly-planned seduction by that grinning neighbour boy. The memory of his grin started to change as she began to recall the aggressive eyes and the ugly names he 'jokingly' called her. She evaluated the long-term consequences and went through a time of intense anger and hatred. The Spirit of God enabled her to get in touch with the darker side of her own life, the living imprint of her seducer. It took her a considerable time to work through these dark memories until she found peace.

Alice entered into a period of grieving about her loss of innocence. She was also upset with her mother for not seeking professional help after the event, for staying silent, for covering it up. She also wondered about the power of God. Why did he let this happen? Where was he at that time? She wasn't satisfied with standard answers. She wanted to find an answer herself. The counselling process helped her face her doubts and questions without a sense of condemnation.

Edgar had come for counselling because of an addiction to food. Soon it became clear that this addiction also masked a religious addiction: a pathological involvement with his church, which only saw him as a very willing and available member. He was always ready to do anything, even at the expense of his own private life and finally his job. When he understood that his image of God was that of a slave driver, he was ready for a new encounter with Jesus as the Servant-King, and he learned about God's unconditional love. When he found peace with God, through Jesus, his initial reaction was one of amazement at his new-found inner tranquillity. Then one night he called me. Incoherently he stumbled over his words, mingling them with tears as he blurted out the story of the abusive relationship with his mother. Somehow, his memory-bank had decided it was now safe to release the locked-up information.

When memories should stay away

The above stories make clear that not everyone is ready to face the question of sexual abuse. It often takes time; a right platform must be created and the survivor empowered to deal with their problems, rather than be helplessly dependent on a trauma specialist.[7]

The only person who has the final say in this question about the search for hidden abuse memories is the survivor. Counselling should help them to make that decision. In fact, I prefer a natural approach: to create a healing atmosphere and teach a person to deal with anything from the past that comes up of its own accord.

If a helper suspects an abusive past the following question should be uppermost. 'If this is true, should I say it now, or just wait, and start working on some of the long-term consequences without sharing the impression I received?'[8]

When Elizabeth sought help, it was not initially about the abuse, but about her inability to forgive. Vera longed for long-term deeper relationships. Alice was shattered by what her mother had told her and confused about her own questions regarding her sexual identity.

In time, they all had to face the past, as the long-term consequences of the abuse became evident. I did not have to wait until the 'Abuse Question' had been asked, in order to help them. I could start to work with some of the problems they manifested, even though I suspected that there was more than they remembered when they first sought help.

Learning as pastoral counsellors to respond to incest memories

Become a learner:

How does one, as a pastoral counsellor, deal with incest memories? In the first place, there is a steady stream of new informative books, both secular and Christian. It also helps to discuss these writings with other counsellors. Even better is to find survivors who are willing to give comments and who can share how they learned to apply the gospel to their personal lives. It means facing the pervasive inability of a person like Elizabeth to forgive her father and to study again the issue of forgiveness as a gift of God, rather than a perverse law. People like Vera, Alice and Edgar also have their own story and need a tailor-made approach in their private twisted world. No standard solutions suffice. Counselling abuse survivors will challenge your own experience of the reality of God. It will create your own questioning, perhaps even like Jesus, with tears and loud prayers.

Differentiate between objective and subjective truth:

The snapshots in this chapter only tell us what the people remembered or what they were told by others. Our ability to remember selectively, to rationalise, to block out facts, to see things which have not actually happened, force many a pastoral counsellor to question the truth of what is told. I find that most pastoral mistakes start here, even before an abuse victim has an opportunity to share their side of the story. The information is too threatening: 'My youth worker can't have done this . . .'

For therapeutic purposes, it is not so important to know exactly what has happened, when, or by whom, but to know that the victim is obviously hurting from something. When factual statements are made which might point to abuse, we should note them down, avoiding any impression of not believing, and let them rest for a while. Often the first memories are still shrouded in confusion and it takes time for a picture to emerge as the fog of denial slowly lifts. Then, when they are able to back up their statements with inner self-assurance, they can face the turmoil which emerging realities create, with adequate strength.

There are at least three reasons why the facts remain lost in the vague contours of a distant past:

1. *If abuse happened many decades before.* The survivor often does not realise that many of the incidents might be distorted through partial denial, fantasies, etc.

2. *If a survivor was very young when the abuse happened.* In this case, since the memories had no words, there are only feelings which float around like information without an address in the memory bank of a computer. Often a survivor will shake their head in unbelief and say, 'This can't be true. People just don't do these things to children.'

3. *If the consequences of admitting early sexual abuse is so devastating that the whole social fabric of a survivor will fall apart.* Eager counsellors, who want to see retribution take place or who fear that the abuse is still going on, might force a survivor to speak up before they are ready to face the devastating consequences. This can result in a recantation of the abuse facts at a later date, leaving the counsellor and the judicial system with a very red face.

Even if the objective truth is not yet clear, we can look for the subjective truth and the signals of long-term effects. Often survivors will want to doubt their own stories, the fleeting memories. They are too ugly anyhow. They will ask if you believe them. It is then that an understanding of sexual abuse problems can help you point out the long-term effects which you factually observe: that obviously something bad must have happened. Then work can start on the effects, even if one does not know exactly why they are there. It is necessary to deal with the subjective experiences first, and counsellors do well to develop the discipline of not jumping to objective conclusions too soon.

It is here that the rôle of pastoral counsellors and police officials differs. Our task is first and foremost to bring healing to the survivor, including to enable them to arrive at an awareness of objective truth.

The distinction between subjective and objective truth might also be a help for those counsellors who are obliged to inform authorities of sexual abuse. Such a conclusion could be postponed until they have more assurance that the seeker of help has some reasonable grasp on reality. To postpone action until they can relate their story coherently will also strengthen the counsellor in the ordeal which often follows public disclosure.

A false-memory syndrome?

Conflicting reports for and against the possibility of a False-Memory Syndrome have recently been published.[9] This syndrome is supposedly an 'induced memory' because of suggestive questioning or through some hidden inner workings in a seeker of help who keeps wondering why the symptoms of abuse exist and keeps trying to discover the person or people responsible for it. The vague feelings keep begging for a concrete answer—a picture, a face.

On the one hand professionals agree that they wish that much of what they heard was not true, but the denial of painful realities which have been suppressed for centuries would not be helpful for anyone and could be disastrous for the victims. On the other hand we need to face the fact that in a culture where proof of guilt is needed before one can be condemned, a hasty judgement could be seen as a kind of social capital punishment. When rape and incest is equal to emotional murder, false accusations likewise are hanging the innocent.

When professionals battle about the reality of what they hear, what can pastoral volunteers do? Through being called to train hundreds of pastoral counsellors I have found at least two important safeguards: apply common sense and stay close to the gospel.

1. Use common sense

This can help us to take the seeker of help seriously about what they consider to be their reality and their need. True or not, if someone even thinks that abuse has happened, then they do have a serious problem which needs our careful attention. One can start to look for the results of what the reported abuse has caused, and aid seekers to begin to face those consequences, which seem to result from that (suspected) abuse. The change of focus from vague facts in the past to the healing of twisted life patterns in their daily lives now will, in any case, strengthen a person.

2. *Stay close to the heart of the gospel*

Pastoral counsellors have a different function and different equipment from psychologists or other therapists. The power of the gospel of Jesus is that he comes to meet us where we are. The task of an abuse counsellor is to develop skills which enable him to be sensitive to the specific spiritual, emotional, behavioural and physical needs of survivors. Objective Christian truth will not be enough. We have to go one step further and speak about a personal experience of the presence of God.[10]

To speak in western mainline churches about experiencing God has always been somewhat suspect, because church history shows us how subjective experiences have caused deep divisions and strife. In the western secular world we are now seeing an increased stress on 'experience'. I believe this is also a major reason why the New Age movement is gaining attention. As churches, we will need to give more attention to formulating a biblical theology of experiencing God.[11]

In this book I try to chart my commitment to basic evangelical faith as well as my understanding that this faith will need a variety of cultural expressions in the language and the mood of today. As I looked for new approaches, I encountered new experiences, new ways of helping counsellees to face reality. I didn't just ask myself or the counsellees if it worked but also, 'Is it biblical?' The answer to that question is not just for me to give. Biblical evaluation also calls for interaction with other believers. For that reason I initially presented these understandings to the College of Counselling and Health Care of the University of the Nations (Youth With A Mission) during a congress in Manila in 1988. Since then, I have used them in teaching many different seminars in Scandinavia, Iceland, Switzerland, Austria, Asia and my own country, the Netherlands. The comments I receive help me to add, subtract and multiply. Because of the effect of the peace of God in abuse ministry, we started to talk about 'powerful peace'.

Powerful Peace: one approach to introduce an abuse survivor to a God who cares

The essence of my approach can be summarised as an under-standing of the biblical concept of the Hiding Place (Psalm 91). It centres on the possibility of becoming so enveloped in the peace of Jesus that ugly realities fade out as his presence filters in. This means that a revelation takes place: 'I am not alone, he is here.' This allows a person to face painful realities. It becomes like a stereo experience: on the one hand is the reality of inner peace, and the memory of the shadows of the past is on the other. The secret here is to focus more on the present reality of the presence of Jesus, with its effects of peace and security, than on the past. If the pain becomes too much, a refocusing *away* from painful realities gives rest, as the focus is once again turned to Jesus alone. Newly strengthened in this peace, another attempt can be made to deal with unresolved issues: 'From peace alone, to peace with pain, and back again to peace alone if necessary!' This becomes a self-healing process which allows the survivor to proceed at her or his own speed.

The experience of the presence of Jesus is in itself a very powerful concept. Often the New Testament calls this an 'infilling' with the Spirit of Jesus, or an infilling with the Holy Spirit. Past powerlessness to stop traumatic events from happening is—according to Finkelhor—one of the major reasons for a sense of powerlessness of abuse survivors in later life. This experience of the presence of Jesus becomes an empowering element, through which the weak become strong. It helps victims to become survivors, and more than that. As missionaries, they enter into the unknown parts of their own secret, deformed world. There they share the good news of the gospel of peace: the internal warring sides of one's personality can find peace at the foot of the cross. Restoration starts to take place as Christ is allowed to rule every part of the inner country of our personality.

Serious traumas have a combined effect on spirit, soul and body. The healing process involves all these areas.[12] I have come to understand that the physical body functions as a recorder, with an ability to register sound, sight, touch, taste and smell. Deep traumas are often linked to specific parts of the body. This is especially the case with sexual traumas.[13]

One of the possibly unique parts of this approach is the fact that Powerful Peace can give a new physical experience to the video-tape in the body. The good memory of a physical touch by the power of God can overrule the ugly memories. This physical touch by the power of God is very much like what we hope will happen when we pray for a sick person. Thus what I am proposing is not very different from what pastoral workers already do when people are sick. It seems to me that this is the essence of what the apostle Paul shared with converts who had been used to a perverted sexual life. They were people who could say, because of the name of Jesus and the power of the Holy Spirit, 'I was like that.'[14]

To apply the word of God in that special world of the abused or—as one could call it—the *culture* of the abused, still needs much more work than I can present at this time. What I write here is one of the many different ways in which people try to help. It is also a progress report.

Abuse traumas: a call for the church to be involved

With a new awareness of the shockingly high incidence of traumas and serious abuse all around the world, we need many more vuluntees who are able to minister wisely, as part of the healing hand of the church, each depending on their limited natural and spiritual abilities. Because I see myself basically as a practical trainer, I look more for a variety of pastoral workers and church members who know what it means to 'love with wisdom' than just specialists. Young people, for instance, can be very effective, because they are so close to young survivors. Also, older people, weathered by the storms of life, need to be encouraged that they can have a very meaningful contribution. The ability both to enter into the other culture and stand firm on one's own cultural values, is needed to survive long-term abuse counselling. The God who calls also equips. I hope to show in this book how this can be experienced. I have found that 'grace-gifts', the special expressions of the Holy Spirit through ordinary believers, can be very helpful as volunteers are involved in abuse counselling. Grace and peace are also two key words in the ministry of the apostle Paul.

The grace of God is not only expressed through those who consciously serve him. There are basic values, which mankind has received through creation and to which one can find a way back, in any culture.[15] In addition, more specific Christian values, embedded in western culture, still have an effect on the values of secular mental-health workers. That gives an opening for co-operation. Any meaningful church-based counselling programme must decide how to relate to mental-health professionals. I co-operate with both Christian and secular professionals, provided they can work within the value-framework of the persons I refer to them. The 'Hiding Place' approach has been quite helpful in preparing counsellees for such professional help. The counsellee is then empowered to give directions to secular helpers regarding their value system.

Such enabling is very necessary, as both pastoral counselling and secular help can become very manipulative if the helper is not careful enough with the fragile individuality which grows stronger in the course of the healing process.

In the Netherlands and Scandinavia there are already signals from mental-health workers who groan under the huge load of abuse cases which threaten to clog the health system. Also the slow recovery rate and the barrage of painful stories could create an 'incest tiredness'. The answer lies, I believe, not in more mental-health professionals, but in lay counsellors, who are supported effectively by professionals. Throughout the centuries the church has inspired and guided volunteers to share a message of hope for both individuals and society.

This message of hope and of how lives can be changed, can

help us not to look away or even deny the reality of sexual abuse, even by members of our churches as well as church leaders. It is still hard to accept that these things happen. Biblical realists should not be amazed. The Bible spells out in detail how perverse mankind can be. This should also prepare us to hear some more grim stories in the next chapter, as we walk with others into the shadows of the past.

Notes

1. Berliner & Loftus (1992) These two experts in the field of sexual abuse admit that they often had opposing views, Berliner as expert for the prosecution and Loftus as an expert for the defence. They give prudent advice in regard to the 'memory problem'. Writing about the percentage of abuse reports that are true, they state 'If we are talking about a clear and specific account from an older child, teenager or adult, we can agree that most are probably true. The percentage question becomes much murkier when one considers ambiguous statements from very young children, claims from severely disturbed teenagers or adults, recounting bizarre elements or "memories" which emerge only after extended exposure to therapy where abuse is suggested as an explanation in spite of the client's lack of memory for the events.'

2. Psychologists in Norway informed me that a very high percentage of the long-term female patients in Norwegian psychiatric institutions (over 60%) have an 'early sexual abuse' history. The example to which I refer also shows a positive interaction between pastoral and psychiatric care.

3. Boulton, Morris; MacEachron (1989)
   My experience in Europe, and informants from Asia and the Middle East, indicate that this is a cross-cultural phenomenon. This includes persistent reports from northern Africa and Asia, as well as Europe, about mothers seducing their own sons, or older sisters their younger brothers. TV programmes both in the Netherlands and in Sweden about male victims have recently resulted in floods of telephone calls and a new openness among men in seeking help.

4. Boulton et al, (1989), David Finkelhor, (1986).

5. Hallgrimur Petursson, 'Hymns of the Passion'; Hallgrimur Church, Reykjavik.

6. Alice Miller (1990) shows how secular helpers have denied the reality of child abuse, because of the need to deny their own pain.

7. Many abuse survivors complain that professional helpers did not

ask the key questions which would have allowed them to share the dark secrets of the past. Many indicate that it was not until the fourth or fifth professional helper was consulted, that *the* question was asked. While an unwillingness to face the question of abuse is to be deplored, one can also turn the question back to the abuse survivor: why were you unable to inform professional helpers of this painful information? Might it be that there were several consultations needed before you found the courage to speak up? Was helper number five so much more skilled or were you more empowered by previous sessions with others?

8. Pastoral volunteers should be even more careful about digging into the past than professional helpers, who, by training and experience, can better deal with the surge of bad memories, once a door is opened to the past. As I will explain in the application of the Powerful Peace approach, pastoral workers have different possibilities: to empower a seeker of help through the 'grace and peace of God the Father and Jesus Christ his Son.'

9. Elizabeth F. Loftus; *The Reality of Repressed memories American Psychologist* May 1993. She gives a clear overview of current concerns about memories which can be induced through the type of questioning by police as well as therapists.

   Les Parrot, in *Christianity Today*, 21 June 1993 gives vivid examples of the questions we face as pastoral helpers, when people who seek help tell us bizarre stories.

10. A.W. Tozer writes in *The Divine Contest* (1950: 21, 21):

    'Wherever faith has been original, wherever it has proved itself to be real, it has invariably had upon it a sense of the *present God*. The Holy Scriptures possess in marked degree this feeling of actual encounter with a real person . . . With him they held a person to person conversation, and a sense of shining reality is upon their words and deeds.

    'Some who desire to be teachers of the Word, but who understand neither what they say, nor whereof they affirm, insist upon "naked faith" as the only way to know spiritual things. By this they mean a conviction of the trustworthiness of the Word of God (a conviction, it may be noted, which the devils share with them). But the man who has been taught even slightly by the Spirit of truth will rebel at this perversion . . . he cannot love a God who is no more than a deduction from a text.

11. This was also the conclusion of the Dutch Council of Churches which released a study on the rapid decline of membership of various Christian denominations. The lack of attention to the experience of religion was cited as one major cause of the lack of cohesiveness between people and their denomination. From clinical experience I would add one more factor: the presence

of a strong 'shame and guilt' factor coming from Dutch culture with its roots in Calvinism. The strong presence of negative religious-based feelings such as shame and guilt prevents for many the possibility of even the idea that religion could have beneficial, uplifting and rewarding experiences.

12. I Thess 5:23.
13. I Cor 6:18.
14. I Cor 6:9–11; 18–19.
15. The creation-based values seem to me to be captured in two Scriptures. Rom 14:17 (righteousness, peace and joy) and 1 Cor 13:13 (faith, hope and love). The desire for these values seems to be manifested in one form or another in every culture.

CHAPTER TWO

WALKING IN THE SHADOWS

Clear blue eyes stared into an infinite distance beyond me. I already knew Helen's story from my co-worker's notes.

> Helen shared some pretty gruesome facts without much show of emotion. As a preschooler, she had been abused for the first time by her father. Then, as her mother divorced and remarried, the step-father just took over and used her too. One of the step-brothers also got involved. By the time she was fourteen, she ran away from home and found shelter, but always at the same price. She cursed her beautiful body and decided it was time to get fat. Then somehow, somewhere, she met a friendly lady who did not ask questions, but gave her a room at a very low rent. But she added a moral tax, 'No boys here, OK? I want you to have one place where you can be safe.' That last sentence triggered off something in Helen. She actually dared to start thinking about security, safety and love. This friendly lady invited her to church. There, Helen met yet more warmth and love. Shortly after this, she became very depressed and suicidal. This shocked her deeply. 'Just when I'm starting to live and experience some warmth and security, my world seems to be collapsing. How can this be; where is God in all this?'

Building on frozen soil

For sometime, I had been asking myself the same question. Others, who seemed to do well for a time, experienced something similar to Helen's experience after opening up to the gospel. I discovered that a group of Christian psychiatrists was wrestling with this issue as well, and they asked me for a pastoral viewpoint. The invitation had been quite provocative: 'Can personal faith be dangerous for your mental health?' In my preparations to speak on these professional questions, a picture grew which seemed to be a good metaphor for the situation:

> Many survivors of serious abuse somehow make it. Their survival system often seems to function well. But it is as if they are building on frozen ground. Personal faith introduces a new warmth, both directly between the Creator and his creation, as well as through developing relationships in a new and safe environment. The rock-like foundation becomes soft as the frozen ground thaws. The house starts to shake. Yet this is not bad news; it means that new foundational values are needed for the rebuilding work.

My co-worker told Helen about this explanatory model. It made sense to her and she asked if she could meet me. Up till then, she had been almost paranoid about any man coming close, including during church meetings, so she always sat at the aisle end of a row of chairs, with the landlady next to her. We had already felt it was time for her to meet male helpers. Part of her healing would be to get used to 'safe men' first, to learn to respond in a relaxed way to the opposite sex. Thus, her request for my help showed she was indeed ready.

I deliberately arrived after her at my colleague's office. This was to give her a greater sense of control over the room and thus increase her awareness of security. She was sitting in her favourite place, with a fluffy stuffed animal—a monkey with a broad grin—on her lap. I knew that she disliked shaking hands, so I greeted her from the other side of the room and sat down.

After repeating the picture in my own words, Helen nodded thoughtfully and asked how she could work on new foundations for her life. It was then that I suddenly seemed to lose her as she stared into the distance beyond me. I didn't hurry with the answer, but started to share my admiration for the way she had coped in life, in spite of all that had happened. I also thanked her for allowing me to be involved, and with a straight face I suggested that I should start with my introductory course:

'How to survive Teo's counselling.'[1] Her eyes lit up with a smile and she was back.

After her question about 'new foundations for life', Helen had just split off from reality and experienced a fleeting moment of not even being in the room with us. This often happens with seriously abused persons, as a way to survive the stress. Her question, or the answer I might give, or just the fact of being so open with me, all could be reasons for this 'splitting' moment. At the same time, she had listened vaguely to what I had said and the implied joke about my survival course made sense to her. So I explained how her emotional batteries might sometimes give a 'low-power' signal or that she might just feel like walking out. That was acceptable behaviour right from the start. She should be in control of what happened in our sessions at all times. I also told her how she could indicate if she felt the sessions were becoming too tense or if she felt it was enough for that session. This approach relaxed her quite a bit. That gave me courage for the next step, to be selectively open about my feelings on what men had done to her. The key would be to be honest without becoming too intense. Still from a safe distance at the other side of the room, I opened up with:

> I am ashamed of what men have done to you. I have wondered what I, as a man, can do to respond. The best thing I have come up with so far is that I would like to suggest that perhaps at some time I could pray for you and bless you.

Pastoral prayer was not something unusual to Helen. I knew from my co-worker that she expected it, so I knew I was not forcing an issue. As a safety measure, I added 'at some time', to give her a way out. She smiled, shaking her monkey as well. We all laughed. Then I told her that there are several ways to pray. One way was just to sit there and pray, but there was also the kind of prayer whereby a hand was placed ceremonially on a shoulder or head. Now I knew that this was normal in her church, but I wanted her to be sure there were various options open. Finally I suggested that there was one form of prayer which perhaps fitted the situation best: to pray like Jesus did as he washed the feet of the disciples. 'Because of all that men have done to you, I would like to kneel down and touch your feet as I pray.' She stiffened at first and then blurted out, 'That's about the only thing you are allowed to touch.' Then she started to weep quietly. As I knelt down and asked for God's mercy, her sobbing increased. Suddenly she slipped from the chair, threw her arms around me, put her head against my chest and sobbed, 'Mamma, where are you?' A silence followed, then she remarked that she could feel my quiet heartbeat. After a while, I gently slid her into the arms of my lady co-worker. I knew that after such expressions of emotion, great embarrassment could arise later, which might hinder her searching for relaxed responses to men. We let her go on sobbing quietly, as the sun seemed to stand still and actual minutes turned into hours.

It was in that silence that my colleague and I realised something had happened to the atmosphere in the room. A new lightness, a sense of the presence of God. Later Helen commented on the tranquillity and peace of those moments. She affirmed how this began something new in her, an emotion for which she had longed, but never known before. That incident opened new doors which my co-worker and her assistant could walk through. Later, Helen wrote, 'Teo, you were the first man I learned to trust. Thank you for coming into my "valley of darkness and death" and being a light to help me find my way.'

Light through the cracks

With Helen's letter in my hand, I wondered about my own involvement in counselling and remembered the words of a Scandinavian film director. He attended one of my seminars and made an interesting observation:

> Whenever I interview actors, I try to get to know them and find out if they have suffered in some way during the struggles of life. If not, they won't act well. Suffering creates cracks through which the real self can come forth. Then, their acting is not wooden, but life itself.[2]

I know about Helen's 'valley of darkness and death' through personal experience—painful memories, as well as the lasting results of them, in the shaping of my own personality. Dark events in my own life had taken on the shape of shadows which refused to go away. It seems at times as if the sun shines from behind and we are walking in our own shadow.

Looking back, I see how amazing it is that a child can learn to adapt to a life of gloom and coldness at an early age. Like many others who suffered traumas, I went into a psychological hibernation, passively waiting for the darkness to break. But that incredible spark of life which separates humans from animals did not give up. The hibernation was not total; some parts refused to sleep and dreams of hope kept calling me not to give up. That's how I learned to create my own 'quiet country'. Those around me did not know about that part of Teo and I did not know how to communicate it either. This secret inner country was rather elusive; I couldn't just enter it whenever I wanted. That inaccessibility caused perhaps more pain than the real shadows of the past. But I had other solutions to this problem; a secret fantasy life which helped me to evade painful realities. These fantasies would work addictively and keep me out of touch with the outer world. At times I sensed that danger. The only answer left then was dark, silent, wordless despair.

When my parents changed from nominal Christians into believers with a personal faith, a new horizon opened up. I saw the reality of God's power, both as he healed my mother from a severe rheumatism with crippling deformities, and as he brought a new kind of peace into the family. Reading the Bible for myself, I discovered that Jesus was not just a distant figure, but real and alive. Experiencing new life myself at the age of about eighteen, I also became aware of a kind of emotional pain. It was like an emotional leprosy[3] starting to heal. The long periods of darkness from the past were hurting more because I was now starting to live. I discovered what I had been missing.

At the same time, the leadership of my very traditional church had increasing problems with me. There came a time when I reflected often on Malachi 4:2: 'But for you who revere my name, the sun of righteousness will rise with healing in its wings. And you will go out and leap like calves released from the stall.'

I felt like one of those calves escaping confinement. Then I discovered what it meant to be rejected by religious leaders. My involvement in Youth for Christ and my personal expressions of faith were unacceptable to our church. When they refused to allow me to partake in the Lord's Supper, my world collapsed. In utter agony I raced into the dark November night, while the storm lashed my face and soaked me to the skin. That's when death appeared as a friend, waiting . . . As I screamed into the night 'God, where are you?' there was no answer except for a growing, rather strange pregnant silence within. Then the message to the church in Laodicea flashed through my mind: Jesus, knocking on the outside of the church door, asking to be let in. I realised Jesus was inviting me to a meal better than the church could ever give (Rev 3:20). There on that night, I had communion with God without bread and without wine. There and then I learned that there was yet another option for escaping trauma: not the fantasy world, nor despair, nor death, but worship. I shook off the lie that death was a friend and chose to live. I also discovered that worship could lead me so much more easily to the secret silent country within, where Psalm 23 became a reality, a rest in God.

As I learned how to respond to other trauma survivors, I saw how important this discovery of the quiet green pastures within had been. Initially, my skills in helping abuse survivors were mostly intuitive. In time I became aware that our human personality is like an onion with many layers. I kept searching beyond the layers of trauma to the untouched core of a survivor. While other helpers seemed to concentrate on the time when traumas started, I looked for the unspoiled beauty. In a sense, I became a passionate explorer of unknown countries, a treasure hunter, a pearl diver. When I met Sarah, this approach took a new turn.

'Now I know how beautiful the trees are . . .'

Sarah had been a long-term inmate of a psychiatric institution as a result of the diagnosis that she was suffering from a severe form of schizophrenia which had not responded to treatment. A pastor, with the help of some volunteers, had somehow convinced parents and medical authorities that they were able to provide her with a protected environment in a family atmosphere. The pastor also told me that he had a deep conviction that somehow there was another girl inside, waiting to be released.

I was asked to help and saw her at weekly intervals. Initially she was very unresponsive. Especially at meal times or during other family activities, she seemed to freeze emotionally. Through a trust which developed, she would open up a bit at times. Thus I saw glimpses of a very strange world. It struck me that she seemed like a one-woman-country with a very strange and private culture. That's when I decided that I should perhaps try to use my missionary gift to see if I could, somehow, enter into Sarah's world view. I attempted to learn her language, imagery and indirect speech. Finally she confided to me that she knew there were microphones in the walls which recorded all she said. So it was wiser not to talk, rather than to let the whole world know what she was really like. Taking her seriously, I suggested that we should take a walk outside in a nearby park. 'There are no microphones there and even if there were, if we walk fast enough, they won't catch what we're talking about.'

I still remember the amazed look, the recognition of being understood. That walk became a very remarkable one. As I commented on the beauty of the environment, she lamented her loss of a sense of beauty. I sensed that she needed hope that life could be different and I felt secure enough to tell her how I became sensitive to beauty again at about the age of twelve. I shared with her how, until then, my life had been only black and white with many shades of grey and how that at times it had caused hilarious moments. For instance, my mother would point to my feet and somehow I would have put on one green and one red sock and never noticed the difference. Yet tests showed that I was not colour blind; I prefer to call it 'colour-indifferent'. Then in the early spring of 1948, my mother suggested we take a bike ride. We lived in one of the most 'Dutch' parts of Holland. The willows on the banks of a small stream were just about bursting with pale green leaves. The sun was about 15 degrees above the horizon, shining in our faces. Then it happened. As we went around a bend, the sun slipped behind the trees, producing a near-fluorescent green haze. 'Look Teo, how beautiful,' was my mother's delighted cry. 'Look at the trees.' It was then that I looked, and consciously absorbed the colours around me. From that time on, my awareness of beauty was slowly woken up and I became much more conscious of colour.

As I related my story, Sarah asked some very intelligent questions about my emotions and my life now, and left me wondering what was really inside her. A few days later, she stormed into my office and shouted, 'Teo, I have seen how beautiful the trees are.' The others in the room wisely decided to leave us alone and for nearly half an hour, there was a radiant, beautiful, totally normal girl sharing what she had seen, how she felt and showing glimpses of her personality we had never known before. We were elated. For the next few hours she still functioned quite well. Then the crash came, as she relapsed into her old twisted world. It took many months before we saw glimpses of the inner Sarah again. Yet the short self-exposure had given everyone hope that there was someone else there; we just needed to find her. After a period of time, she recovered enough to live her own life, in a somewhat protected environment. I have lost track of her, but I will never forget the image of that radiant girl who broke through the walls of outer indifference.

Walking in the shadows of others does have a dark side to it. To be invited inside also means being confronted with untold horrors, and discovering what people can do to each other. It affirmed to me what others have observed, that 'the only beasts are humans'. It is incredible what people can do to each other. Yet we must face up to this painful reality. I discovered this more as my ability to deal with this pain increased. It seemed as if people would smell the difference and dare to open up in ways I had not known before. The capacity to enter into these shadows is linked to a capacity to face reality.

William Glasser (1965) has explained how a sense of reality is needed for mental health. But how *can* one look into the burning fire of cruelty, devastation and endless pain without being blinded?

Staying sane in a crazy world

Mental health work can be dangerous for one's own health! As someone has suggested, perhaps job advertisements in this field should carry a sticker similar to the warnings to smokers on a packet of cigarettes! This warning seems to make even more sense, working in the twisted world of sexual abuse. When I share with students what I have learned from helping several hundred incest victims, the obvious question is always asked, '. . . but how do you stay sane?' I admit that there are times of despair. I believe that I have only been able to go on by focusing on my initially instinctive search for this unspoiled inner beauty in the survivors, rather than the blinding flames of demonic cruelty.

My own life 'in the shadows' was one part of the training in communicating with seriously hurting persons. One of its consequences had been a nearly constant despair on two counts: firstly, that I could not express the feelings which were inside, and secondly, an inability to observe accurately the emotions of others. I had a serious communication problem. Looking back, I have come to the somewhat paradoxical conclusion that my inability to communicate verbally has been a key in becoming a counsellor! Not understanding what people were really trying to tell me, I often found myself praying, 'Lord, what is really going on?' The intuitive responses, often triggered by what I can only describe as 'help from above', repeatedly set me on the right track.

My initial formal training had nothing to do with counselling. After secondary school I became a medical technician and went to Bible school for a two-year practical training as a missionary. I met my wife, Wil, during this time and we realised we would have to wait to get married until she had finished nursing training. To bridge this time span, I was able to turn my military service into a volunteer assignment as an army medic in Surinam, a former Dutch colony between French and British Guyana. There, I also had my first missionary experience. When Wil had finished her training, I returned home for our wedding. Soon after this we enrolled in a three-month intensive course in the Summer School of Linguistics, outside London, before being assigned to work among the poorest of the poor in north-east Thailand. As we worked with leprosy patients we learned about despair and hope in a totally different culture. We were also invited into the private fears of these animistic, rural people: the dread of ghosts and demons. I learned about the ugly ceremonies they conducted to escape from the grip of evil. This showed me the lengths they would go to in order to seek peace. But I also observed the tender love of a family-based, private ceremony. Close relatives would gather around someone who had undergone a severe shock, to comfort and encourage, and to call back the fragile personality which might have fled in the process.[4]

This caring for each other, in times of need, was very evident in the church family as well. I had the privilege of learning from Thai church leaders who were Christians long before I developed a personal faith in Jesus Christ. For them, prayer to Jesus replaced the call on the spirits. The desire for inner peace was answered by the encounter with Jesus, who *is* our peace. I discovered also that I could use this method to help people who were gripped by fear of demons.

In time, I was asked by fellow missionaries how to relate practically to the animistic Thai. Several missionary doctors also encouraged me to develop my budding gift for counselling missionaries. They introduced me to helpful literature to answer my probing questions. In 1972 I was asked to speak at a missionary conference on 'emotional healing'. It was a new expression in the evangelical world, which I had never heard before. Someone gave me a book about it. I had planned several days to prepare my talk. My office was a tiny storeroom in which we had installed air conditioning. Locked away from the outside, it was as if an inner curtain was drawn. But there was also a Presence, which took me by the hand and helped me consciously face my past. For three days I wept through my life history. As layer after layer of my emotional onion was peeled off, there was also that Presence which comforted: Jesus, an experienced specialist in pain and trauma himself.

Even as a child, the fear of death was not something new to me. Several times, I had faced death directly. As a refugee fleeing various areas of battle, we had been shot at indiscriminately, machine-gunned and bombed. Once a crazy pilot saw some children playing in a meadow, and decided to do some 'rabbit hunting'. My friend was shot in the hip, my brother hid behind a birch tree, which caught the bullets. I ran home screaming. Bullets were flying all round me, but miraculously I was not hurt.

Some time later, when the fighting became worse, we were in the middle of a bombing raid. My mother was too ill to go to the bunker again and she told my brother and me, 'Come and sit on the bed, then the bomb will hit us all at the same time.' I still remember how we huddled together. I was shivering. Then my mother said, 'I will pray.' I remember that prayer in our family was only in standard formulas, before and after meals and when we went to sleep. I don't recall any expression of a personal faith by my mother before this bombing raid; perhaps that's why this scene made such an impression. As she started with the Lord's prayer, she suddenly switched to normal talk, sharing her heart's cry for us, pleading for safety and committing us to him. Suddenly a total change of atmosphere took place. My shivering stopped. I calmed down. Looking back, I realise that this was my first encounter with the 'Hiding Place'. The God of peace touched an area deep within, which shielded me through the ordeals that soon followed. One short crazy moment in particular has been indelibly etched in my mind.

A towering soldier looks down at a seven-year-old boy. 'Where is your father hiding?' He pulls a pistol and places it against my head. 'Speak up, or I shoot!' Seconds of silence turn into an eternity. Inside me an icy resolve erupts: 'I'd rather die . . .' Then I scream at the top of my voice. My mother races out of the house, sees what is happening and lunges at the soldier with a hail of words. He turns around and walks away, head down, ashamed. The icy cold inside me remained, however, and from then on I knew what death was.

After the soldier left, we had a few more days of peace. My father had already disappeared. When they came to pick us up, I became a silent onlooker of the ugliness which followed. After a few weeks with my mother in a concentration camp I was torn from her arms and taken to a children's home. She was trying to encourage me through the open car window. The last thing I heard was her scream as the car drove over her foot. It would be a long time before I would see her again. I don't recall that I cried, then or later. The freezing cold inside me had done its work, suppressing the raging fire of anger and resulting in a sullen retreat into inner silence. The formation of an outer personality, which was calm and at ease, but which masked a sleeping volcano, had already taken place.

This calm exterior and a totally different inner world lasted until I was eighteen. Then, all alone, just reading the Bible, that same peace which I experienced during the bombing came again. A slow process of healing started, as Jesus became alive for me.

Little did I know then that these traumatic events not only deformed, but also produced great beauty. Once I saw an artist look at a twisted piece of wood. He described the beauty inside, waiting to be released. It was then that the analogy struck: that's me! Twisted wood can have beauty! In spite of the onion-like layers of abuse which covered my life, there was a precious protected part waiting to be released. Looking back now, I believe the wait was too long. With just a little competent help, I could have recovered so much earlier. As I meet other trauma victims, my own past makes a bit more sense. Perhaps this is the fire behind my passion to help, to go just one more mile. There are moments when even those closest to me find this intensity hard to understand.

At times I still come across another onion-layer of unresolved pain. I am not specifically looking for it. I have decided *not* to look for wounds, but to live in the present, to accept that healing is a process. It is 'life from above being poured into us'.[5] I need co-workers (volunteers and professionals), who give me input on how I am functioning and growing. Above all, I need relationships with a variety of other believers. Normal church life is also a place of restoration for abuse counsellors!

Churches involved in healing

William Glasser who, as a secular helper, attempted to include community life in the treatment, stated that mental health depends on three Rs: a clear view of Reality, personal Responsibility for one's behaviour, and solid values about Right and wrong. The wisdom of this is self-apparent. To face reality, to have courage to take personal responsibility for one's behaviour and to have solid values, is quite a challenge. The apostle Paul in his pastoral letters about church life stressed that one needs to learn this from and with others in community. He points out how churches can be involved in healing by providing a healing atmosphere. The church has a potential which secular services cannot provide; people meeting, not because of their problem, but from a desire for relationship irrespective of what one's problem or background is.

Many of the counselling services which mental-health programmes offer are either on the basis of individual treatment, or given to groups of people with the same problems. The use of group therapy for abuse victims, for instance, gives them a chance to meet others who have also been through the same ordeal. They learn to open up and communicate that which was previously taboo. Churches can offer that, but also something else: the availability of 'community'. If nothing else, abuse victims need a social network in order to learn how to make and maintain healthy relationships, and I would hope that churches can provide a healthy family to those who have never had that before.

I also believe that churches can co-operate with local mental-health authorities. The increased cultural diversity in western Europe affords better opportunities for this. If Muslims can request a culturally-sensitive approach, then Christians can also be seen as a cultural group. I have found that such a presentation of the Christian faith—as Christian culture—avoids a discussion as to whether that faith is true or not. That is not the task of secular helpers to decide. By accepting the reality of Christian culture, secular workers can avoid violation of our values, even if they differ from their own private views.

Churches should also co-operate with mental-health authorities or professional Christian counsellors outside their own circle for their own survival. I observe how some church leaders, who seriously want to serve their members with good pastoral care, at times have to devote most of their energy to some of the toughest counselling situations. If they are also very evangelistic, then much time will have to be spent ministering to the emotional problems of those they attempt to reach. An increased ability to help pastorally will also attract more people who need help. This then becomes a vicious circle. It is also a reason why some pastors become rather edgy when individual pastoral care takes the central place in a church. There are other tasks and functions that are just as important, such as the need to share the art of Christian living to whole groups through preaching and teaching.

When our pastoral help seems insufficient and counsellees do not progress as we expect, we need to be honest and refer them to others. After all, God has more gifts than those that are available locally or even inside the church. The God of creation has given gifts, even to those who do not acknowledge him personally.

Healing communities

In a community which aims at helping abuse survivors, there must be a place where painful realities can be faced; this is the key problem. Abuse survivors often do not know how to talk about it, because of the consequences. The abusers often discredit the victim in such a way that they can be sure the victim will not be believed. So what can one do?

One approach that a sensitive church leadership can take is to invite trusted outsiders, who are available to hear 'confession'. I have often served in such a capacity and at times will take along teams of trained and trusted counsellors whose only task initially will be to listen and encourage anyone who needs it to follow up such a confession with more pastoral or professional psychological help.

The opportunity to 'be close to others who are strangers' might be one reason why some young people join an international youth organisation such as Operation Mobilization or Youth With a Mission (YWAM). The new relationships often give them a chance to unburden their need, to find understanding and to leave the past behind! I met David at a YWAM Discipleship Training Course. Twenty young people aged between eighteen and thirty were eager students. They came to this course to be trained in evangelism. 'To know God and make him known', was the motto which someone had painted on the wall of the lecture hall. I was asked to teach basic counselling skills. 'They will go for about six weeks to bars, nightclubs and parks to meet young people,' the letter of invitation had stated. 'They will work with the only church which is left in the area; all the other churches have fled that part of the inner city.' The participants were a lively group of young people. Laughter and seriousness went hand in hand. On the second day of the course David asked to talk privately. He had understood the practical reasons for writing a letter to speed up the counselling process, so he already had one in his hand when he came in.

David was ten when a good friend of the family seduced him for the first time. It lasted until he was thirteen. Then one day he felt such revulsion that he literally kicked the abuser when he once again tried to touch him. Several years later he discovered that his father knew all about it, but that he had been blackmailed. The 'good friend' had made a loan, which they could not pay back. David was angry with the abuser, and with his parents. (Where was mother in all this?) He told us that it had taken him time to learn to understand his parents and to learn to forgive them. He was still struggling with that 'uncle' who had, in the meantime, disappeared from the scene. 'I will deal with that in time as well,' he wrote, 'but my immediate question is a practical problem. Before I came to the course, I fell in love with a girl. When we became more physically involved, I usually got a tight stomach and became nervous. I have gone through therapy and understand the link with the past. I still like the girl, but realise that I have to deal with this before I can go on.' David's willingness and ability to talk, the sense of commitment to God, and his openness to the small prayer group of fellow students all worked together.

Reflecting on what I did to help David, I can only say that I came into the harvest of what many others had prepared, including secular counsellors. I explained to David how our body remembers what has happened,[6] and how there is a link between body, soul and spirit; how our bodies can acquire new memories of love, power, life, and of fire as well as tranquillity. Then there was a worship time in a small Lutheran chapel. David came to the altar and knelt down. Several of his friends came along. Then we prayed. I still find it hard to express all that happened; it was so personal, so fragile. The only thing I can say is that the presence of Jesus became very real. For a long time, David lay silent in front of the altar. Later he shared how something physical happened to him, as if streams of life washed him clean. 'I literally felt like Isaiah who had fire touch his lips. You know what he forced me to do orally. Well, for the first time now, I know my mouth is clean.'

The type of help David needed was probably best given in a committed community where he not only experienced the warmth, love and understanding of counsellors, but was also exposed to an intensive retraining in social interaction with the community of students and staff. This community life also forced David to face some traits he had developed, which were good for survival in the past, but detrimental for keeping friends in new settings! It took several months of honest evaluation, a lot of patience and loving confrontation, to show him what he was doing and how he could change these patterns. It was a joy to hear how he joined a team of young people to work in refugee camps in Asia.

Into all the world

Amnesty International, Norway's Redd Barne, Foster Parents, World Vision, TEAR Fund and other organisations have done much to alert us to the level of physical and sexual abuse which is going on around the world. There are simply not enough professionals to help the millions of refugees, the tens of thousands of torture survivors. But we can teach them to reach out to others. There are many ways in which abuse survivors need to be helped. The encounter with the Holy One, the healing of spirit, soul and body from the evil of the past, is a dimension which secular forms of helping can't provide and where the church is challenged to overcome our revulsion to the stories described above, to get in there and to heal in Jesus' name. To enter into the different world of the abused, we first need to learn more about some of its realities.

In the following chapters I will work out more of what I have learned, as a pastoral counsellor, about sexual abuse, and how to help from the perspective of the Christian culture. Not many pastoral counsellors in Europe have done this yet. What I am writing is, I hope, just a starting point for further discussions and new studies. In order to encourage such a discussion and cultivate new skills in helping, we should first give attention to some basic definitions and concepts of the lives of the people who live in the 'world of the abused'.

Notes

1. As abuse survivors have an insistent need to have control, I start out with teaching them how to maintain control over the counselling process. After all, as pastoral helpers we do represent 'power' and this can cause negative reactions before we have even had a chance to show that this will not be yet another abusive situation.

2. This thought also seems to be reflected in Paul's observation about his own ministry when he says, 'Let light shine out of darkness,' II Cor 4:6.

3. We started our mission work in leprosy ministries and discovered how leprosy can kill the nerves in such a way that one does not feel actual pain, even when one can see the blisters of burns.

4. S.J. Tambiah. *Buddhism and the Spirit Cults in north-east Thailand*, Oxford Press, describes such a 'sukhwan ceremony' in detail, a traditional ceremony which involves the animistic spirit world.

5. In John 3 Jesus explains to Nicodemus how this life needs to come from above. He enlarges on that concept through the teaching of our relationship with him in the metaphor of the vine and the branches. Also Romans 5:5 points to an infusion of life into us from God.

6. 1 Cor 6:18.

CHAPTER THREE

STARTING POINTS AND DEFINITION OF CONCEPTS

Traumas in general and incest trauma in particular

We can describe a trauma as an event which results in a devastating violation of a person's being and personality. Certain events cause a lasting, painful remembrance. These events can be spiritual, emotional and/or physical in nature. Such events create a 'reaction of intense powerlessness' and result in an acute disorder of one's life.[1]

A *spiritual trauma* can be caused by a deep religious disappointment. For example, you could be convinced you will be miraculously healed, and then the miracle does not happen. I sometimes meet young people whose unfulfilled hopes and expectations cause spiritual wounds. They have 'received a promise' from God that they will marry a particular girl or boy, and then someone else carries off the person of their dreams. When tragedy strikes, the agonised cry of 'Why didn't God intervene?' can also be a real spiritual trauma.

An *emotional trauma* can include, for instance, the breaking of a solemn promise of secrecy by a friend; or adultery, your partner rejecting you in favour of someone else. The lingering fear which, months after a robbery, can still cause panic reactions and sleep problems. Children can experience the consequences of the death of a close relative for a long time, if the parents and/or carers of the child do not allow them to go through the normal mourning process.

A *physical trauma*, such as physical maltreatment, bombing, shooting, a road accident, can all leave their mark—often literally.

Child sexual abuse is the abuse of a child for the sexual gratification of an adult or a significantly older person. However, where sexual violence is concerned, an age difference is not part of the definition.[2]

Incest is commonly used to describe the overstepping of boundaries of sexual propriety by a close family member.[3] A basic characteristic of incest is the abuse of power. More often than not it is a mixture of spiritual, emotional, social and physical power. In recent years the concept has been enlarged to include people who are supposed to take care of the child: more distant relatives, babysitters, neighbours, teachers and religious workers, etc.

Child sexual experimentation is a factor we also should mention, as I often get questions from concerned Christians who wonder if they were abusers or abused as a result of sexual play. There is a form of sexual play, exploration and experimenting by children, even within the family, that is different from incest. Not that this is always without problems. But the major element of incest—misuse of power—is lacking. I have known a few situations where the biological age of the children involved was not so very different, but the younger brother or sister was emotionally less developed. In those cases, the use of power and authority is the decisive factor in calling this 'game' incest.

Incest, child sexual abuse, victims, survivors or . . . what's in a name?

In this book I will use the word 'incest' for both close-family member sexual abuse as well as by carers. Also, the phrase 'child sexual abuse' will be used where this is applicable. In the previous chapters I have used the words 'victims' and 'survivors'. I try to differentiate here, at the request of those who feel that the title 'survivor' is more respectful of who they truly are. To be labelled 'victim' for the rest of one's life focuses too much on the (past) helplessness inherent in the word victim. One of the main aims of helping victims is to see how they were very creative in dealing with their abusive past and how that creativity, their way to survive, holds keys to freedom from past traumas. I have tried to limit the use of the word 'victim' to situations in which victimisation is obviously the focus.

The choice of the words 'victim' or 'survivor' also has pastoral implications. To be a survivor includes an element of praise. They are still alive, in spite of all that happened. This positive outlook helps in directing a person to hope and to life beyond survival.

The discovery of incest and child sexual abuse by feminists

The feminist movement was among the first to draw attention to the fact that so much incest and early sexual abuse occurs with girls. Incest became, in that context, an expression of anti-female culture. We are now a few years on, and it has become evident that women can also be abusers.[4] I know personally of female abusers such as mothers, sisters, babysitters, Sunday School workers, kindergarten teachers and nurses. As far as we know at present, there are fewer female abusers than male. Or is the cultural revulsion towards female abusers so great that they know better than to confess, and the repression of their failure is therefore much stronger? Are female abusers 'caught' less easily, especially where very young children are concerned?

Variations in response to trauma experiences

Not everyone responds with the same intensity to a traumatic experience. There are people who, for a variety of reasons, do not seem to show any observable after-effects of traumatic experiences.[5] Different researchers indicate that it is not the objective fact of what happened, but the subjective experience of the child that determines the damage. This also means that a realisation at a later date can still cause an after-shock. Thus a girl who was abused at the age of eight came back for renewed help when she entered puberty. It was then that it dawned on her what had happened.[6]

Obviously there is a difference between abuse within the family and abuse by a carer such as a teacher. In the latter case, the child should be able to get all the support they need from parents. Some carers tell a child that their parents approve of this kind of behaviour, so that the child then distrusts their parents and becomes a prisoner of silence. Also there is a difference if the abuse is a violent rape by a stranger or by a carer. The child knows at once that the violent action is wrong. The subtle abuse of carers makes them an accomplice and causes feelings of guilt and shame.[7]

The effects of the stress caused by a sexual trauma are not the same as with other forms of trauma. Sexuality is so interwoven with the personality that a rape can be considered to be emotional murder. This can also be seen in the link between war and rape. The Old Testament laws place rape in the same category as murder and called for capital punishment. The experience of rape as an adult is devastating enough. However, many adults have already acquired sufficient emotional stability to work through such a trauma over a period of time. The inner resilience and stress-capacity which have been built into the adult personality allow a good chance of recovery. An incest trauma in a child, however, has drastic results:

—The development of the child is still in full swing, which means that the resilience is not yet sufficiently developed. The dependent relationship of child to protector/child-rearer should change gradually into a relationship of equals. The normal course of events is that a child outgrows the sphere of dependence on carers in order to lead its own life. The universal, creation-based centrifugal force in a child causes it to grow towards independence from former carers. But the sexual relationship works as a glue.[8] It binds people together. The clash between the centrifugal force and the binding force creates havoc in a child's emotional development.

—The sexual experience is awakened traumatically. What was intended to be an act resulting from adult choice is now functioning in an unripe way. I have noticed that of the homosexual and lesbian people I have met, practically all experienced sexual abuse as a child. These children never had the chance of a free choice of their sexual preference.[9]

The damage is yet more destructive if:

—There were several abusers.
—There was danger to life.[10]
—Long-term abuse took place during several developmental stages of the child.
—If other carers did not give wise support at the time of discovery.

Add to all this the fact that there are some children who are abused within a religious setting, and you can see that just to think of God will make them feel nauseous. In brief, as far as the different kinds of trauma are concerned, incest trauma is in a category of its own. Sufficient reason to give special attention to helping survivors of incest.

Incidence and prevalence of child sexual abuse

The actual amount of child sexual abuse is still uncertain. The statistics which we hear only tell us what people can remember *and* are willing to talk about. Berl Kutchinski's 1994 report (Institute of Criminology, University of Copenhagen), gives a summary of what is presently known in western countries. This report states:

> child sexual abuse in the *general population* (as recorded by adults who answered questionnaires or interviews) show that between 10 per cent and 40 per cent of the female and between 5 per cent and 20 per cent of the male respondents have experienced at least one incident of child sexual abuse during childhood or adolescence.[11]

The variations in statistics are also a result of different definitions of child sexual abuse, age limits etc. In any case we see that there is a real problem. How much of the abuse is done by church workers is not clear. About sixty persons in Norway alone told me about sexual abusive acts by church workers. In my own country it was much less; not that I believe that it happens less, but perhaps the Dutch also need a visitor from another country before they can open up.

Child sexual abuse and incest is only one area of trauma

Statistics for 1991 from the Dutch National Telephone Line for Children show three times the number of requests for help in connection with physical maltreatment than for incest.[12] Some workers correctly point to the need to remember that some kinds of child molestation are almost as bad as incest.[13] But the question is: to what extent does physical molestation of a child occur as a result of sexual aggression on the part of the abuser? And that brings me into the arena of psychiatric presuppositions.

My experience is that the pastoral approach we use for child sexual abuse and incest also works well in cases of serious physical maltreatment. Briere (1992) and others are also identifying common elements which can be found in *all* forms of child maltreatment. Briere observes that what we have often called problem behaviour by abused children really should be respected as a creative lifestyle developed from a need to survive. This creativity, when properly understood, can become a great tool in the treatment programme.

Forms of incest

1. Brute force

'There was a terrifying monotony in his behaviour. First the tension in the family began to mount, and then he began to drink. Then I knew what was going to happen and learned to wait in resignation until he came to my room. He put his big hand on my throat, although I don't believe anyone would have intervened if I had screamed. Then, in my thoughts, I went on a "journey" to beautiful countries and lovely beaches until he had finished.'

I hear this kind of story over and over again. Brute force is used. The child learns to wait helplessly until 'he has finished'. Now that we hear more and more about men who are incest survivors, the question arises whether you can speak exclusively of an anti-female cause for this violence, or whether there is something else.

I have the impression myself that 'despising weakness' plays an important role; that is, the experience of power, in which sexual urges in the abuser cannot be denied or refused by the victim. That would also explain why there are female abusers. In cases where victims become abusers, one could suspect a drive to overcome the paralysis and victim role of the past, as well as the need to relive former abuse from a position of power.

2. Subtle force

'Father was never home. The neighbour had retired. He was always so nice. We often played games such as "Ludo" or dominoes. When I was beaten up once by a boy, he was the one who comforted me. I still remember clearly how he pressed me to him and touched me in places where no-one else did. I was shocked, but he was so nice. One thing led to another . . .'

Misuse of power can also happen subtly, through careful manipulation, trying to sexualise a child. For instance, I know of a paedophile who took more than a year to work himself into a family in order to seduce one child after the other. He admitted that the excitement of working himself into the family was almost as exciting as the ultimate 'victory' over the children!

Sometimes it also happens that a father's moods are the reason why a girl learns to give in to his sexual desires. The child sees how her mother suffers under his (sexual) violence. If she 'co-operates' and is nice to him in a particular way, then the pressure on her mother is lessened. The thought of a pacified father can exert a subtle manipulation over a child, and so there are daughters who thus sacrifice themselves for their mothers' sake. When they seek help later on, they are left with guilt feelings because they chose to go to father 'voluntarily' and let him have his way.

It needs to be made clear right from the start that the child had no other choice in this subtle, manipulative procedure. The father is always responsible. As an adult, he should have known better and not assented to his daughter's attempts to relieve the pressure.

'I was never threatened. But my mother was. From my bedroom, I could clearly hear the rows and the beating. Afterwards, he sometimes came and sat with me, and shared that he really wanted to leave. But that for my sake they didn't want to get a divorce. I saw how he calmed down when I touched him. Mother would look at me gratefully the next day and thank me for pacifying father so well. Once it was so bad that she sent me to my room together with him. "The tension is so awful, you go and calm your father down. It's bad for his heart." '

3. Incidental incest

From the results of research, I get the impression that secular counselling has much contact with the serious kinds of long-term incest.[14] In my pastoral work a different picture emerges. Seventy-five percent of the people who ask me for help have had an 'incidental incest experience' (once or just a few times). This seems to leave an inheritance of negative memories with many of the same long-term effects as the victims of long-term abuse. The damage was worse where the religious background emphasised the feeling of shame after incest. And this became even worse if the child was given no chance of sharing with good carers. The healing of incidental incest is sometimes easier, because the personality has not been exposed to sexual violence on a long-term basis. But on the other hand, the persistent feelings of shame can leave a permanent scar.

'I was twelve. Father was away again for his work. Mother had become very nervous. She asked me to sleep in her bed. I woke up with her hands on my chest. She stroked me gently. I liked it and let it happen. Then she touched my private parts. I felt uneasy, and only then did I recall how this was discussed at school. I jumped out of her bed and ran to my room. She did not come after me, nor did she speak about it. I made sure it never happened again, always locked my room at night'. To an outsider, this just might have been a one-time stupid act of a lonely mother. To the boy it was a bombshell, especially because they never talked about it. The problem was not solved and it festered on, influencing his relations with girls.

4. 'Non-touch' incest

Incest is not only to do with direct physical touch. It is evident that living in an incestuous atmosphere can itself cause serious problems.[15] We mustn't forget the other children in a family! Even though nothing may have (yet) happened to them, the sensual atmosphere in itself has a formative influence. Porn, dirty talk, lack of privacy, visible sexual activity by the parents, all have their influence. Then it can happen that a child indulges in fantasies about sex, absorbs the atmosphere of power abuse that it senses in the home, and learns to apply it at an early age. In the fine line between fantasy and reality, a child can occasionally imagine that 'something is going on with me', while the father fiercely denies that anything happened.

In such cases, however, I still hold the parents responsible for the sexualised atmosphere and the conclusions of the child— even though objectively speaking they are being falsely accused. 'Yes, I admit there was porn in the house and that I sometimes teased her about her developing body. I admit that we were careless and that our house had thin walls so that she could hear us in the bedroom. But really, Teo, I've never touched her. What she's saying about me isn't true.' Clear blue eyes looked at me. What could I say? I was reminded of the text, 'They sow the wind and reap the whirlwind' (Hos 8:7). He was guilty of the consequences of his own behaviour.

5. Step-parent incest

The rapid increase in the number of divorces has also created a new problem. While previously the biological father was often the abuser, sexual abuse by a step-parent or mother's new boyfriend is now also common.

'We were really happy when my mother came home with a new boyfriend. The allowance we had to live on made it impossible for me to belong to a sports club, let alone go horseback riding. The boyfriend brought his money with him. He was very friendly and jolly. When my mother suddenly had to go away for a few days, he came to me and began to touch me. He was very direct. "Your mother is a nice woman, but I need more. If you'd rather not, then I'll leave." It was a very thinly-veiled threat. I saw myself having to leave the sports club, and I was just beginning to enjoy riding. So I gave in. It lasted two years, and then he suddenly disappeared.'

Who did it?

Quite a number of people who responded to my writings in Dutch and Danish told me that they were not aware of sexual abuse. They didn't know that they had been physically abused, yet they showed many of the symptoms which abuse victims have. I caution against digging in the past in order to find out the 'who did what and when . . .' by pastoral workers. At times non-sexual abuse surfaces as people become empowered to face reality. Then later on, concrete memories which can be proven may surface. Others continue to feel that it happened but have no clear facts. Symptoms of sexual abuse as listed in various books on this topic cause some to wonder about themselves. Even when there is no memory of abuse they conclude 'I am sexually abused'. This might be one explanation of why the statistics about early child sexual abuse show such variations. The normal drive for revenge pushes people into investigating their past. The fear that other children might still be abused by the same, as yet unknown, person pushes them still harder. The danger is that under these severe psychic pressures an 'answer' is found: the culprit is named. We do want abusers to be caught, be held accountable and where possible helped to change, but the urge to find out facts can actually hinder the healing process which is needed to face the consequences of such a confrontation.

Types of abusers

There are various descriptions of abusers in the professional literature. Most of them focus on male abusers. As we now begin to realise that findings about sexual abuse by female offenders is on the increase, I appreciate Anne L. Horton's descriptions which avoid the gender issue:[16]

(a) the sexually addicted: always searching for new victims;
(b) occasional abusers: people under stress, who relieve their tensions through sexual violence now and then;
(c) opportunists: people who only abuse children when there is a good opportunity.

Incest even in Christian circles

'He was the one who baptised me as a baby. He started to abuse me when I was nine and pronounced the blessing at my confirmation. His hands offered me the cup at Communion and gave me the bread. Now I can no longer sit through a Protestant church service. If I feel a lack of relationship with God, and especially Communion, then I go to the Roman Catholic mass. The priest knows all about it; he is the one I confess to and I'm now gradually beginning to see light at the end of the tunnel.'

'I come from a non-churchgoing family. In my search for the meaning of life, I ended up in a church youth group. The youth leader told me about making a personal choice for Jesus, and I made that choice out of a real sense of conviction. Shortly afterwards, he seduced me. But the biggest blow was when I realised that ALL the other girls in the youth group had the same experience.'

I wish that these were the only stories I had ever heard, because then I could still be justified in thinking, 'Well, there is the occasional criminal exception.' However, there are no research findings which reveal that incest occurs in lesser or greater measure among Christians than in other people. Religion can be used to gloss over or minimise incest. Through religion, an authoritarian atmosphere can also arise whereby parental power is limitless.[17]

The reaction 'It can't be that bad' is understandable. Until recently, the medical/psychiatric world was just as sceptical. But nothing surprises me any more, except the grace of God and the fact that both of the women mentioned above have kept a personal faith in God and through that very faith now help others. It surprises me less that there are many who, because of incest in religious circles, don't want anything more to do with organised religion. But I have only met a very few who are no longer drawn by religion.

Do we really want to know?

There seems to be a pattern: if you don't *want* to know what is going on then sexual abuse, even in the church, will go unnoticed. Pastoral workers who become equipped to help abuse survivors tell me that after their courses and seminars, people just come to them for help. That willingness to consider the painful reality was for me too, a basic condition for getting involved in helping. Until 1985, I had come across two incest cases; since that time, hundreds have followed.

The brief sketches above are merely fragments of the stories of incest survivors, but even this will be shocking to the many who have never known the facts before. What a different world! For incest survivors themselves reading about the experiences of others is a painful reminder of what they have tried to leave behind.

Specific traumatic events or life in an atmosphere of chronic trauma both influence the way we respond to events around us; it colours our life. Military airplanes fly regularly over our town. Children of refugees from Bosnia, who came to a centre close to our town, threw themselves at once under the table . . . Their experiences created a different world than most of us can imagine.

After centuries of silence in both church and secular circles, secular workers have in recent years done much to break the mysterious silence of the 'incest world'. In pastoral work too, we have shut our eyes to this world for too long. Sexual abuse survivors treat the world around them using a different perspective than others. To understand that is one way in which we can help child-sexual abuse survivors. I discovered that again yesterday, as a tearful woman informed me that she needed a divorce. For over a year she had been unable to let her husband touch her. I explained to both of them how normal her inability and his despair were. Naturally they wanted to know what they could do to change. I showed them the way to first learn to understand the lifestyle, the responses, without despising themselves; respect for who they were now, as a starting point for ways to change. We prayed together for a 'missionary gift' for the husband, to be able to cross the invisible barrier to that 'other world' of his wife.

Pastoral helpers can also obey the Great Commission to go into all the world. Jesus gave us the task and the equipment to cross every social and cultural barrier. Those barriers are actually more within ourselves than in the other. We will need eyes to see and a sensitivity to recognise what is going on.[18]

Because of these recognisable patterns of behaviour of abuse survivors, one can speak of a culture of abuse. What that world looks like is the theme of the next chapter.

Notes

1. *Trauma, Dissociatie en Hypnose*, Onno van der Hart (ed.). Smits and Zeitlinger 1991.
2. Berl Kutchinsky, *Nordisk Sexologi*, March 1994, Dansk Psykologisk Forlag.
3. Lev 18:6.
4. Carlotte Davis Kasl (1989), also Ruth Mathews' study about 100 female sex offenders in *LEAR'S* February 1992.
5. Peter Snijders, unpublished doctoral study, University of Utrecht, 1992, quotes Kleber and Brom (1989) who after a review of 25 publications concluded that about 20 to 30 per cent of the persons who experienced a serious psychotrauma, actually develop long-term stress manifestation (Post Traumatic Stress Syndrome), such as sleep problems, intestinal problems, panic reactions, etc.
6. As I have a long-term relationship with the family, I expect that when she becomes romantically involved she will ask for some

more help. Jan Hindman and Beverly James stress how in each developmental period a seriously abused child will probably have a need for re-facing the reality of the past in the light of that life-period. Often I see how abuse survivors have an emotionally more-difficult time when their child enters the age period during which their abuse started.

7. Fear of violent responses of the abuser as well as shame also can make children prisoners of silence. Last week a friend called me to ask advice, as his fourteen-year-old daughter had finally started to tell him about the rape by her physical-education teacher. The man is also a karate specialist and threatened to kill her or a relative, if she talked. For one year she had been too emotionally paralysed to open up to her parents.

8. Mt 19:5, I Cor 6:16.

9. The issue of homosexuality and lesbianism is a complex one. I am not saying that it always is caused by early sexual abuse, only that this is my clinical experience. It is amazing, however, how feminist-oriented writers, who have done so much ground breaking work in the incest-field, so easily refute any meaning to such a connection (as in *The Courage to Heal* by Ellen Bass and Laura Davis).

10. Jan Hindman (1989, 1991) makes a convincing case for uncovering the myth that violence is a significant indicator of trauma. She points out that when an abuser is violent, a child will more easily realise that the abuser is wrong or criminal. It is the gentle and nice abuser who really can confuse a child much more.

11. Nordisk Sexologi 1994: 12:51–61.

12. Marianne Janssen, 'Nine hundred children talk over the 'phone about molestation;' *De Telegraaf*, 4 April 1992. See also John Briere's (1992) landmark study on the common elements of various child-abuse traumas.

13. The American researcher David Finkelhor (in Briere 1992:xii), cites statistics (Sedlak, 1991), which indicate that: 'sexual abuse constitutes only about one-sixth of all child abuse reports, only half the incidence of physical abuse.' Finkelhor also deplores how an over-concentration on sexual abuse diverts research to a very specific and limited area only, rather than to look at the overall impact of childhood abuse on adult life.

14. Frenken and Stolk 1987.

15. Briere (1992) Fossum & Mason 1986.

16. Anne L. Horton et al, 1990.

17. Imbes & Jonker 1991.

18. Phil 1:9.

CHAPTER FOUR

THE CULTURE OF CHILD SEXUAL ABUSE

Culture is common to us all, but how do you define it? What is Dutch culture, or English or American? One of the reasons why recent discussions about integration of immigrants is so problematical is because we find it so hard to define our own culture; what it is and what it is not.

Culture can be seen as the integrated system of learned patterns of behaviour, ideas, and products characteristic of a society.[1] For most of us culture is only what you see on the outside. Less visible are the fundamental norms and values which give shape to our behaviour and ways of life. While our personality is formed, we are spoonfed 'culture' by our parents and those who care for us. The way that they see the world and face reality[2] sets a pattern for us.

Children exposed to an abusive environment at first consider what happens as normal. 'That's just how life was', said Peter to me. 'When Dad came home, one of us would always be beaten up. We did not know better. Only when I was married and discovered from my wife what her normal life had been, did I start to realise that something had gone quite wrong. My automatic responses to her were so macho, it became more and more repulsive to her. Fearing a divorce, I went for help and then discovered how twisted my view on life was.'

Culture, a social fingerprint

The Creator has put laws into creation which make each one of us very unique. The fingerprint is one of the signs of each person being different. There is also an inner urge to indulge and express this kind of uniqueness. An urge for growth, for space and freedom, works as an outward bound centrifugal force. God's original plan was that the whole world should be populated as a result of this inner drive. This centrifugal force is balanced by a magnetic force (more formally called a centripetal force). It binds people together in experience, choice and way of living. Culture experiences both forces: a social glue that keeps a group of people together and a force which fosters diversity. Thus people form new associations, fellowships, businesses, migrate, etc. The two forces at work are also evident when people marry: they leave home and form a new family unit.

Experiencing new things and crossing barriers is usually something we want to share with others. Thus people with the same experience sense an attraction to each other. Businessmen who continually live abroad or caravan-dwellers are all examples of non-localised cultural groups. Those who suffered in concentration camps, or abuse survivors, likewise form a recognisable group because of their experiences.

The binding force of culture is reinforced by rules of rejection: it tells us what is not 'us'. How these forces interact can differ greatly. Because sin came into the world through mankind, culture has also been infected with the power of sin. Thus the culture of a group also becomes twisted by sin. God's creation gift, culture, can then turn into an oppressive group-atmosphere. In this way nationalistic fervour can result in a refusal to allow a marriage with someone from another, hated group. The ethnic struggle in Central Europe teaches us how deeply ingrained these rules of rejection can be. If you compare today's map of Europe with that of eighty years ago, there's not a lot of difference!

The imprint of abuse on a child

Children who grow up in an abusive environment face:

1. Emotional chaos

In the last chapter we saw already how sexual relations create a strong binding influence and how the need to grow away from parents and caretakers is frustrated by the binding force of sexual relations. Ambivalent feelings of disgust and attraction keep them bound to their tormentor like Siamese twins.

2. Emotional deprivation

The Dutch psychiatrist Anna Terruwe identified the Deprivation Neurosis:[3] the result of lack of emotional food and affirmation with the consequent absence of self-worth and lack of emotional growth. Its sufferers manifest many problems which resist traditional psychotherapy.

3. Social deprivation

To prevent others from discovering what is going on, a closed family system evolves, with strong rules about silence and secrecy. The secret world which binds such a family together also hinders a child from absorbing values which they otherwise might observe in others. This increases the effect of the shaping power of parental values.

4. The danger of repeated abuse

A friend of mine was asked to care for a child who had been sexually abused. One night he read her a story. She obviously liked it and made happy sounds. Then she started to grind her little bottom in the lap of her foster-parent. My friend widened his legs, the girl slipped on the floor. As she looked amazed at him, he stated, in a neutral tone: 'We don't do these things', and continued to read!

Abusers often misread children's body language and developing sexuality. They put a meaning on it which the child does not intend. In this case, fortunately there was a wise adult, who knew how to respond. It does show the risks of placing an abused child in a family which has not understood these processes!

5. *The danger of becoming abusers themselves*

The attempt to master a trauma through reliving it over and over again is one way through which abuse survivors get control over their life and emotions. This can also result in actually reliving the child abuse trauma by becoming an abuser! There is also some evidence that victims of *parental* sexual abuse have a greater risk of becoming abusers themselves.[4]

Child sexual abuse and incest create a culture of their own

As feminists started to speak about incest, abuse-survivors started to talk and write about their experiences. When they met each other, there was a sense of affinity.[5] Certain patterns of behaviour emerged. Recognition of the effect of abuse resulted in listing of a variety of symptoms. Medical personnel, psychologists, social workers and teachers were alerted for danger-signals. While it seemed helpful in the beginning, the danger of symptom lists is that many of the medical/psychological symptoms also occur in other problem areas.[6] As a pastor and trainer of lay-counsellors, I realised the need to stay within the pastoral field of knowledge and see if somehow a pattern of behaviour, values and attitudes could be established.[7]

Major landmarks of the culture of abuse

I have found eight landmarks which help me to recognise 'incest country':

1. a survival lifestyle
2. a dysfunctional relationship style
    The American researcher Finkelhor has brought four specific personality adjustments to light.[8]
3. a traumatised perspective of sexuality
4. a pervasive sense of distrust (betrayal)

5. a paralysing sense of powerlessness,
6. a realisation of being markedly different from others (stigmatisation).

   Finkelhor points out that traumatic sexualisation is the major difference between the consequences of incest and those of other severe traumas. The combination of traumatic sexualisation with distrust, powerlessness and stigmatisation reinforces the toxic effect of each of these, ultimately resulting in yet two more major trends in the culture of the abused:
7. a pervasive sense of shame
8. an addictive behaviour.

As we get to know this culture of abuse better, I expect that we will see more specific signs. From a pastoral point of view I have found these of significant use.

Variations in response to the culture of sexual abuse

Male and female responses

Boys often seem to respond differently from girls to early sexual abuse. Boys are often said to act out their frustration, while girls turn inside, causing internal damage to their personalities. I wonder how much of this is cultural conditioning. The high number of incest victims among prostitutes might indicate that there are also many girls who are acting out. Also, the increase in reported abuse by female offenders might suggest that gender is not the most important factor for acting out or turning inside.

Introvert and extrovert aspects

I have found it helpful to differentiate between people who respond as introverts and those who respond as extroverts. The introversion/extroversion factor has to do with the way information is dealt with. Introverts have a quiet, 'inside' way of processing information. They need time to think and reflect before they respond. Extroverts need to talk, to express themselves, in order to think. They process the information outside of themselves in relationship with people or things. Most people are not pure introvert or extrovert, but a mixture of the two, and this can change with circumstances or in the course of time.

We will now look at the eight landmarks of 'incest country'.

1. A survival lifestyle

Problem-focused and emotion-focused ways of coping

The way children cope varies. They learn from their environment, but it also has to do with their personality make-up. The older the child is when it suffers pain, the more it will try to discover ways to cope. Researchers Lazarus and Folkman[9] differentiate between problem-focused and emotion-focused ways of coping. In problem-focused coping, a child attempts to change the situation or the problem (like attempting to wriggle free when an injection is given). In emotion-focused coping, a child attempts to control the outcome of a situation by the use of emotion (like crying, kicking or the anticipation of a promised sweetie). When the situation is overwhelming, a child will tend to choose emotion-focused solutions.

Denial

When problem-focused methods don't work and emotion-focused efforts wear out because of the intensity of a situation, yet another coping mechanism starts to work—denial. One schoolgirl was a normal, effervescent young woman during the daytime, but from the moment she got home she became the second wife of her foster-father. The young girl, who was an orphan, simply switched lifestyles and denied the other reality in order to survive.

Mental absence

Through various 'mental absence' techniques, one can cope better with reality and avoid the pain of memories.[10] When tensions become too high, one's mind wanders off to better places. When such evasions of reality are needed frequently because of the bad circumstances, and fantasy is either too tiresome or insufficient to kill the pain, mental nothingness, staring into emptiness, can be a place of escape. Pastoral volunteers can learn to discern quite early how traumatised persons switch off, escape, split away from reality. When a child cannot escape, it can learn to deny reality and go off in a fantasy world. When lovemaking in adult life brings up ugly memories, one can 'depart' inwardly and, for instance, go shopping, or count the nails on the ceiling or books on the shelf.

Creating your own pain

A survivor can drown the existing pain through intense emotions (self-mutilation, various kinds of addiction, suicidal behaviour, or seeking intense feelings). In time, intense emotions can change into numbness. Pain is bad, not to feel anything is worse! As one girl described it, 'When I slash my arms with a knife, then at least I have the feeling I'm still alive . . .'

Accommodation to the wishes and needs of others

Accommodation to the pressures around is yet another form of survival strategy in abuse survivors. This can be seen as a denial of one's own needs, for the sake of peace, in order to avoid even more serious consequences if one says 'No'. This denial can take an extra twist in committed Christians who, by denial of their personal needs (thus escaping the pain of reality), constantly pour out their lives for others, causing a 'saviour complex'.

Suicidal tendencies

Paradoxically, the battle to survive is often laced with moments of such despair that death can become a temptation. Most incest survivors I know have shared with me how, at one time or another, the will to live was so strong, but living so impossible, that the urge for life slipped into reverse gear and they became suicidal.

Introvert and extrovert responses to a survival lifestyle

Stoic silence as a way to survive is the preferred survivor-style of introverts. This silence can be filled with anything between happy fantasies and dark, inner emptiness. The latter takes the form of a trance-like state in which one loses time. Extroverts often take charge of a situation through noise and laughter. Where introverts tend to accommodate, extroverts become manipulative in order to achieve their goals by any means. Introvert Christians with a survival lifestyle also turn more easily to mystical, inner experiences than do extrovert persons. Extroverts with a survival lifestyle in Christian leadership positions are prone to becoming authoritarian, while introverts tend to let themselves be used and ruled.

2.   A dysfunctional relationship style[11]

Some families are like a tin of spaghetti. The relationships are all enmeshed and the family system is 'canned'; there is no way out. Nor would they know how to get out, even if the tin were to be opened. In such a family system individual development is limited due to vague, unclear relationships and lack of individuality. The lack of boundaries fosters a tendency towards an abuse of power. In some cultures one family member, usually a male, considers it normal to bully the rest of the family. Such abuse can also be very subtle, through quiet manipulation or the use of an illness. In general we can describe such a family as dysfunctional.

When religion is important in a dysfunctional family, even religious values can be used for spiritual abuse. Survivors of sexual abuse within a Christian culture often report that they were forced to co-operate with the abuser, or otherwise God would punish them. There are also non-religious abusers who seem so gentle, so attentive and so involved with others in society, while at home they show a completely different side to their personality.[12] The cover-up of such differences calls for secrecy.

In a healthy functioning family, power is used to the benefit of the whole group. They aim at mutual growth, allowing a balance between individuality and togetherness. To use the words of Jesus: leadership means servanthood.[13] While there can and should be strong convictions, there is an attempt to foster 'unity in diversity', with increasing freedom for individual growth as children grow up, with a warm support (rather than indifference!) to make their own choices.[14] From a biblical point of view, healthy families also have a lot of grace, as they encounter failures or sin with a willingness to forgive oneself or each other when there is a wounding of relationships. Honesty is a strong antidote against dysfunctional patterns in which appearance has a higher value than truth.[15]

Most descriptions of dysfunctional relationship patterns indicate three positions or roles: an abuser, a victim and a helper.[16] The relationship of the abuser to the victim is based on blame, while the victim feels guilty about making the abuser do what he does. The helper faces a sense of pity and enables the victim to continue to suffer the abuse, through the support they give. The victim responds with blame or guilt feelings to other persons, becoming the abuser in a relationship which is manipulative or uses the 'poor me' approach which induces pity and brings action from another enabler in that situation.

When these three roles are the only 'normal' life a child knows, it can be understood that there will be shifts from one position to the other. Thus a child in a divorce situation can turn abusive to one or both parents. The parents, feeling sorry, can feel and act like a victim, allowing the child this abusive role. This model also explains how it is possible that victims of sexual abuse can become abusers themselves, either within the family or with younger children. In time some of them turn into adult molesters of children.[17]

I find the 'three positions' triangle of relationships too limited for pastoral use, as it does not account for the place of the social context of a church community which an abusive family attends. A quadrant of relationships seems to express more what happens in pastoral situations.

If it denies reality or adopts an aloof attitude, a church community can become a part of the problem. Many abuse

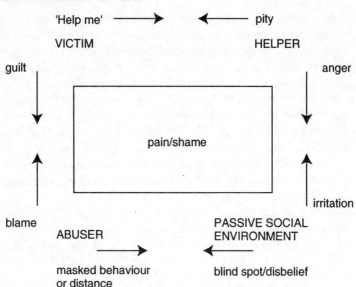

The quadrant of relationships in a church community.

survivors have testified to the fact of how painful it was when important persons in the church refused to hear what they were trying to say. As I stated in my dedication of this book, for a long time the church had no eyes to see or ears to hear what happened to victims of sexual abuse among their members. Usually when it *did* know, there was a lack of courage to act.

It is likely that religious-oriented but abusive families will choose to attend churches where values and customs are abusive as well. Those who prefer social distance will choose churches which are not too intimate. This will help them to keep the family secrets and avoid confrontation with their lifestyle. The social environment can function as a supporter of an abusive family system, such as a Sunday School teacher who observes physical signs of abuse and only prays that the Lord will change things. Or a family doctor who should have seen that the child was in unusual distress, but just prescribes sedatives. But let us not condemn too fast. There are very cunning abusers. One of them went to the pastor to complain about the 'silly stories' his daughter was telling about inappropriate touching by the pastor. Naturally the pastor was upset, but did not speak to the girl about it. When the girl finally broke the secret of the abuse she was suffering from her father, the pastor accused her of 'just making up stories'. The father had effectively pulled the pastor into the dysfunctional relationship system.

Dysfunctionalism: the abuse of power

At the root of the problem in dysfunctional systems is the abuse of power, either brute force or subtle manipulation. The over-powering presence of the abuser makes it difficult for a child to grow up into a mature individual. When we look back again at the relationship quadrant, we can see how the parent-helper position can mean that a mother will attempt to keep the

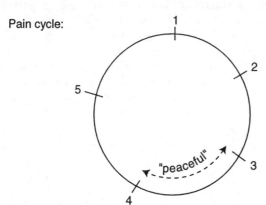

Pain cycle:

1. Warning signs
2. battling and losing
3. abusive behaviour
4. new promises of better behaviour
5. growing inner tension

The period between 3 and 4 is seen as more peaceful by the family

Pim's family cycle of pain.

dysfunctional family going, even if she suspects incest. Where would she turn if she decided to walk out with her children?

Pim, son of an alcoholic mother, once showed a counselling class which I taught his 'family cycle of pain'.

It had become a recurring pattern. The relative quietness of the family was marred by a tense undercurrent. It only appeared to be calm. They all knew that mother was going to drink again. They could almost figure out when she would be back on the bottle again, even without the tell-tale signs(1). The tension would build up as mum was really fighting hard, but losing(2). Then the binge period started(3). Then there followed a period of repentance and sorrow. Mum would ask for forgiveness, pray again, take them to church, tell them to be good. New promises were made and peace was restored briefly(4). Tension grew, as the battle to stay away from the bottle increased(5). Holding up the illustration in the group, Pim asked us when we thought things were most peaceful in the family. Those who guessed correctly were all from dysfunctional family systems. Pim told us 'things became manageable when mum really got drunk. It was awful, but at least the tension was broken. As she sobered up and wallowed in her sorrow, we had only a short time before things became tense again! She would shower us with empty promises.'

Pim felt that he could not take it anymore. Although he was only fourteen, he took the initiative to seek professional help for himself. His mother was very angry about him breaking the secret. He then felt very guilty. That is a normal experience for anyone who attempts to break loose from a dysfunctional relationship. Everything in this abusive relationship system will attempt to keep the old patterns going. 'Yet, I realized that every time Mom was hitting rock bottom, she would count on me to get her out. I had become her crutch. After I asked for professional help, she really went into a depression, but that was also the first time that she even became willing to discuss her problem with a social worker'. In the triangular picture of abuser, victim and helper, the only way out is by becoming the abuser. The girl who starts talking about the abuse is the reason that the family breaks up. That's how the family system looks at it and she feels it too. For many, this open break is not possible. In the quadrant there is yet another exit, perhaps less brave, less radical, but more possible for many, the quiet way out. They can quietly withdraw from the system, through a natural exit; an early marriage or opting for an education or job which makes leaving home a natural event. This was the choice of Albert, the son of an alcoholic father and a victim-mother who suffered much physical abuse. Albert decided to stop being his mother's saviour and left home for an out-of-town job, immediately after graduation from secondary school.

Albert dealt with his past and tried to start a new life with a clean slate by leaving. Pim stayed on, braving the occasional outbursts of his mother for bringing out the dirty family laundry. When he turned eighteen, he too felt he had to leave his parental home. The church he attended knew that he had brought the case to the welfare office. They were less understanding than his pastor. Mothers warned their daughters about Pim, 'He doesn't come from a good nest.' He was branded with a stigma.

Dysfunctional families, from generation to generation

Pim and Albert felt attracted to people with the same background. Albert's wife was an incest victim. Their church suggested that the best thing was to close the door on the past and not to think too much about what had happened to them. He ultimately became an alcoholic.

Dysfunctional churches

'Birds of a feather flock together.' People who grew up in a dysfunctional climate often seek that atmosphere even socially, such as in a church or a group of abusive friends.[18] Albert's church stressed denial of painful realities. Pim couldn't cope in his dysfunctional marriage. Rather than receiving compassion, he was reprimanded when it appeared that the marriage was breaking up.

In dysfunctional churches, there is often a good chance for those who seek sex with children to become trusted people who can easily get close to children. Members of dysfunctional churches often have an authoritarian style of family life. This frequently results in either a less well-developed sense of self-worth and will development, or it creates an emotional vacuum which the child attempts to find in someone else. Both aspects work in an abuser's favour!

Dysfunctionalism: conditional love

Manipulation is the lifeblood of a dysfunctional relationship and it turns expressions of love into a barter arrangement: 'If you do this for me, I will do that for you.' This gives some the idea of their 'right' for sexual gratification, even by using a child! The next morning the girl finds money in her coat pocket. 'I can't imagine how I could, but I used it, Teo. I just accepted it'.

Dysfunctionalism: lack of boundaries

A dysfunctional family is like a house with thin walls. Whatever happens in the other rooms (the lives of the people in the family) influences the others deeply. The unwritten rule is then that one should feel what is expected without having to be told.

Dysfunctional development of the will

Abuse survivors often show signs of suffering from a will-power problem. They developed their will in pleasing others. A selectively-developed will develops in situations where a child managed to do exactly what they wanted in particular areas, but had to submit completely in incest situations. I know of incest survivors who, as long as they gave in, were able to wind the abuser round their little fingers in other matters.

The broken will occurs where a child experienced a normal development of the will as a toddler, but later on became involved in an incest situation. They are aware of the possibility of their own will, but they cannot exercise it, as any attempt to use the will is crushed again and again. Some who are in a healing phase appear to be hard, stubborn and rebellious. Each of these forms of will development has to do with the urge to survive.

Dysfunctional families and those helping them

Being sensitive to the needs of a client can make a helper very soon feel that he or she is responsible for the well-being of the person seeking help. It can also be satisfying to be needed. One question has helped me to deal with the emotional pressure of having to 'do' something to alleviate a situation: 'Whose problem is this anyhow?' What should they do; what are the limits of my responsibility? It is here that teamwork becomes very important. Teaching pastoral volunteers to respond in such situations, I have learned that giving right principles to avoid such dysfunctional traps is not enough. One needs a different attitude, which is the opposite of the power abuse; a spirit of servanthood.[19] Such an attitude becomes the fountain from which the right actions can flow.

Introvert and extrovert responses to a dysfunctional relationship style

I have the impression that dysfunctionalism tends to create extreme 'will' responses. Obviously, an extrovert, because of the expressiveness of that personality trait, will either be in constant trouble, or they will try habitually to create an atmosphere of normality and to cover things up through jokes, excitement and activity. The quiet introvert can become even more silent, or turn deliberately extrovert, but this is a kind of acting. That is what happened to me on a missionary retreat in Saigon in 1972. During some of the sessions there was a powerful manifestation of the Holy Spirit. It was then that I discovered a quiet, even shy side to myself, and noted how the extroversion evaporated. I will never forget how at the same time some rather quiet and dignified missionaries turned pretty extrovert!

3. Traumatic sexualisation

The growth of the sexual identity and sexuality of a child takes time. The natural process is cruelly interrupted through incest. Much preparation is needed before the seduction of a child can succeed; the child mustn't give the game away, the right time and place have to be found, the breaking of the natural taboo in both abuser and child takes time, etc. The incestuous abuser does not therefore cross barriers immediately. There is a vague no-man's-land between a normal hug with the right feelings and a touch which produces shame. The moment comes, however, when the child knows 'This isn't right.' But by that time it's often too late. The child within is, as it were, 'killed' and an adult experience of sexuality now determines the further development of the child. You can view this as a gauge; the setting of the sexual thermostat in a negative framework. Sexual feelings and negative aggression forge a link. At a later age, a friendly embrace with strong arms from a boyfriend suddenly can cause a wave of nausea.

Introvert and extrovert responses to traumatic sexualisation

Both introvert and extrovert survivors often have problems with deeper relationships. Introvert people react by taking a more reticent approach to sex. This can have its effect at school, in forming friendships and love-relationships. The body is seen as an enemy. The natural physical responses produced by sexual stimulation are often seen as betrayal of the body: 'My body did what I didn't want!' Extrovert people can respond in exactly the opposite way. The earlier breaking through of the natural 'shame' boundaries can mean that they don't realise when those boundaries are being crossed again. Or a person goes further than he or she actually wants. Such a person often gives confusing signals to the outside world. This can be expressed, for instance, in indecent clothing and behaviour and in the continual need for sexual experiences.

As a child's awareness of sexual identity develops during the maturation process, problems can arise regarding sexual preference. If abuse took place, then I would tend to believe that the child did not have a chance to choose.[20]

4. Betrayal

A child needs trustworthy people in its growth towards adult-hood. Sexual border-crossing by an abuser is a betrayal of that trust. People in authority have turned out to be untrustworthy. Distrust of adults is thus common sense!

Introvert and extrovert responses to betrayal

Trust and encouragement from care-givers in the growing years of a child are needed in order to cultivate a healthy self-confidence as well as a healthy distrust. Not everyone can be trusted! The pain of the loss of trust often causes an abnormal need for privacy. Introvert incest survivors often appear shy, stand-offish and distrustful. Fearing loneliness, the intuitive warning signals are ignored. Then they enter into the most unlikely relationships! Extrovert survivors can react in exactly the opposite way and display a 'what does it matter' attitude, or danger signals can cause excitement and overconfidence: 'I can handle this'. Excessive self-confidence can lead to one dis-appointment after another, and ultimately to great uncertainty. Extrovert survivors watch carefully what happens around them, and in childhood this mental alertness can help them to get good marks at school. Driven by fear of failure, quite a few abuse survivors I helped lost their drive for studies as a result of the new freedom they found. It took time to find positive reasons to pick up the studies again.

Introverts deal with emotional tensions and uncertainties by freezing their feelings, and/or transferring their attention to safer topics. The extroverts are forever taking on new projects but have difficulty in persevering with them. Introvert incest survivors have a tendency either to keep their distance from people in authority or seek them out! The latter may be because they need someone who is wise and who gives the strong leadership that they lacked as a child. Extrovert survivors see people in authority as a challenge and are thus often considered rebellious. This rebellion may be a desperate attempt to say 'no'—something they were not in a position to do as a child.

Driven by a need to maintain control, relationships often

suffer. When control becomes impossible in a relationship, they distance themselves. Then the relationship is either broken off or there is a fierce, but often illogical, conflict. The need for control is often seen by others as a critical attitude. As I teach this in my courses many a pastor has suddenly understood some of the painful conflicts with their church members.

5. Powerlessness

The physical/sexual feelings, the emotions produced by betrayal, the threat of violence, the fear of discovery by others, the fear of pregnancy in the older child, the intense sense of shame together are overwhelming. This increases the sense of powerlessness to stop what is going on. A 'learned powerlessness' grows: whatever you try, it doesn't change the situation. The victim, in an effort to survive, gives up all resistance and allows anything to happen. Even if the child could, in fact, run away, it doesn't.

The need to avoid conflict can even result in the child shadowing the abuser and actually copying all that he or she does. In this way, abusive character traits can also be taken on. Sexual abuse is violence expressed in a sexual way. This may also produce criminal behaviour in survivors who have not dealt with their past.

There may also be a link between the powerlessness of abuse survivors and deeply-ingrained feelings of guilt. Some researchers believe that this powerlessness is unbearable for a child, and that 'power fantasies' can therefore arise, indeed, that they are common. Within such a fantasy the child victim will often think up schemes to punish the abuser. They then choose to be 'better' than the abuser by not using this feeling of power; by not acting. This false sense of power creates a pervasive sense of guilt; 'I could have stopped him.'[21]

An exaggerated sense of responsibility can often be observed in adult survivors of childhood abuse. Children, by nature, think all too easily that they are the cause of any problems their carers have, and incest survivors experience that even more acutely.

Abusers often tell a child 'You're so beautiful; that's why I have these feelings', so some survivors may try not to be beautiful by over-eating. Others, possibly in an attempt not to mature physically, curb their growth by eating far too little. If we remove that exaggerated sense of responsibility by pointing out that the abuser is solely responsible, then we are left with a dilemma. A sense of responsibility is part of a normal self-consciousness. If you are not responsible, does that mean you're a nobody?

Introvert and extrovert responses to powerlessness

Introverts often react like puppets. In this way they try to avoid tension as far as possible. That doesn't always work, and in that case, their aggression turns inward. An introvert abuse survivor can quietly brood about the possibility of suicide. The more extrovert survivors might be more expressive, finding ways of venting their aggression by taking it out in open self-destruction or being destructive to others.

6. Stigmatisation

The feeling of being different from the others is one of the characteristics of a survivor. A deep feeling of shame can reinforce the loneliness normally experienced by modern man, including children. This 'being different' reinforces a natural feeling of shame. To know that you have been 'used' sexually greatly decreases your loss of self-esteem. I have had to counsel couples who had real compatibility problems. The loss of self-esteem had made a victim choose to marry 'below their class', as if they are 'damaged goods' which can be sold at a reduction! That again can cause problems during the time of healing. They wonder, 'What have I done? Why did I marry him/her? If only I had married someone else . . .' And because partners do not understand the incest culture and the marriage isn't going so well anyway, the chance of divorce is high.

In order to escape the tension of stigmatisation, survivors sometimes deny facts about the past or explain them away as fantasy. This denial can be conscious (the price of confrontation is too high) or unconscious (the pain is too great). The other extreme is an opposite reaction whereby they cannot let go of the past. Their whole personality is then based on their incest experience and healing would mean the need to lose the security of their old identity.

Introvert and extrovert responses to stigmatisation

Introverts often seek isolation, in order to keep their own lives under control and to prevent power abuse. Extroverts can react in the opposite way and draw attention to their being different by weird behaviour.

7. A pervasive sense of shame

Fossum and Mason state that 'a pervasive sense of shame is the ongoing premise that one is fundamentally bad, inadequate, defective, unworthy, or not fully valid as a human being'. They distinguish between guilt and shame. Guilt they define as the more mature response of regret due to failure of personal values.[22]

The feelings of shame which come because of sexual violation or incest are not the same for every seeker of help. How people respond seems to relate to the size of a 'reservoir of shame': the feelings of shame gained through cultural values, through transfer from generation to generation, or through personally-felt failures. Abuse victims have often such intense feelings of shame and guilt that we need to look into this with more detail.

Cultural shame: a husband in some parts of Latin America cannot hang the washing outside when his wife is ill. He needs to ask a lady neighbour to do this for him.

Family shame: families can be gripped by an intense feeling of shame. Becoming pregnant before an official wedding was for a long time a terrible experience in strict Calvinistic circles. Such parents often have a relationship problem, because that child reminds them of the deep sense of public shame.

Personal shame: to be 'a child of shame' can cause a deep personal sense of shame. An individual shame can also occur when a person does not measure up to their own standards. In Asia I was introduced to a whole new experience: young people who failed their exams and were unable to face the outside world. Some would lock themselves inside the home, sometimes for years, refusing to meet anyone. Others would run away or choose a whole new set of friends.

Guilt has to do with the judgement by others or oneself. From a biblical point of view there is true guilt, condemnation based on biblical values; and false guilt, where other values play a role. When the apostle Peter was eating with heathen, he hastily left the table when legalistic Jews came in. They would condemn his behaviour, a clear example of cultural guilt feelings.

The power of shame

I believe that the power of shame can be so strong because it is linked to a basic element of creation: to be a person, to have an identity. This identity had boundaries in the Garden of Eden, with the potential for illegal border crossing and the need to resist this. Several defence mechanisms were dormant, among them a natural shyness and the ability to feel pain. After the fall of Adam and Eve, these defence mechanisms were activated. Becoming aware of the male and female differences, shame and pain were activated. Fossum and Mason aptly call shame 'a deep pain in the soul', when we have been seen weak and fragile, and experienced rejection, scorn, humiliation. For Adam and Eve a new need arose; to hide their deepest selves. New problems came into being; they had to decide to choose to share their lives, to unite their two individual worlds, to deny that between them there were boundaries. It was a choice to 'uncover' in private, an intimate relationship, which is not to be seen by others. The privacy of these moments creates an extra bond. This choice to be bonded, or as Luke describes the words of Jesus 'to be glued together' is one of the fundamental forces in creation which influence relationships. When such natural boundaries are violated, the natural reticence is wounded;

shame feelings take over.[23] 'We don't discuss the dirty laundry with outsiders' said the mother when father was released from jail and they moved to another part of the country. 'It is nobody's business what happened. Dad had his punishment; if people know he won't get work'. The young boy understands and obeys; he learns a new pattern: shame-avoiding behaviour. Later he tells his son the same principle: 'don't talk to outsiders about family matters'. From generation to generation, shame-avoidant behaviour becomes a pattern.

The power of shame in sexual abuse survivors

I believe that survivors of sexual abuse have a special problem with shame:

a) Even small children can have a sense of shame. The first forms of shame are not sexual: that seems to start at about school age. Before this a child can feel a sense of shame when it becomes the centre of attention or suddenly discovers that someone is looking.[24] Shame in a child can also result from a sense of natural inadequacy when it compares itself with adults. Then feelings of shame have a developmental reason. When a child is sexually abused, a marked lack of emotional growth is often the result. As an adult, the 'wounded child within' continues to carry these developmental shame feelings; even when the mind tells them that nothing is wrong, they *feel* that they are wrong.

b) When an abused person also grows up with the understanding that we are persons unworthy before God, the spiritual shame becomes even a greater burden.[25] Abused persons often have a strong need for privacy. Some therefore are bothered by the idea that 'God sees everything'! As Christianity also teaches personal responsibility, this can cause deep problems. Unable to separate the responsibility of the abuser with personal responsibility, strong feelings of guilt result. At times pastoral counsellors can mess things up even more, by inducing feelings of guilt in survivors.[26]

c) When growing up in a survival and dysfunctional lifestyle the difference from other families can cause a deep shame. The need to keep some dignity forces people to hide the truth. If a person also has a traumatised perspective of sexuality, the combination of psychological, social, emotional and spiritual effects of shame create a toxic potion which invades the whole personality. This sense of shame involves the body in a special way.[27] It seems to me as if shame settles in every cell of one's body. This observation has led me to seek pastoral methods that touch the whole personality as well as the body.

8.   Addictive behaviour and shame

The intense shame experiences of abuse survivors call for drastic ways to avoid the shame. When something does take away that feeling of shame even for a moment, then this gives a great release. Fossum and Mason show how this relief lays at the root of addictive behaviour. The hidden reservoir of shame plays a role here. It can be filled with shame from former generations. A woman who asked for help finally understood why she had reportedly suffered intense shame responses from birth: she discovered that her father was also her grandfather.

An accumulation of unwise acts, disappointments and failures can all add to our shame-reservoir. Then a single shame-causing event takes place, wounding the soul. That happened to me when I was seven. There were many festivities in our village when Juliana became our new queen. I was known to be the fastest runner in my age group. I knew I was going to get the first prize in the 100 metre dash. After only a few seconds I was far ahead of the others. Then the elastic of my shorts broke. The watching crowd roared with laughter. Grabbing my pants I raced on and came second. For many years I have battled with an urge to check my belt when I stand up in public. The shame event and the laughter of the crowd had resulted in automatism: crowd, feeling of shame, checking my belt! Now I also know why I experienced such an intense reaction. There was at that time quite a hidden reservoir of shame as my family had suffered public humiliation for a variety of reasons. This is only a simple example of how addictions grow. As I work as chaplain to the staff of a Christian Psychiatric Hospital for Addictive Behaviour, it has become increasingly clear how shame and addictions are linked.

Recognition of the culture of sexual abuse, but no memories or facts

In Chapter Three I mentioned how there are many people who tell me that they recognise many of the symptoms which I describe, but do not recall abusive events. This absence of clear memories leads to a lot of uncertainty. It can result in either searching desperately for facts, or doubts about the reliability of their own feelings; 'I must be imagining this'.

One possible explanation for these feelings can be a transfer of the shame-avoiding behaviour mentioned above and abusive values from generation to generation.[28] 'Now that I am older and have a daughter myself, I realise that Mom always had a sharp edge to her voice when she detected some improper behaviour. Once I was playing with my dolls. Suddenly she walked up to me and shouted "close the book", pushing my legs together. I was exposing myself. This "close the book" became a secret signal anytime she thought I was careless. Now I realise that a lot of feelings of shame came from her own fear that I would be abused as well.' Such parental behaviour can cause second generation incest victims: a person who has not actually been a victim can take on the feelings of a parent or other close relative.[29]

I have found that this has helped people who feel that they have had sexual abuse experiences, but have no recollection of facts. The explanation of a possible trans-generational incest can prevent a person from suspiciously combing the past and viewing the normal affection of parents or carers as incest! The feeling of abuse can then be given attention, while the absence of clear facts can be left alone. The pastoral approach to sexual abuse will be the same anyhow, whether facts are uncovered, or none ever at all. My experience in helping abuse survivors does show that this approach can lead 'in time' to factual recollection as memories surface after wounded emotions have been healed and abuse-affected behaviour changed. This healing empowers a person to let suppressed issues come to the surface. I have found that the preoccupation of such persons with the 'who, what and where' is not helpful in the healing process. As I stated before, it can actually make the bonding with the abuser even stronger. To place feelings before facts in these situations means also that one can start with the healing process straight away.

Giving priority to the feelings experienced by a seeker of help also gives them a greater sense of power. The facts can't be changed, but how I feel about life and how I choose a different behaviour is within reach. The explanation of second-generation incest could also point to one of the causes why abuse victims can become offenders. The dysfunctional, abusive values have been internalised from youth. When other factors become involved (alcoholism, high stress, resentment, etc.) abusive potential in an abuse victim is more easily awakened than in people who do not have such a dysfunctional background. Just as children of alcoholics know that they should be careful with alcohol, those who grow up in a sexually abusive environment should understand how the culture of abuse has affected them. They can also be prime candidates for becoming great pastoral volunteers, helping those who did experience abuse as well as offenders. After all, the gospel gives us hope for both.

Abuse survivors and offenders are 'hidden people'. They need those who dare to cross cultural borders. That was the example of Jesus as well as the challenge he gave to his Church. How this can be done is the subject of the next chapter.

Notes

1. Hiebert, 1986.
2. Berger and Luckman (1966).
3. Conrad W. Baars and Anna Terruwe; *Healing the Unaffirmed, Recognizing Deprivation Neurosis*. Alba House, New York, 1976. They recommend an affirmation therapy, which keeps in mind

that the person lives in two worlds: the actual world outside with all their responsibilities, and the inner world of the unaffirmed child. They developed affirmation techniques including behaviour which normally they would have wanted to do as a child. I only started to read about the work of Dr Terruwe during the final editing of this manuscript. What fascinates me is the fact that she sees a definite difference in the way that female sufferers of Deprivation Neurosis need wise physical touch, while younger male patients need more 'verbal touching'. In the chapter on the Practice of Powerful Peace I will indicate how this experience of a physical touch can also happen through a spiritual encounter with the peace of God.

4. *Lear's Magazine*, Feb. 1992.
5. This is one factor behind the success of the Incest Support Centres in Norway, which stress the need of survivors helping survivors. 'Not the specialist who comes with the power of head-knowledge, but a specialist with the knowledge of experience meeting another.'
6. Frequent lumbar backache, general feeling of tension in the body, insomnia and the accompanying tiredness, reduced appetite. Sometimes loss of smell-sensitivity, the feeling of a band around the neck, problems with touch. Displacement-eating (the creation of pleasant feelings through eating, accompanied in some people by the need to vomit intentionally so as not to get fat). Or the opposite: purposely staying thin by eating little. A feeling of uneasiness when someone stands behind you. A 'dirty' feeling, and the need to wash constantly (hands, abdomen). Insecurity, few personal barriers. Loss of memory, forgetting specific periods of one's life. Problems on hearing male runners panting (similar to when the abuser was sexually aroused). A continual feeling of tension in the stomach, insomnia, vague fears, nightmares, anxiety. Addictive behaviour, including religious addiction.

   Suicidal behaviour without concrete suicide plans and a reckless lifestyle are also often mentioned. One wonders if reckless behaviour in young people, for example in sexual relationships or in traffic, should always be attributed to inexperience or carelessness. These doubts are reinforced by my experience with active Christians, where I sometimes also meet with reckless behaviour, along with an attitude of 'Well, if anything happens to me, I'm going to heaven anyway.' Death is mistakenly considered to be a silent friend who waits in the wings, not as an enemy who must be unmasked and ultimately destroyed (I Cor. 15:26). In the grave, we cannot praise God (Ps. 115:17). Premature death, brought about be recklessness, cuts short the fulfilment of God's plan in us.

7. Pastoral volunteers can learn to recognise the symptoms of depression, suicidal tendencies, insomnia, phobias etc. The question is: what do you do with this information? For counsellors without a training in psychology, I believe the approach of 'incest as culture' gives points of contact. Learning to observe and analyse cultural patterns corresponds more with our own experience, as well as a biblical mandate (Rom. 12:1, 2). The study of incest, then, can be along the lines of viewing the incest culture as a cohesive unity of origin, personality, living and working situations, as well as religious conviction and a person's dreams (or nightmares!). This approach also requires less theoretical knowledge to achieve good results anyway. The cultural key is easier to use than working with psychological concepts and therapies.

8. Finkelhor, David. *A Sourcebook on Child Sexual Abuse*, Sage Publications, London 1986.

9. Christine Eiser 1990.

10. Carol Poston describes very lucidly the phenomenon of 'being absent' in *Surviving Incest* (Poston & Lison 1990). Ensink (1992) and Putnam (1989) indicate to what extent this can have an effect in distorting daily life and disintegrating the personality. An extremely moving account can be found in *Courage to Heal* (Bass & Davis 1988), where Annette describes how, as a child and a believer in Jesus, she survived satanic rituals.

11. Charlotte Davis Kasl gives some very helpful observations about 'what successful couples seem to know' (1989: 143–148). She gives a good picture of what is not dysfunctional and this can help us to face the impact of dysfunctionalism even better.
    1. Functional couples had adult models of caring relationships.
    2. Successful couples maintain separate identities.
    3. They view their marriage or partnership in terms of 'us'.
    4. Although they do everything they can do to make relationship work, they know they can survive without it.
    5. They accept change in themselves and their partners.
    6. They maintain basic trust.
    7. They have a sense of humour about themselves.

    Healthy couples listen to each other, think about what their partners tell them, take what they heard to heart, and make changes.
    8. They have the ability to say: 'I made a mistake, I am sorry'.
    9. They expect and weather hard times.
    10. Sex flows from a caring bond.
    11. Sex is a barometer, not a thermometer, of the relationship.
    12. Sex books and props are not generally used.
    13. The relationship gets priority time.

14. They try to make decisions to please both partners.

15. They are involved in some form of service to others.

12. Barbara Oliver's story in *The Healing Relationship*, (with Marsha Utain) 1991, and the landmark study of Dutch authors Imbes & Jonker in *Godsdienst en Incest* shows us that non-religious abusers can also appear very motivated to be socially or politically active.

13. Mark 10:44.

14. See also Malachi 4:6 where the prophet indicates that a country can not continue to exist unless there are heart-relationships between parents and children. It is in the family where this should be 'caught', by example and taught through loving correction. The initiative for such heart-relationships and the responsibility to initiate this is with the parents. Lack of heart-food results too often in persons with an adult body, but a retarded emotional growth. Increasingly this seems to become the major pastoral problem: adult bodies with infantile development in the area of personal responsibility and the experience of adult emotions.

15. The healing power of truth is also affirmed by William Glasser in his approach to Reality Therapy and May's provocative study on addictive behaviour: *Addiction and Grace*.

16. Various studies show this interaction in the form of a triangle. I was greatly helped in my understanding by the work of Utain and Hindman, as referred to in the literature list.

17. The *LEARS Magazine* report quoted earlier indicated that when the parents are the abusers, a child has a higher risk of becoming themselves abusers. This can be explained by the fact that the damage done through broken trust and the patterns set by parents are so much deeper than when a 'kind uncle' (or aunt), outside the direct family circle is involved.

18. Arterburn & Felton, (1991) and Johnson & Van Vonderen (1992) give many examples of how dysfunctional churches attract dysfunctional persons, but also how dysfunctional leadership creates and needs dysfunctional systems for itself. The authors give many practical suggestions of what can be done to escape the oppressive atmosphere without throwing one's personal faith overboard.

19. Phil 2:1–5.

20. Traditional committed Christians with homosexual or lesbian tendencies have a hard time with the words of the apostle Paul in Romans 1, about homosexuality and lesbianism. Paul does describe a reality in his day which I believe is still the case today: there are people who worship creation rather than the Creator himself. The idea which Paul seems to convey is that when one slips from Creator to creation worship, one is actually 'loving those who are like you, created beings', thus one worships

one's own kind. Down that slippery slope, it results in an inability to have a love relationship with someone of the other sex. It appears to me that the tension which there is and will be in an intimate relationship between Creator and creation is related to our ability to stand the tension between intimate male and female relationships. Those traditional believers I have met who have self-stated confused feelings and questions about their sexual orientation, are NOT for the most part worshipping creation as the highest, but have chosen to worship the living God. Whatever the source of their need, it is something different from homosexuality as in Romans 1:26–7.

21. According to Nicolai as quoted by Snijders, Peter *Incest, enkele aspekten en demensies*, unpublished doctoral thesis, University of Utrecht 1992.

22. Fossum, Merle A. and Mason, Marilyn J. *Facing Shame, Families in Recovery*, Norton & Co, London, New York 1986.

23. The link between shame, pain and boundaries can also be seen in the intense reactions which cause war. The uninvited crossing of borders causes a national outrage. The same is true with the current problems people feel as massive numbers of migrants settle. New cultures, new smells of cooking and different lifestyles invade the normal experience.

24. *Encyclopedie van het Christendom*, Katholiek deel, Elsevier 1954.

25. Sandra Wilson (1990) sees biological shame as the natural response of observing the difference between a child and an adult. The binding shame is the feeling of inadequacy which parents affirm in children through blaming, lack of affirmation, or other forms of abusive treatment. The biblical shame is seen by her as 'a healthy response' due to the differences between God and us and our separation through sin. I have trouble with the phrase 'biblical shame', as shame itself has elements which are destructive. The 'fear of the Lord' might be a better expression to stress the awareness of the fundamental difference between us and our Creator. A biblically healthy response to shame is the immediate coupling of shame with grace, resulting in an absence of shame feelings.

26. Some pastoral counsellors stress repentance in order to be able to meet God. Thus the fact that a child responds with anger to an abuser, or has thoughts of hate and a desire to kill, is pronounced as guilt and then the victim has to ask for forgiveness. I find such a stress on personal guilt quite abusive and a travesty of the gospel. The manifestation of the kingdom of God precedes repentance (Mark 1:15). Abuse survivors need to meet first the 'goodness of God which can lead to repentance' (Rom 2:4). The conviction that

they did anything wrong demanding confession should grow out of that personal relationship with a gracious God.

27. 1 Cor 6:18 indicates the effect of sexual sins: also when there is sin against a person, the impact of what happens is also quite intense.

28. This doesn't mean that every incest survivor automatically has to turn into an abuser. Less than 50 per cent of known abusers report that they were abused in childhood. If the father or the mother is the abuser (rather than other carers), this incidence shoots up much higher. Finkelhor (1992) reports that 70 per cent of the male offenders he studied knew that they were abused as a child. Of those, 50 per cent had been abused by the father and an astounding 44 per cent by the mother! See Finkelhor in *Lear's Magazine*, February 1992.

29. A similar phenomenon has been recognised in children who were born after their parents were released from concentration camp after World War II.

CHAPTER FIVE

MISSIONARIES IN THE CULTURE OF ABUSE

When western tourists go to Third World countries, the impact of unfamiliar sounds, smells, customs and social conditions can be quite a shock. An air-conditioned bus and hotel windows will provide some protection. From such a safe distance it is easy to have pity. We can even become experts in watching. Arriving in the 'Culture of Abuse' can cause similar experiences. We can watch through our 'cultural bubble'. We seem so close, yet we don't touch the real issues.

Cross-cultural understanding

Biblical concepts need to be translated into the heart-language and culture of people. Translation is more than just finding words of equal value. It is also the search for concepts which have the same effect on the readers now as the effect then. Also the way we behave might fully express biblical values in one culture, yet the same behaviour in another culture might be offensive.

Sharing the gospel with abuse survivors likewise calls for understanding of the deep feelings which certain behaviours, concepts and words can create. A friendly embrace, now so common in my country, can freeze an incest victim. When the father is the perpetrator, the idea of God as father easily causes revulsion. To use the word 'Father' for God in prayer might make one cringe.[1] If abuse survivors have problems with God as father or Jesus as a male person, I usually suggest they think of the image of a dove. After all, the presence of God was manifested to Jesus in that way after his baptism in the Jordan. Missionaries and new believers together learn what the Word means, and how that meaning is made practical in that specific culture.

The great missionary Paul showed us a way. His letters to different people in different cultures repeat core-issues which he finds important. Working with abuse survivors I too had to find new ways of communicating and use a picture language which would make sense to them. Concepts which make incest victims cringe, such as the 'father' idea, or the words 'forgiveness' and 'honour your parents', needed to be recast in ways that do not lose their original meaning. In my approach I have attempted to use some of those core-issues which the apostle Paul seems to have used as a foundational undertone in all his writings. Although there are more such 'biblical anchors' than I can share in this book, the most important ones which I have used are concepts such as grace, obedience, peace, the 'rest in God', Maranatha, 'in Christ', forgiveness and 'unity in diversity'.

Grace and peace. In the introduction to each of Paul's pastoral epistles, we find the heart of his pastoral approach. The fact that all his letters start with a similar phrase shows us its importance: 'Grace and peace to you from God our Father, and the Lord Jesus Christ.'

Grace is an expression of God's goodness which we receive but cannot earn. The linguistic relationship between the words 'grace' and 'laughter' also make it possible to translate 'grace' as 'God who smiles'. Grace is also linked to the understanding that we are responsible for our behaviour and that there are consequences of what we do. Grace means that Jesus has taken the consequences of our failures and sin. This binds grace to the message of the cross. It also helps us to have another look at suffering.[2] Through grace there is room for the heartcry. 'Where was God, when this all happened? Why didn't he stop my father from abusing me, when I asked him to intervene? How can he be almighty and let me suffer like this?'[3] Grace is also linked to the resurrection of Jesus. The video-tape of our memory of abuse experiences can be recorded with another experience: the same power which raised Jesus from the dead is at work in our mortal bodies.[4] I myself still face the consequences of past events in my life. It helped me to accept this when I realised that the marks of wounds were not taken away from Jesus when he was resurrected. The burden 'nobody knows the trouble I have seen . . .' can become lighter because Jesus is alive and well, praying for us with outstretched wounded hands.[5] Through this, Jesus shows us his solidarity with us. He is waiting for us until we are all together, before the physical marks of his sufferings fade out and the glory of God will be the central focus of our attention.[6] Grace seems even to be needed for the saints in the New Jerusalem, who now can experience God as he is. They must have noticed the pain in the heart of God because of the suffering of his children. They wonder how long he still can be gracious before he avenges them.[7] This stress on grace, the unconditional love of God, is a help for survivors who have lost trust, who know mentally that they are not guilty, but who carry emotionally a sense of badness and feel alienated from their bodies. Rather than trying to continue to 'brain wash' them from the lies of abusers, another truth can become stronger and touch them deeper: God smiles at me!

Obedience. There is a strong relationship between grace and obedience, our loyal response to this goodness of God. This link must be stressed, because obedience is a tough word for survivors. With the painful experiences of the breaking of their will in the abusive past, grace becomes a healing agent: God expects and allows us to make our own choices. Then he graciously gives us the power to do what we choose to do.[8] It is here that the words of Jesus to the disciples, 'teach them to obey', show his insight into the human condition. Obedience can only be learned, and one needs grace to achieve it.

The peace of God. The peace of God is something he longs to give us as a free gift. The war with our Creator can come to an end. This peace is not the absence of war, nor just a pleasant, calm feeling, but an expression of the presence of God. Peace is not 'it' but 'him', a person. Jesus is our peace. Through a personal relationship with Jesus we can experience the fruits of peace, but there is also such a thing as the gift of peace. Just as Jesus sent his disciples out with the greeting of peace, the Shalom blessing,[9] we can bless one another in the same way, or wish them well. As a 'royal priesthood' (1 Pet 2:9) it is our task to be a force for blessing in the world. This truth had a tremendous effect on the self-image of the believers in Paul's day. A slave could be a royal child. That new outlook changed their perspective on their own lives and those of others. They were on a mission, roving ambassadors of another kingdom! They proclaimed that war between God and man is unnecessary. They themselves were called to manifest this kingdom reality with 'grace and peace'.

Rest in God. The writer to the Hebrews challenges everyone to seek that attitude, to live with an inner tranquillity, never mind what happens: a 'rest in God'.[10] Such an attitude empowers abuse survivors to relive the pain of the past. It is this rest in God which I see as a biblical answer to what others try to achieve through hypnotic means: the creation of a 'safe place inside us'.[11] Rather than using such approaches, pastoral workers have powerful metaphors and tested truth to help an abuse victim to come to an inner rest, the Shalom of the kingdom.

Maranatha. The word 'Maranatha' highlights an important part of the message of Jesus: the kingdom of God. Closely linked with this kingdom message was the expectation of the coming King, and a strong emphasis on experiencing the presence of God. Maranatha has a double meaning: a prayer 'Come, O Lord,' and an expression of faith, 'The Lord is coming back!' In both cases the stress is on the coming of Jesus, both in our situation now and also later, to bring justice and righteousness.[12] The importance of Maranatha can be seen in the way that this word has been retained in the liturgy of the early church. The meaning is deepened when we study the development of its use. In Old Testament times the king would travel through the land to dispense justice where needed. A herald would go before him, blowing the trumpet, warning the people 'The King is coming'. Then the roads would have to be prepared, the holes blown by wind and rain would be filled. The stones, once thrown away as the field was cleared for sowing, needed to be removed. The king could actually see and feel how obedient people were by the smoothness of the road. Those who were mistreated were waiting for the king. Others would encourage them and say 'The King will come, there will be justice'. It is in this context of conflict that the apostle Paul uses this Aramaic word 'Maranatha' in his letter to the Corinthians.[13] The message of ultimate justice helps survivors not to despair too much. There will be a final accounting. God will avenge!

The use of Maranatha in New Testament times also indicates the intensity of the expectancy of believers that Jesus would be with them, as he promised, even though they would not always see him.[14] He gave power, authority, special gifts and even special signs and wonders, in order to lend power to the pro-clamation.[15] The fact that his kingdom did not become visible at once was, I believe, less disappointing for those believers than some theologians today think. After all, they had the possibility of a manifestation of Jesus, through united prayer, in one form or another.[16] How they would experience this would also be related to the cultural setting in which they lived. We still see that today. African believers often are moved to dance. The youth culture is moving away from verbal expression to a video-clip culture of a massive barrage of sound, spectacular visual impressions and movements. Other cultures prefer silence.

In Christ. As experiencing God is also a very subjective matter, we need some form of evaluation. How do we know that it is truly God and not our own imagination, or even worse, a manifestation of the adversary of God?[17] Pastoral counselling needs a solid theology of 'experiencing God', as the healing process of sexual abuse involves emotions and physical aspects as well. The apostle Paul used the 'in Christ' concept to give our experience of faith a sound footing. He was intimately acquainted with Jesus' message of the kingdom of God. Mis-sionary Paul had a problem in translating this kingdom concept in the political setting of his time however. How could he speak about 'another kingdom' and not be seen as a revolutionary? Missionaries face this problem all the time; what words do we use for atonement, salvation, or sin? One cannot just think up new words for everything. Existing words and concepts need to be borrowed, cleansed and packed with biblical meaning. How otherwise can one in Papua New Guinea explain the concept of the 'lamb of God', when lambs are totally unknown? I believe that Paul decided to use an existing religious phrase, 'going in your god'. It described a religious experience: the possibility of a mystical contact with one's god. Usually this was sought in isolation. Paul used that word in a new context and packed it with kingdom content. The ancient individualistic but also occult connotation of going 'alone in your god' was changed into a more communal experience. The fleeting mystical experience enlarged into a permanent state. Paul uses the objective truth about God—as he knew him through the Old Testament, through Jesus and through personal revelation—in order to 'patent' the subjective content of going 'into your god'. The meaning of this concept doesn't depend upon individual experience but on objective reality as we know it through the word of God. Rooted in the objective reality, Paul considers it as certainly possible and necessary to also have a personal experience of God. This 'doctrine of experience' is linked to the Old Testament experience of 'God who reveals himself in the temple'. In the New Testament Paul links this with our bodies as 'a temple in which God lives himself'. As in the Old Testament temple, we too have a very special place which God has reserved for himself, a holy of holies. It should be occupied by no-one but Jesus.

With the 'in Christ' phrase, Paul initially avoided unnecessary political problems. But a conflict was brewing. Political power had much to do with origin of birth or status and the Emperor himself was considered to be of divine descent. He demanded to be addressed as a god. According to Paul, however, ordinary slaves were also 'his offspring' (Acts 17:28). Everyone was a priest![18] As slaves found spiritual freedom, the authorities lost their power, that is, fear. That made them force the issue; bow to Caesar, or face death. The power of the spiritual freedom which these slaves faced shines through as we read about the heroic stand many took and accepted death rather than return back to a state of spiritual slavery.

Spiritual Freedom. The spiritual, inner freedom which Paul preached then is also an answer for people who live in dysfunctional families or cultures and who do not have a chance to break free socially. At least they can become free spiritually, even while stuck in a dysfunctional family or church. Spiritual freedom can be the beginning of the dissolution of a dysfunctional system. Spiritual freedom of abuse survivors empowers them to face reality, even if they are still stuck socially. Too often I observe how people break free from their dysfunctional families or churches, only to cluster with other survivors to be in an even more-limited circle of people.

Forgiveness. Forgiveness is a tough word for most abuse survivors, often used as a whip, insisting that they shape up and 'let the past be the past'. At times even an abuser can use it and tell them how bad they are, because they don't forgive. The whip can also be internal, with the survivor blaming himself.[19] The result of all this is that the word forgiveness can cause an allergy, a revulsion. When working with abused people we need to understand this and be sensitive in how we share biblical teaching on forgiveness. Forgiveness in New Testament Greek comes from the root 'to release'. We can continue to focus on the abuser and, through it, continue to be bound to him. To release means that we can focus on the future, on our own choices, even when abusers refuse to admit what they did, or belittle their responsibility for what really happened. Key concepts linked to forgiveness are repentance and confession. The issue of forgiveness cannot be seen apart from the biblical teaching on righteousness. In the next few pages I will return to this topic.

Unity in Diversity. Unity in diversity is also a theme which is a powerful healing agent for abuse survivors. They know they are different. They are marked by their history. The difference can become an advantage, rather than a burden. The gospel shows how different people can learn to live in peace. I have met believers in many different cultures. What strikes me is that you can see everywhere the same transformation of the personality through the impact of the gospel. The fruit of the Spirit has an effect on the believer. Key concepts such as grace, forgiveness, peace, happiness, and righteousness through the Holy Spirit are immediate points of recognition which underline the mutual experience of unity.

Cross-cultural counselling

Understanding the culture of seekers of help enables us to see better the struggles which people face in their specific situation. To communicate, we need also to get acquainted with the cultural forms as well as the deeper meaning behind a custom.[20] Missionary Paul was able to quote national poets in his proclamation of the gospel.[21] When he wants to say something negative about the cultural habit of Cretans who believe flattering stories all too quickly, he wisely quotes a local prophet: 'Cretans are always liars, evil brutes, lazy gluttons.' And he adds delicately, 'This testimony is true'! (Tit 1:12). He also understood the need to find positive points of contact, such as 'the unknown god' for which he found an altar in Athens.

Ethical evaluation of one's own culture

The apostle Paul spent years after his conversion learning how his own values needed to be cleansed.[22] Our own norms and values play an important role in how we look at other cultures. An American missionary who settled in the Netherlands was shocked to discover that the believers were smoking and drinking beer or wine. We were amazed by the way that his wife used makeup. Judgemental attitudes hindered our interactions. My own strict upbringing made me gasp when I visited him in his home: a painting of a half-nude young woman decorated the wall of their living room. The topic we discussed was quite serious, but I admit that I did not give him my undivided attention!

   Helping abused persons also requires an ethical evaluation. What is good in their culture? What should be purified? Which elements should be rejected? To be able to do this, we need some specific values as the foundation for our evaluation. The Bible does provide universal values and I would like to share a few which I have found helpful.

Universal values

The Bible tells us that every culture is under the influence of sin. The sin principle started with Adam and Eve. Sin has infected humanity, like 'a blight has infected a tree'.[23] Thus human associations, tribal groupings, churches, businesses, etc. are likewise infiltrated by sin. These don't need deliverance, but cleansing. Culture can be influenced by demonic forces in such a way that it needs deliverance.[24] The gospel tells us that God has not forgotten his creation. Jesus came into the world as the greatest missionary of all time, leaving behind a kingdom to withstand this realm where evil forces reign. Our evaluation also needs the concept of hope: the gospel can penetrate every culture and then change that culture from within, where necessary.

The apostle Paul has given a firm foundation for cultural freedom. He was furious when Jewish Christians tried to impose their Jewish culture on non-Jews.[25] When he was required to answer practical questions about customs and cultural notions, he used as starting-point the values of the kingdom of God: 'righteousness, peace and joy in the Holy Spirit.' (Rom 14:17). These values reflect the character of the God of the Bible. As Creator, he has placed these values in every human being. It is not hard to recover these values, even if they are twisted by sin. Thus the universal desire for righteousness can, twisted by sin, become like a 'spirit of litigation', where everyone sues everyone. The desire for peace can be twisted into an addiction, drowning our unrest. The desire for joy can develop into a hedonistic culture, where pleasure is the highest value.

The values of righteousness, peace and joy become even more clear when we contrast them with their counterparts. Righteousness goes together with wrath. God is angry when there is unrighteousness. Anger about unrighteousness is also both natural and necessary for us. Peace, the inner yearning for 'Paradise lost', the desire for the absence of strife and a sense of harmony and unity, is also a shadow of God's nature in us. Its counterpart is unrest, the sense of disharmony and fragmentation which also belongs to a normal response. Similarly, joy and sadness belong to each other and are likewise an expression of the Creator in us.

The gospel shows us a way to redeem the original values, to see them cleaned from sin, as we learn to walk in obedience which is rooted in the experience of his grace.[26] Before we dare to look at other cultures we need to face our own, not only out of humility, but also because of blind spots which prevent us from seeing our reality. It is here that I believe inter-cultural relationships become so important; we need people outside our culture to help us see the blind spots. It is here that equality between helpers and abuse survivors becomes a possibility. Their sensitivity to power abuse will soon signal inconsistencies in your own principles! Such assistance quickly becomes a mutual exchange of insights which is good and necessary,[27] because, as survivors, they have been exposed to one-way communication long enough.

Evaluating culture

Culture is God's gift to humanity, enabling people to survive and to thrive together with others. It is amazing how people adjust to a variety of circumstances. I still recall the taste of the delicious gravy my mother made in wartime—lightly-burned flour, water and salt. The abused deserve admiration for their creativity. It sounds paradoxical: can there be a positive side to a life of struggle for survival, dysfunctional relationships, traumatic sexualisation, betrayal, powerlessness and stigmatisation? And if there is, can these positive factors then be used in helping survivors of sexual abuse? Indeed, survival strategies learned, such as the fear of power abuse and the need to respect privacy and individuality, can be very useful later in life, when one has shaken off the incestuous past.

The presence of the King

Missionary Paul focused not just on kingdom values, but on the presence of the King.[28] Some of these presence-related values are righteousness, peace and joy as they are biblically defined.

Righteousness

Abuse survivors often manifest a very keen sense of righteousness, and easily become enraged when they meet injustice. Although they have had to swallow too much injustice themselves (acquired powerlessness), they react violently when others suffer injustice. The craving for righteousness also has to do with the need for vengeance. We are created in God's image. He avenges, and so we too have a need for satisfaction, for revenge. This is one of the pillars of justice in society. Inasmuch as a person can be held responsible for his own behaviour, then the consequences have to be borne accordingly.

Rage is a justifiable reaction to injustice. Abuse survivors have to learn to be 'angry, but without sin' (Eph 4:26). After serious abuse there is a natural urge for revenge. This urge is biblical, as God has placed that in mankind. In the Old Testament there were precise rules about how this revenge could be applied. Tragically, this need for revenge is denied by many Christians. That misunderstanding, combined with what I mentioned earlier about a wrong view of forgiveness, means that many Christians torture themselves with the thought 'I can't forgive, nor do I really want to.' In order to find a way out of this, it is necessary to:

1. Appreciate this need to satisfy the desire for revenge! In secular life, it is one of the foundation stones for fines and punishments by law.[29] From a biblical perspective, revenge was never to be denied or suppressed! This would place the Old Testament instructions against the New Testament teaching. We are now offered another way to express our

need for revenge. We are invited to leave the revenge to God, who can do it better than we can! Just as we can sell an unpaid bill to the debt-collector, so our revenge is transferable to God. He cashes the bill with the offender on our behalf.[30] That then releases the survivor. Otherwise the unfulfilled desire for revenge binds the survivor to the offender! If God then decides to be gracious to the offender anyway and not strike him dead, that is his business. After all, we cannot stop God being gracious. Where would *we* be in that case?

2. Forgiveness is one of the great basic Christian values which has both blessed and tortured the conscience of people who felt unable to forgive because of what they suffered under the actions of others. As we saw before, forgiveness includes the concept of turning away from the offenders. This is an important aspect to foster healing of the past. The focus of our problem is not *what* was done or even *who* did it, but what we felt happened.[31] To forgive then becomes a healthy choice to focus on one's own healing rather than on the person who hurt us. Usually abuse survivors have carried the needs of everyone else on their shoulders. To learn to break that habit is an essential part of the healing process.

As victims struggle with the biblical command to forgive, we need to stress its impossibility! Only God can forgive. That was the lesson Peter had to learn when he thought he had understood Jesus' teaching on forgiveness.[32] For us forgiving is something unhuman. But God wants to share with us the power to learn to forgive. Grace precedes obedience. As Christ is in us, he can radiate forgiveness. It is not our achievement, but his work in us. Learning to forgive is a process, which begins when we pray 'God, teach me how to forgive'. It is debatable whether forgiveness should be anything more than 'turning one's attention away from the abuser and leaving justice to God' if the abuser does not confess.[33] Biblical righteousness demands that each person takes responsibility for their actions. Even if there is confession by an abuser and spiritual forgiveness is possible, this does not excuse that abuser from the legal consequences of his or her actions!

My experience is that abuse survivors, when equipped with a right understanding of righteousness, revenge and forgiveness, can much more easily turn their attention away from the abuser and thus break free from the emotional bonding to them. Some even, with time, acquire an attitude of empathy, arising from an inner freedom and power.[34] Thus it becomes possible to say 'I have forgiven, I am free'.

The relationship between forgiving and personal responsibility is also a problem for the victim at times. A child often has an inflated idea of what it can do, or should do. Thus when abuse cannot be stopped it feels a personal responsibility and, with it, guilt and shame. Especially when abuse still happens in the early teens, this can become a problem. I have found it helpful to state that '. . . even if you are one per cent responsible, then Jesus has still paid for your sins . . . But before you can come to that conclusion, you will need to experience grace and peace so that truth can surface and be faced. Now shame is colouring your perception. You need to refocus away from shame, to peace.'

Peace

We saw earlier how important peace was for the apostle Paul. He only had the Old Testament, which firmly links righteousness with Shalom.[35] The need for this Shalom is evident as we look at the situation of abuse survivors. Many hurting people respond at once to the need for justice and become angry because of unrighteousness which they experience or see happen to others. They don't hesitate to face a confrontation. Abuse survivors knew about anger when they were abused. Unable to express it then, they learned to escape confrontations. They were powerless anyhow. The patterns set in early childhood, in response to sexual abuse, have become 'fast lanes'. Certain trigger words, actions, smells or events can cause a sudden flashback. Only recently has there been more attention given to the biological effects, which become imprinted in the nervous system. It can be understood that later stresses and lack of peace are thus magnified by such an early conditioning.[36] The consequences of abuse, such as a difficult sexual relationship with a partner, can compound the problem and increase the unrest. Thus our emphasis on experiencing inner peace and calm, as well as peace in relationships, often finds a willing ear. Thus the biblical meaning and experience of Shalom is a very good place to begin helping abuse survivors.

The absence of peace is not just a spiritual or emotional phenomenon. The body remembers as well. Negative experiences can influence our emotions and thinking. It is possible for the peace of God to affect the body.[37] As physical healing of deep emotional traumas is pivotal in the helping of sexually abused persons, I need to go into more detail about this.

The differences between spirit, soul and body, and their connection with each other, become clear if we see these words as various descriptions of a relationship. The spirit is the description of an unique relationship which we can have with God. By nature, we are spiritually dead, like cut flowers; still beautiful, but no longer connected to the plant. 'Revival' means recovering a relationship with the origin of life, God himself. The peace of God at work in our spirit results in a restoration of our relationship with the Creator. That it is a process is affirmed by the apostle Paul, who expresses the desire of countless others, to know God better.[38] This results in worship, whereby our attention is concentration on who God is.

The soul is that part of our being that has to do with who we are, here on earth, in our situation and particular culture. The way we worship God is determined by our culture. That's why there are so many different churches and groups with different worship forms. That's good; it's all part of 'unity in diversity'. We need all the variations in experiencing God through different cultures, as the apostle Paul says, to understand the content of God's love.[39]

The peace of God is not only a spiritual and emotional issue, but aimed at the body as well. The abuse survivor has a burn-mark of the abuser on their being. The darkness, the demonic nature of that touch, the memories of abuse are linked to the deep emotions which there were at that time and the body-responses during these events. Thus the body has its own capacity to remember. A certain smell, for instance, can instantly recall feelings or memories from the past. Working with hundreds of abuse survivors, I have found that a physical healing is needed in order to break loose from the consequences of sexual abuse. Through a Shalom experience, the body receives a new memory, stronger than what happened before. The sense of shame is countered by a new awareness; Christ in my body. That peace can also be experienced physically is not always stated very clearly in evangelical teaching. We find this expressed in 2 Corinthians 7:1, where we read that we are urged to cleanse our own spirit and flesh from anything that contaminates. The 'flesh' here is not to be denied, put to the cross, but to be purified. And it becomes even clearer if we compare with with Romans 12:1–2 and see how changes in thought-patterns have to do with the way we use our bodies! We can go further than avoiding a negative use of the body; we can also put our bodies to positive use—the body, a temple of the Spirit of God. In the next chapters I will give more details about how to implement this practically.

Joy

People who suffer much also develop more easily the gift of humour. I see humour and joy as the other side of the coin of sorrow. They compensate for the grief they have suffered. Just think of the Jews and their proverbial sense of humour. Likewise joy can help survivors to cope with their grief. This natural capacity for humour is overshadowed in survivors by the complex forms of misery that crush them. By encouraging humour, however, we can promote a 'stereo experience': laughter with tears. This increases their ability to bounce back, which is so necessary during the hard work that has to be done before the past no longer dictates what the present and future will be like.

When anger, sadness, and unrest cannot be expressed, the focus of life can be set on seeking fun. Given the right opportunities, this can result in an addiction to emotional highs. This understanding gave hope to Andrea who wrote:

> I always wondered why I started to look for sexual experiences when I was a teenager. Now I know. I tried to choose a life where I had fun when I wanted. I hated my body for having pleasure feelings while being raped. Thus I chose to have good feelings and made sure that I always got involved with married people, as they just wanted sex, not a deep relationship. I did not want the trouble of anyone falling in love with me. When I was on drugs, I felt that I had the best time of my life. It helped me to forget and to live for that moment only.

Experiences of righteousness, peace and joy through the Holy Spirit

When we speak about experiencing God, we need to place this within a biblical context. Jesus promises a manifestation of his presence as a result of our united Maranatha prayer.[40] We saw earlier how such manifestations are, by definition, cultural expressions. The culture of the abused makes some people very alert; the need to control their lives results in a high attentiveness in school. They get good grades and praise. Such affirmation spurs intellectual development, while their emotional life is starving.[41] They are so tired of twenty-four hours per day thinking that they relish an emotional awakening. Others are emotionally worn out. I see this especially in abuse survivors who have gone through many alternative treatments, meditation techniques, or attended charismatic meetings in the hope that they would get better experiences. Such persons need a more mental presentation, without any challenge except of what the word says about righteousness, peace and joy. Any emotional expression makes them pull back. Some did not have a chance to develop mentally. Those around them either did not give much attention to cognitive development or they considered the child as stupid. Emotional experience is their starting point. As their unfulfilled emotional needs become satisfied, their study results improve greatly. (That's actually my story as well!) Whatever the case, the gospel opens up a way to be understood in the situation where the seeker of help is.

Alex was always told by his abusive step-father that he was stupid. He believed it and became a silent, solitary farmhand. His gifted mind did not get much positive attention. He expressed himself in violent and emotional ways. When he became a personal believer in Jesus, a change took place. A perceptive counsellor noticed his keen questions and encouraged him to take evening classes. He needed this mental challenge and was encouraged to study the Bible not just as devotional reading, but to see the beauty of its design, the way different books of the Bible came into existence and to understand the historical and cultural background. That gave him a firm mental framework to face some hidden deep-seated emotions later.

Janice was the oldest of a family of seven. She learned to deny her emotions. Her mental development received all her energy; she had to use it to stay away from an abusive father. Her whole life consisted of planning the smallest details. She achieved excellent results in school. As a secular university student she found Jesus as her Saviour through Youth for Christ. Her stress on Bible memorisation became an obsession. She needed to back off from a formal approach to the word of God and was encouraged to read-and-pray through the Psalms of David. This allowed her to let her emotions harmonise with the poets. As her drive for control became less, she also felt much less need for good performances in her studies and even stopped for a time. Only after she had developed more emotionally was she able to go back.

Because abuse survivors often have problems in forming deep long-term relationships, the subject of experiencing a personal relationship with God usually is also a problem. Particularly because the emotions have been so shocked, there can be a long period in which the emotions are apparently superficial, causing a sense of loneliness. To stop seeking relationships is paradoxically the biblical answer to loneliness. The acceptance of the emptiness is the beginning of fulfilment. Then we can ask Jesus to come into this experience of loneliness and learn to be alone with God. I found much help in the words of the prophet Isaiah and chose to study the names of God to survive in the loneliness, which I felt like a dark cloud.[42] To know how to deal with loneliness prepared me better for learning to relate with others. I became less afraid of not being understood, of being rejected. After all, there was still a God who would be there anyhow. The story of Hosea is a poetic expression of the way God deals with his wayward people, how he leads them into the desert of life, into loneliness and then meets them there. The adulterous wife of Hosea is confronted with a husband who does not give up and finally she is restored to him.[43]

Abuse survivors need hope that life does not have to be as it was; that their families can change and be at peace as well. Even among Christians I have found a kind of pessimism; we live in violent times and that is how it will be. I see two arguments against this pessimistic thinking, one from anthropological research and one from biblical understanding:

1. This peacefulness is actually a more natural state for our societies and the anthropological research of Howell and Willes affirms that it can be found in practice.[44] The natural hunger for peace in people can be tapped into as a source for change.
2. The ultimate result of the peace of God at work in spirit, soul and body should be that this so influences our environment that we are sources of peace in our society. The divine gift of 'grace and peace' can empower the natural urge for peace, to see 'peace as a rational and active construction of cooperative beings' state.

The missionary life: surviving and thriving in two worlds

To be a missionary means to live in two worlds. This demands a large dose of flexibility. When the familiar environment has gone, a normal reaction to such a clash of cultures is to reject the new culture; we call this culture shock. A critical attitude is the result. The new world is always viewed through the old glasses. Or the opposite can happen: everything in the new world is 'better than what we had at home'.

This lesson from missionary experience is of vital importance as we enter into the culture of the abused. The initial experience can be shocking, but normally one learns to cope. Some need to back off and return home to less conflicting situations. There are a few principles which can help to cope with culture shock and become effective in another culture:

1. The missionary gift

Not everyone has the same natural talents or spiritual gifts. Some businessmen who are highly successful in their own country cannot adapt to a new culture. They don't feel at home. The inner barriers are too high. Yet there are others who cope extremely well in other lands. They have a natural flexibility. They enjoy the encounter with other systems and values, and settle easily.

When Jesus gave the commission to preach the gospel 'over the borders' he also gave extra promises of power and special spiritual abilities. For crossing borders, there is the missionary gift: the capacity to feel at home in another culture without losing your own. I believe this is also vital for helpers who work 'over the border' in the culture of abuse.

2. A multi-cultural personality

Encountering other cultures gives a widening of horizon, but also changes us permanently. 'Whoever increases knowledge, increases sorrow'.[45] A sense of alienation, of being different, an inability to connect again, is often the complaint of missionaries who suffer 're-entry shock' when coming home on furlough. Many an abuse counsellor experiences the same. How can he share details with outsiders, even if he could do so, without breaking confidentiality? Who would understand? This loneliness is a pain which is quite similar to the stigmatisation of the abuse survivor. The helplessness which a counsellor faces when excruciating traumas are relived, the sense of shame about what people do to children, the rage of betrayal when you find out who the abusers were, are all factors which help us to be at home in the culture of the abused. There is a need to come to a cultural peace, to accept this type of life as a gypsy, moving from one culture into the other. It can feel like rootlessness. At times abuse counsellors will need to stop and 'go on furlough'. Yet, the formation of a multi-cultural personality, one which can be at home in any culture, will be needed if abuse pastoral care is a life-time commitment.

3. An inner peace

Skilled professionals often show an uncanny sense of when just to be there, in silence; when to respond; when to show their feelings; and when to start talking. This inner peace is more than an inner tranquillity if it is based on biblical truths. Pastoral volunteers, aided by the peace of God, can also be sensitive.

Missionary Paul knew by experience how important it was to have mental and emotional protection. He describes this 'peace of Christ' as a defensive wall. When people ask me how I cope with the facts and the emotions of abuse counselling, I often refer to this wall of peace.[46] It allows me to manifest God's peace, even while inside I groan, hurt and am very upset simultaneously, as I listen to the horrid stories which survivors have been waiting to share for so long, but did not dare. Attention to the theme I mentioned earlier of being 'in Christ' is important here: who you are in Christ, what your objective status is, irrespective of changing situations. Jesus referred his disciples to the need for this kind of spiritual anchor: 'However, do not rejoice that the spirits submit to you, but rejoice that your names are written in heaven' (Lk 10:20).

This inner peace will be especially needed when the missionary in the culture of abuse faces some of the toughest questions of life, 'Where was God when I needed him? Why did he let this happen?' In the next chapter I will try to report on some stages of my own pilgrimage in search of an answer.

Notes

1. The problem with the word 'father' might have been one reason why the apostle Paul suggests the name of Abba to the believers in Rome. Fathers of that day could do what they liked with their children. They could apply—unprosecuted—the worst kinds of corporal punishment. They could sell their child as a slave or prostitute and even kill it! No wonder Paul says to the new believers 'You can call him "Abba"'—the term of affection that Jesus used when he prayed!
2. 2 Cor 12:9
3. See Chapter 8 for my own attempts to find an answer to this perplexing question.
4. Rom 8:11
5. Heb 7:24, 25
6. 1 Cor 15:20–28
7. Rev 6:9–11
8. John Bright, in *The Kingdom of God* (Nashville 1994), stresses the relationship between grace and obedience. It is here that many pastoral workers with a traditional evangelical background fail in practice. Too quickly they introduce the concept of obedience. But obedience without grace is nothing more than legalism and easily turns a religious system into a spiritual abusive system.
9. Mt 10:12
10. Heb 4:1–12. The link between the rest in God and the power of the word of God is evident. For an abusive survivor the fear of death, the shame, the helplessness, distrust and all the other intense emotions have become a very physical experience. To learn to 'rest in God' needs to touch the bone marrow!
11. The whole idea of hypnosis as part of treatment causes great alarm among many traditional Christians. They see in it a link with the use of 'transrational' forces, or psychic powers which originate from the hypnotist. To allow one's being to be so deeply influenced by another person is seen as very dangerous and unbiblical. When the hypnotist also represents a different belief-system or even is involved in the occult, it is at times seen as a 'foreign invasion' from which one must be delivered. Jeffrey Masson (*Against Therapy*), has shown how the belief systems of the helper deeply affect the seeker of help. This concern about power abuse is not limited to these traditional Christians. I know a secular, feminist psychologist who has used hypnosis in the past but has decided to discontinue this, because of the 'abuse of power' factor, to which feministic psychology has sensitised her.

    To be fair, we should also point out that the possibility of the abuse of pastoral power demands that we ask ourselves what is the difference between hypnotherapy and authoritative pastoral pronouncements or the pastoral use of 'guided imagination'. I know trustworthy psychologists who, as Christians, have no problems with the use of guided imagination. I myself am concerned about its use and the great possibility for abuse which this creates. The same is true with 'simple relaxation exercises'. The minute that this results in an 'inner blankness', an emptying of oneself, there is a great danger that we enter into a self-hypnotic state. The issue at stake here is the locus of power; who is in control. I have observed how powerful influences of ideas, statements of parents, pastors or other care-givers ('you are no good'), the diagnosis of a doctor, an encounter with a fortuneteller or witch, can have such an impact that deliverance was needed: a restoration of one's own freedom from dominion of that influence. This has made some unduly afraid of any experience. Yet Jesus promised us a peace, not like the world can give us. A firm fixation on the presence of Jesus, in spirit, soul and body (1 Thess 5:23), on the other hand, can prevent unbiblical experiences in mass meetings, in church or in private meditation, as we then can accept that God will not give stones for bread.

What I attempt in this book is to point out that there is the possibility of a genuine experience of the rest in God, because God himself has promised it. The Bible does not limit the type of experiences that God gives. The apostle Paul even describes something what might have been an 'out of body experience' (2 Cor 13:3). What the Bible is firm about is that the experience can be of the wrong sort, from sin-infiltrated self-life or occult, God-opposing forces, as well as of the Holy Spirit.

Biblically valid experiences can never be 'organised' in a counselling session, and thus it can never become a technique. God manifests himself in his own way. Initially, for many in the Bible and still today, such a manifestation can be rather disquieting in the beginning! A kind of positive apprehension is helpful if one is not to become too callous about an encounter with the Holy One. The Bible calls this 'the fear of the Lord'.

12. Oscar Cullmann (1959). Also John Wimber who, as Associate Professor in Fuller Theological Seminary, together with Peter Wagner conducted a course in 'Signs and Wonders' and who introduced me to the writings of George Eldon Ladd and others, who restated how to understand the kingdom of God for today.

13. 1 Cor 16:22. The expectation of God's presence in conflict is also a direct reference to Mt 18:15–19. When the Bible uses the phrase 'two or three', it usually is in the context of (potential) conflict. When Paul, heavy-hearted as he must have been to rebuke his

children in faith so strongly, summarises the conflict in a few lines, he is compelled to use the word Maranatha; 'Come, O Lord'.

14. Mt 18:19–20; 28:18–20
15. Heb 2:4
16. Mt 18:19, 20
17. Gal 1:8
18. 1 Pet 2:9
19. Jan Hindman *Just before dawn, From the Shadows of Tradition to New Reflections in Trauma Assessment and Treatment of Sexual Victimization*, (1989) and *The Mourning Breaks* (1991) Alexandria Associates, Ontario, Oregon. Lewis B. Smedes, *Forgive and Forget, Healing the Hurts We Don't Deserve*, Harper & Row, 1984.
20. Augsburger, David W, *Pastoral Counselling Across Cultures*, The Westminster Press, 1986. Hesselgrave, David J, *Counselling Cross-Culturally*, Baker Book House, Grand Rapids, 1984.
21. Acts 17:28
22. Philip 3:7
23. J. Sidlow Baxter, *Christian Holiness Restudied and Restated*, Zondervan, Grand Rapids, 1977
24. To name just a few; female circumcision in Africa, the widow-burning in India, the birth practices in north-east Thailand or the way euthanasia is being encouraged in the West.
25. Gal 2:11–14; 3:1–3
26. 2 Cor 7:1
27. The urge in abuse survivors for righteousness, to make abusers accountable for their deeds, might be one of the great contributions to a renewal of biblical theology. Over the last decades we see more and more the effect of humanistic values which seek to understand, and therefore often excuse, wrong behaviour. Also insurance policies and inability of governments to enforce laws have made a dichotomy between our behaviour and the consequences we face. I see a direct link with the upsurge of Buddhism in Europe and this development. Buddhism teaches strongly the relationship between cause and effect, the law of Karma. Just as the Enlightenment helped us to see that the child was not a miniature adult, and the feminist movement opened our eyes to the sexual abuse of women, I suspect that Buddhism will force us once again to restudy the biblical teaching of punishment, hell and damnation, as well as God's way to escape this.
28. Ladd, George Eldon, *The Gospel of the Kingdom*, Eerdmans, Grand Rapids, 1981.
29. Rom 13:1
30. Rom 12:19

31. Seminar notes, Beverly James, James Institute, Post Office Box 148, Honaunau, Hawaii 96726 USA.

32. Mat 18:21–35

33. There are miracles of forgiveness, where parents could forgive the murderers of their children and where relationships became restored. Corrie ten Boom writes vividly about her struggle to forgive and reach out to the people who tormented her in concentration camp. While there is a choice to be open for such an infusion of love, the actual experience is a gift of grace, which one can not make happen.

34. Rom 12:20–1 speaks about heaping burning coals on people's head. I often just felt like doing that! The meaning of this phrase though, has been lost since the invention of matches. In the days of Paul, it was essential to 'keep your fire burning'. The fire-pot, usually carried on the head, was an important element of daily life. To keep the fire burning was an art which children learned. If the fire died it was shameful. To heap burning coals on someone's head actually means to relate to their shame and do something about it!

35. The prophet Isaiah links righteousness with the biblical Shalom, which included harmony and prosperity as a community: 'The fruit of righteousness will be peace; the effect of righteousness will be quietness and confidence for ever. My people will live in peaceful dwelling-places, in secure homes, in undisturbed places of rest.' Is 32:17, 18

36. Gerald May gives an excellent summary of these biological aspects in *Addiction and Grace* (1988). Carol Hartman (1993) writes about her findings in the neurobiology of trauma in *Information Processing of Trauma*. She concludes her study with the following remarks:

    'The implication of this biological understanding of trauma and information processing for treatment underscores the necessity of reducing arousal thus lessening the dissociative processes. Once this is done, primary learning can resume. Treatment and research can now be directed to cognitive and physiological interventions as well as holding constant the social/contextual activities that support the healing potential of the therapeutic relationship.'

    It appears to me that here a classical understanding of physical healing, through prayer, can be an application of the above-mentioned principles. At least I observe how the Powerful Peace approach involves also a physiological element of arousal reducing, in which a survivor learns to face reality, protected by the peace of God. This peace then helps the survivor to learn life-skills (primary learning), which they could not absorb before this.

37. 2 Thess 5:23

38. Phil 3:10
39. Eph 3:16–18
40. Mt 18:19, 20
41. See the previously-mentioned works of Dr Anne Terruwe and the Deprivation Neurosis.
42. Is 50:10–11
43. Hos 2:14–17
44. Not aggression, but peacefulness is shown as the basic, creation-given, 'sociality' of mankind. This would fit in well with the biblical understanding that we are created according to God's image and reflect his character, which includes peacefulness. As sin came, aggression took over but, as the authors show, this is not the case everywhere. It is here where we see also the power of 'fallen culture' and the slow pocess of change which the gospel has brought. Partly, as Schreitner (1985) has shown, this is due to our lack of understanding of our own cultures, as well as those cultures to whom we bring the good tidings of peace. My observation from working with missionaries is that many see a western aggressiveness and doctrinal fighting mood as aspects to be aspired to.
45. Eccles 1:18 (RSV)
46. Phil 4:6–9

CHAPTER SIX

WHY, GOD?

Judy stared at me with empty eyes, then they flashed with anger. 'Why did he do this?' Then silence followed. Much more softly she added; 'When I remember, I cannot really believe there is a God.' The beastly events she had just related to me still lingered in the air. I just nodded my head and stayed silent.

A pastoral approach to helping sexual-abuse survivors must face the senselessness, the 'why?', which screams through the empty corridors of a life that has become like a haunted house. As countless poems, novels, paintings and other art-forms wrestle with the paradox of the suffering of innocent people, we suffer the limitations of words, parables and images.

Historian Jeffrey Burton Russell challenges religious answers and states 'No answer is credible that cannot be given in the face of dying children.'[1] As Christianity does not focus on religion, but on a Person, he should answer! Is God silent because we can't hear him due to the screams in our own heart or is he speechless in the sight of suffering?

Let God speak for himself

One girl nearly shouted at me, 'I have prayed my head off trying to understand. If he is almighty, then why didn't he stop what was happening? Where was He when I needed him?' In one of the earliest parts of the Bible, the book of Job, we can observe that even God himself allowed Job to be enraged with him. No thunderbolt came down when he raised his fist to God! When we have no words, God has demonstrated that there is a language where words are not needed, the language of just 'being there'. The friends of Job just sat there with him in silence for seven days, while Job cried out for justice. What they said after that doesn't even seem that important. But at least they helped Job to become angry with them and in this way vent his emotions on 'friends' he could see, while the Invisible not only was silent, but seemed to be out of reach. It appears that Job is not only arguing with God, but with himself as well. Chapter after chapter we read the monologue of a tormented person talking to a God who is silent. Then something happens. The Absent One reveals himself and starts to speak. A monologue becomes a dialogue.

Twisted images of God

At some stage in pastoral counselling, I encourage a counsellee to seek out God personally, through prayer. But before you advise a person to make a serious effort to improve relationships with their God, you'd better find out who that 'god' is. Suppose you send them back to a tyrant![2] Through listening and wise questioning we can learn how seekers of help think and feel about God. The concepts and words they use with bitterness, such as 'to surrender' or 'father' can be noted. Expressions which seem to carry a more neutral or positive value give us a key to enter into their religious vocabulary. Sometimes it is possible to switch to another language they know, rather than use an expression which would cause revulsion. Or one can seek together more neutral words which somehow can carry the same meaning.

While images of God might be twisted, a pastoral counsellor can, just by being there, be the beginning of a process of untwisting the image of God.

Not what you say, but what you are

There are many people who choose to be right there where
people suffer terribly. The Sisters of Mercy, started by the
Albanian nun, Mother Theresa, are well known. So is the
Salvation Army. The tens of millions of refugees in the world
are served by many organisations. Youth With A Mission is one
of them; hundreds of volunteers spend part of their lives in
desperate refugee situations. Scores of them have made this
work a life calling. As I observe such people, I see their private
battle with the agony of innocent suffering. The one common
factor they manifest is that they refuse to walk away from the
problems. They are there with those who suffer, even if they can
give nothing else. I learned through this that it is not so much
what you say, but what you are, as you stand next to someone
who suffers. I have observed that exposure to suffering can
make one harder and closed, or open and transparent.

The Greeks and the Jews in Paul's day scoffed at this teaching of suffering and weakness. Western culture is built on the
attempts to escape suffering. The German theologian Helmut
Thielicke commented that the inability to translate the gospel
into our culture today can be seen best in the avoidance of
developing a theology of suffering.[3] As we are trying to help
those who live in the culture of abuse, we need to develop such
answers for ourselves as well. There are insistent questions
which refuse to go away.

Towards a biblical theology of suffering

A biblical theology of suffering evolves out of our interaction
with the word of God. Due to limitations of space I can only
touch some of the more frequent questions which abuse
survivors face.

One unexpected incident set me on track. I was very angry
about something. As I reflected on Psalm 4:4–8, the sentence 'In
your anger do not sin,' struck home. I felt that my anger was
justified. But I could not call it 'righteous anger' because I was
too well aware that my anger was still tainted by some rather

ugly thoughts. I then decided to ask God to cleanse the sinful elements out of my anger. As worship grew inside, I sensed a strange stereo-feeling: worship and anger. Then a thought flashed through my mind about the anger of God. A strange prayer followed. 'Lord, I am still feeling angry about what they did; is there something you are angry about as well?' Unexpectedly, an answer thundered inside; 'Yes, I am angry; my people in Ethiopia are being killed by the thousands and nobody is lifting a finger.' Now I had not been thinking about Ethiopia at all. It was then that I realised the spark of inspiration and suddenly I found myself praying with a sense of anger, power and urgency, which gave me a new perspective on intercession. Since then, I have learned to use other emotions as well, as a starting place to ask God for his heart about people or things. This is also how I started to consider the idea of God's pain. Could it be that God still has pain today?

One can take many philosophical or religious roads to find answers about suffering. I have chosen, with countless others, to accept what God says in his story about why God sent Jesus to become a human being, to become the Word; to speak for the Father. Looking at the divinity of Christ will not suffice; we need to face the Man, a carpenter, speaking the language of common people; a man who was misunderstood, misquoted, manipulated, abused and terribly tormented before he died.

When God lacked words about himself, he spoke the language of the Incarnation, he became flesh and blood. He became like us. A Dutch carol says that 'even the Christmas manger was a cross for Jesus'.[4] As a consolation for many abused, Jesus knows what it means to have a nail hammered into his body; the crucifixion as a mock-rape. His suffering did not end at the cross. He sees a whole world in suffering and it hurts him.

God's pain

The idea of the pain of God surfaces at different times in church history. More recently it was again brought to the attention of the church by the Japanese theologian, Kazoh Kitamori. In the aftermath of the War, he finds consolation in his *Theology of the Pain of God* (1946). He bases it on Jeremiah 31:20, where he concludes that God suffered for Ephraim and suffers for his people. He stimulated my understanding as we worked with leprosy patients who had lost the sense of pain. I began to realise what a wonderful creation-gift pain actually is. Without pain, we would all be like leprosy patients, unaware of how our body hurts. Pain is a warning signal, a call for action.

God speaking through pain

Because of the message of the cross we dare to look at the pain of others. As we listen to seekers of help to learn, we become more sensitive, respond better, hear what is not said, and grieve. The one who hands out the medicine also takes a good dose for himself! At such moments our words can take on a deeper content as Jesus comes in and brightens up the scene. Suddenly, common words take on a new glow because another Light shines through them. Can there be anything more awesome? It is then that the joy of the Lord can lift our heart and bring laughter, even in the midst of suffering.

God's struggle in a broken creation

In a provocative exegesis of Job, Donald Capps[5], Professor in Pastoral Theology at Princeton Theological Seminary, USA, shows how God's answer to Job bears no relationship at all to the long discourses by Job's friends nor the bitter complaints of Job himself. It is not that these discourses are futile, but that God himself seems to wrestle with the question of innocent suffering. Capps suggests that God seems to be saying that he understands that our suffering is terrible, that he allows us to feel our own hopelessness and to express it. Reading the pages of Job's heart-cry, it appears to me that God is saying, 'Go on Job, I'm listening, I am here.' Job's repeated question is, 'Why me? What have I done that you pursue me like a hunter?' When God finally speaks, none of Job's questions are answered. God starts to walk with his friend-in-pain, and points to him the beauty of creation and how death has come into it; how it twisted nature and how death, which he abhors, becomes a part of the food chain. Then God challenges Job with his problem. Does he have an answer to the hunger of the young lion, or the birds of prey? Doesn't he understand that in order to feed them, there must be innocent victims?[6]

With stunned silence Job saw at once how pieces of the puzzle fell into place. He knew the story of Adam and Eve, of the suffering which came in the world, and that paradise was lost because of evil. But Job also knew of a promise of ultimate victory, as God announced Satan's final doom; 'Your head will be crushed by the seed of this woman, while you will strike his heel' (Gen 3:15). Adam and Eve were confronted there and then with the fact that their sin would bring suffering to another. The waiting for the Promised One had started then. The reality of innocent suffering is vividly illustrated as God kills some innocent animals to provide Adam and Eve with clothing to cover their shame. Then innocent Abel is killed by Cain. Evil seems to reign, but the ultimate victory is promised. God's reasoning about suffering seems to satisfy Job. Traditional translations from the Hebrew give Job's final exit line of the epic story with '. . . I retract . . . repent in dust and ashes.' (Job 42:6) Capps, however, notices that Job was already *in* dust and ashes. This brings him to consider an alternative translation which he claims is both linguistically correct and gives much more sense to the exegesis of these final lines of Job: 'I have heard of you with my ears, but now my eyes see you. Therefore I despise myself and repent *of* dust and ashes.'[7] Job discovered from God's answer that there was no need to put on dust and ashes! Job now understands that there are innocent people who suffer. Because of the Fall, a basic flaw has come into creation. That was not God's will, but his rules of the game couldn't be changed any more. God became limited by his own rules.

God's decree: a limited use of power

God gave mankind the principle of authority as a creation gift.[8]
When sin entered into mankind, authority was also contami-
nated with sin. Servant-leadership became autocratic despotism.
Powerful rulers and their subjects discovered that the abuse of
power was destructive. Thus in Daniel's day they already knew
that a country cannot exist long if the laws are changed all the
time! The absolute king needed to be limited in the use of his
power, while yet maintaining his 'absolute power'. In an
attempt to establish fairness and stability in legislation, I
believe that the rulers of the Medes and the Persians somehow
took a leaf out of God's code of law. There were some very
special rules that a ruler could make, but then they would be
irrevocable! This would make the powerful ruler subject to his
own rules. Thus it happened that the mighty king could find no
way of preventing a good man like Daniel from being thrown
into the lions' den.[9] This story exemplifies the problem that God
faces. He has ordained certain principles of authority and
power. Evil, as personified in Satan and the demons, is still
around. Mankind suffers from a fatal flaw, a basic defect; evil
has infected mankind as well. One of the fundamental principles
of God's laws is that each person is responsible for his own
actions.[10] They have the freedom to make choices. One of the
consequences of that freedom is that wrong choices can be
made and that innocent people suffer as a result.

One can be forgiven for drunken driving, but one has to live
with the tragic consequences of the resulting accident for the
rest of one's life. Evil will hurt innocent people. A world
without innocent suffering means a world where everyone
does what is right because of an automatism which makes
them behave correctly.

When God created the world, Satan had already fallen. The
Creator must have known he was taking a risk when he made
Adam and Eve; they too might fall. He fixed the rules of the
game, and seemingly lost, as Adam and Eve disobeyed. God had
decided to play fair and send the most beloved expression he
had of himself—Jesus—to abide by and suffer under those same

rules. Thus Jesus suffered innocently and died on the Cross. The snake did strike the heel of the Seed, but he crushed its head. Jesus put to shame the powers of evil.[11] Light is stronger than darkness; goodness will overcome evil in the end. He arose from the dead to finish off the battle. An apt analogy is the invasion of the continent of Europe in June 1944. On D-day, the backbone of the Third Reich was broken. But VE-day could not take place till eleven months later. In between D-day and VE-day more soldiers died than in all the preceding years together.[12] This is why Jesus encourages us to evangelise; the decisive victory has been won but many will be hurt before the war is over.

The weakness of God

The Greeks had problems with Paul's presentation of a crucified God.[13] They were looking rather for a 'Rambo' type of God. They could not grasp Paul's message that the highest aim was not a flow of logic delivered with unmatched wisdom, nor healing, powerful manifestations or miracles of all sorts. The greatest miracle of all was God's grace to come himself, to manifest himself, where we are. The paradox is that those Jews and Greeks who responded to the message of the crucified Christ experienced also resurrection power, an infilling of the Spirit of God that included an infilling of power and wisdom. So why this stress on weakness, why all this attention to the apparent defeat on the cross? God knows how power will be abused, that 'powerful people' will seek more power and abuse more people! God knows how religion can be manipulated in such a way that it effectively controls people according to the wishes of those manipulators. But by placing the message of the cross centrally, there is a chance that power will be used for the good of others! While religiousness can go on without the cross, the cross itself continues to be a stumbling block for power-hungry, abusive leaders.[14] When we attempt to help sexual abuse survivors and especially those who have been abused in a religious setting, then we need to understand this apparent 'weakness' of God.

God in our weakness

The idea of the weakness of God was not only a stumbling block for those whom the apostle Paul attempted to reach, it is also contradictory to western views of who God is or should be. Helpers who talk about a good God, about his power and care, will have to face these issues. As one Jewish friend who read this manuscript, wrote in the margin 'To praise God but not to ask about Auschwitz is religious hypocrisy.'

The Bible shows how the suffering of the innocent causes a deep pain in the heart of God. He reaches out to us with grace, with unconditional love. Just as with Job, the battle is about our response. Is it a response of a puppy to its master, or can we achieve the level of the unconditional love of God himself—a love which Satan implied was impossible for Job to achieve?

In the battle about suffering and unconditional love, God gives us some extra tools. The essence of God's nature is love.[15] God promises to pour out his own life and love into our hearts through the Holy Spirit.[16] That assures me that we don't have to 'work up' love, but there is power in the love that God gives.

The price of power

In jail and troubled, when even former co-workers wondered what sin Paul had committed that caused God not to release him as he had done for Peter, Paul writes the immortal words: 'I want to know Christ and the power of his resurrection and the fellowship of sharing in his sufferings, becoming like him in his death, and so, somehow, to attain to the resurrection from the dead'. (Phil 3:10, 11)

Even after all the healing we go through, and after receiving all the blessings there are, there is still a Friend who suffers with a broken world. As his friends, we are invited to be in touch with a suffering God, then we become linked to a never-ending source of power. As I have attempted to respond to that invitation, a hidden resistance to suffering softened. Pain about my own abusive past, which had been hidden for many years, was awakened as well.

But what about prayer?

Laurie, an 18-year-old, tearfully shared with me how she prayed to God 'Make Daddy stop doing this to me.' Yet the abuse went on and on. Her defiant eyes had a burning quality as she added 'Why didn't he answer my prayer?' I was speechless, the desire even to attempt an answer evaporated. Finally, with new vitality, as if a great burden had been lifted, she broke the silence and simply thanked me for 'being there' and left.

Dr Helen Roseveare was a missionary in Africa when a revolt placed the missionaries in the hands of rebels. In a TV programme, she told us how she was raped, how she prayed, and how it nevertheless went on and on. At the same time, there was the strange awareness that God was there with her, not leaving her alone in the ordeal. She also shared how it took months to recover, to weep, to grieve, to be angry, to be restored.

Does prayer make any sense? My battle with this question has even made me wonder whether to skip this whole chapter. Then I realised that it is precisely this battle which we face as counsellors and which belongs to the theology of suffering. Perhaps there will come a time when I can state my answers more articulately and precisely. For the time being, I will have to be content with the following answer for the Lauries of this world:

> Jesus prayed in Gethsemane, 'If it is possible, let this cup pass,' but also 'your will be done.' And we can pray in the same way during our ordeals. God has the power, but he also has a plan. That plan seems to me like onion-skins. There is a hierarchy in the plans, the desires of God, as a 'master builder'. One of them is the principle already stated that, as sin has entered into the world, there will be innocent people who suffer.

Prayer does influence situations. I was twice in mortal danger in Thailand when prayer supporters in the Netherlands (where it was night at that moment) woke up with the words ringing in their ears, 'Get up and pray; Teo's life is in danger.' On both occasions I did indeed experience supernatural help, including on one occasion a manifestation of angels to protect us. There were other times when things went wrong and where I can only say that we prayed and nothing happened, but God did come into our situation. Sometimes just as a quiet wind, at other times, especially when I was emotionally bruised and sore, through friends who chose to stand with me.

Suffering and children

The relationship between prayer and a theology of suffering thus seems to be implicit in the words of Jesus, 'Your will be done.' But how do you explain this to a child? How do we reply to Jeffrey Burton Russell's challenge that 'no answer is credible that cannot be given in the face of dying children.'

I am not going to try to be a lawyer for God, but rather let him speak for himself. The Bible says that angels watch the face of the Father, presumably for instructions as to what to do when children are abused.[17] What that means I can't explain. Is the tremendous drive for survival due more to divine empowerment than to a forceful character? Is the way that children dissociate a part of his gift to survive? Is their 'flight into beautiful fancy' perhaps inspired or even rooted in another supernatural reality? One abuse survivor, who felt she was taken by angels into a safe place when the abuse started, told me about her struggle with God not to have to go back to that body after the abuse was over. She begged God to be allowed to stay with him. Even now, as a mature Christian, this is still a sore point between her and God. Based on the freedom that Job had to pour out his anguish and questions, I have encouraged her to be honest with God about it. While I can see that she is of great help to others who are abused, that doesn't really settle what for her is still a lingering question.

God's presence and our incomplete theology of suffering

Intrinsic in any theology of suffering will be its incompleteness. For me, implied in this 'weakness' of God is the understanding that God still weeps. That he still seeks to bring salvation to mankind, as he did thousands of years ago. The Bible affirms the possibility of a special manifestation of God's presence in our misery.[18] Previously I shared how Maranatha, the expectancy of God's presence, has become a theological anchor for me in the midst of the many emotional storms which abuse-ministry creates. Maranatha also became a firm centre in my incomplete theology of suffering. The link with suffering was strengthened through its liturgical use in the Holy Communion. Meditating on the suffering of Christ, the priest would pray 'Come O Lord,' and then turn to the congregation with the elements of the Communion, exclaiming 'The Lord has come: Maranatha.'

The Maranatha prayer has proved to be of particular value in abuse counselling. Jesus is revealed as the Word, through sacraments and through preaching, in private and group prayer and in a quiet walk, alone in the beauty of nature.

The return of the Lord, the *parousia*, can also be an encouragement. Abuse survivors often battle with a need for revenge. I believe this is a natural response which should not disturb us too much. The 'revenge psalms' of King David are pretty eloquent! When we face the need for revenge the Bible gives us an interesting answer; turn the case over to him. He can carry out vengeance better than we ever can! This helps us not to sink in the swamps of bitterness. It also relieves abuse victims from the warped sense of responsibility for their tormentor, which is often seen. In time they might become ready to realise that abusers can escape God's vengeance if they accept his grace and, as a result, repent and take responsibility for their actions.

But it doesn't make sense!

I find it hard to make sense out of much of the suffering I meet. Philip Yancey[19] helped me a bit with his observations.

Suffering and pain give us a chance to re-evaluate our relationship with God and thus enable us to seek an even-deeper relationship. If we can accept that premise the burden of senseless suffering is (somewhat) lifted.

Those who suffer often harbour vague doubts about personal responsibility of what happened to them. Job might suffer innocently, but these people ask 'Am I suffering because I have sinned?' After all, most of us will not readily compare ourselves with the righteous Job. The realistic believer might not have any difficulty at all in finding some reason for judgement! Yet the story of Job teaches us that the first question for everyone is not 'Have I sinned?' but 'Do you love me anyway?' Only when we can respond positively to this love question is the right 'love-environment' present, where we are ready to hear a possible rebuke about our lifestyle, wrong actions or outright sins. The apostle Paul refuses to accept rebuke for himself without such a manifestation of the presence of God.[20] Right words plus his presence can bring life.[21] Therefore, even if we suspect that sin is a possible cause of our problems,[22] God's first question is 'Do you love me anyway?'

Some people lose their faith as they seek answers about suffering. Mine has increased, because a personal God came into my world. I see him coming time and again into the lives of others. That person, Jesus, has not left us to deal with the difficulties of life alone. He went to be with the Father and to use his power from the throne of God to help us. He is still actively engaged in ensuring our welfare.[23] There is a battle going on between good and evil. It is a battle in which God has accepted a handicap. His almighty power as Creator is far greater than the power of Satan, who is a created being.

Losing faith

There are those who, in the search for answers, come to the conclusion that it is all senseless and decide to stop believing. Yet I have discovered that such decisions can be made on a grave misunderstanding. When a person is in great stress, often there is a reversion to a lower emotional age. Just remember the last time you responded childishly! Children deal with trauma in a different way from adults. The adult mind and the immature emotions thus can get into conflict. The small child does not know how to read the Bible, nor is it interested in doing so. The words and concepts are beyond its understanding. The mature mind feels guilty and sees it as a sign of spiritual deterioration. It is then that a spiritual coach can be a support, someone who becomes a foster-parent, who believes for the child and prays for it. Through wise counselling and reflecting on what is happening, the stress can subside and it is then that I often see faith grow again. Postponing judgement can thus provide a time of restoration and reflection.

Not only abuse survivors can battle with a feeling of loss of faith. Abuse counsellors too can face the same questions. Being exposed to an avalanche of abused persons seeking help brought me to a point which I first thought was the beginning of burn-out. Bible reading for personal devotions become harder and harder, although it worked fine when I prepared a sermon or teaching. Then one day it dawned on me that my devotional reading was being put on a divine fast. It seemed as if God wanted to remove childish understandings of him and create an emptiness which he could fill with more mature insights.

God is interested in the abused person. How that interest works out is the theme of the next chapter.

Notes

1. As quoted by Lance Morrow in an essay on Evil in *Time*, June 10, 1991, p. 41.
2. Gerard W. Hughes (1985).
3. Yancey p. 9 'After an extensive tour of the United States, the well-known German pastor and theologian, Helmut Thielicke, was asked what he saw as the greatest defect among American Christians. He replied, "They have an inadequate view of suffering." ' Was it a cultural blind spot that Thielicke saw this defect only when he travelled in the USA? What about European realities?
4. The romantic picture we have of a baby wrapped in swaddling

clothes has a darker side to it. Like all infants of that time, Jesus was wrapped up tightly for weeks and months, unable to move. That doesn't sound very pleasant to me. But this does mean Jesus can identify with all children who suffer early traumas.

5. Donald Capps (1990).
6. Job 38:39–40
7. Capps p 159
8. Rom 13:1–5
9. Dan 6:6–16
10. See Ezek 18
11. Col 2:15
12. Oscar Cullman (1959)
13. Acts 17:32
14. 1 Cor 1:23
15. 1 John 4:16
16. Rom 5:5
17. Matt 18:10
18. Matt 18:20
19. Yancey Philip, *Where is God when it hurts* Zondervan, 1976.
20. 1 Cor 4:4–5
21. 1 Cor 5:1–5
22. Is 1:2–9
23. Heb 6:19, 20; 7:24–25

CHAPTER SEVEN

CAPTIVES OF A CULTURE

Repressive church structures and the relationship to sexual abuse

The Bible speaks about the Creator and how he is still active within his creation.[1] The forces he infused into the creation, by his commands, are powerful. There is the drive towards expansion, 'fill the earth', as well as well as the magnetic force which causes people to associate. As the delicate balance between these two forces is disturbed people become alienated, individualistic or are packed in tight groups. Some churches are like shopping malls, others offer the stifling packed pressure of a 'racist group' or a religious sect. In many people both forces wrestle with each other: 'How can I escape?' and 'Where do I belong?' Creation forces, which were meant to be a blessing, become a curse.

Power abuse has proven to be a basic condition for sexual abuse and incest to take place. Thus we can understand that abusers seek social relationships where this abusive atmosphere is normal. Those in the system develop a blind spot for power abuse, including sexual abuse and incest. When emotional and spiritual abuse is already taking place the step towards physical and sexual abuse is easier to take.

Gaining understanding about such dysfunctional patterns brought a major shock to my own convictions about church life. I discovered how I had been at times a part of such settings, trying to help emotionally or spiritually abused persons to cope. I did not realise that the cause of the problems was not just a case of 'a brother who abuses power', but abusive patterns in the foundational identity of a church fellowship or a Christian organisation. As I questioned what could be behind such developments, I noted the following:

1. An addiction to power

Looking behind the scenes of many different Christian activities, I discovered 'religious addictions'—actions which were fuelled by shame and social pressure, guilt feelings and manipulation, rather than unselfish love, 'grace and peace', or respect for individuality. Those who are trapped by such a system change easily from the victim position to that of an abuser.

2. The need for ' closed' fellowship

The change from village culture to city culture is not an easy one. The city with individualism, lack of social cohesion and the fast pace of life is just too much for some.

A closed group offers something attractive; there is more intense personal interaction. Everyone knows everyone. Lonely people see the benefits. In the village there are clearly visible and functioning authority structures which are established. In the city you have to earn your position, and you can lose it. Especially in the newer 'free churches' which seem to blossom while more-traditional churches lose ground, such a village-culture church offers a fast-lane for some people to become a part of the village power structure. But then the disappointments start. To belong, one needs to conform to the public standard; if not, one is subjected to gossip or exclusion. Dysfunctional churches and Christian organisations talk about fellowship, but in fact are closed groups where individual borders are easily crossed. This does not foster a climate for true friendship. High public values and low achievement of such values, creates an inner emptiness which is behind sexual addictions in general.[2] The well-publicised reports about some public figures and their failures are only a part of what we know.

Breaking loose from repressive structures

We cannot just tell someone in a repressive structure to get out. New family relationships and social networks don't just grow on trees. Even with all good intentions on the part of a welcoming church to be God's family, in practice it's not easy for culturally-displaced people to form new social relationships. The message of Jesus shows us that it is possible to experience inner freedom first, before steps are taken to break loose from an oppressive social structure. In addition we should point out that 'in the world' it is not a picnic either. We see an increasing amount of power abuse in work situations, not least because of the scarcity of jobs.

The example of Jesus

Power abuse by leaders was also normal in Jesus' day. Shortly after his birth, Joseph and Mary had to seek asylum in Egypt. It makes you wonder what effect it had on Jesus when he heard about the children slaughtered by the soldiers of Herod because of him. When his parents settled in Nazareth, Jesus grew up in a Roman-dominated land. For thirty years, he was out of the limelight. After an 'empowering' through the Holy Spirit, he dedicated himself to helping the oppressed, the sick, the poor and the orphans. He had a message for people who were suffering under power abuse. Inner freedom was available for everyone, even when social freedom was not. However, this inner freedom undermined the position of those in power. The conflict between these two systems took him ultimately to the cross.

The example of Nicodemus

This inner release has to do with a personal acceptance of the message of the kingdom of God. Nicodemus, one of the more educated people of his day, came to Jesus at night and was one of the few of whom we know that had a personal, lengthy conversation with Jesus. Nicodemus seemed to be aware that things had not gone so well with him, even before birth. We do not know if he refers to a situation in which his parents were or if he felt that he, like David, was conceived in shame.[3] His wishful statement lingers painfully in the air; 'No chance for me to get back in the womb of my mother and have a better start'. Then Jesus shares a whole new perspective, which is a message of hope for those who know that they were conceived in shame. Jesus tells of how a different law—that of the kingdom of God—can permeate our whole existence when we receive life from God, a 'life from above', 'not by the will of a man nor of the flesh, but born from God'. As I counselled a woman who was conceived in incest (her father was also her grandfather), these words to Nicodemus started to bring new life. She could not deny where her biological life came from, but she received an infusion of divine life. At times I have felt like a midwife, being present as 'life from above' flowed into the abuse survivor, giving a whole new perspective on their identity, their heritage and their future.

The message of the apostle Paul in a period of political and religious power abuse

Paul also stressed the priority of inner freedom to a society where slavery was as socially normal then as the high debts of today that are making people virtually slaves of the bank. The message of Jesus and the power of the Holy Spirit resulted in individual changes, even for child abusers.[4] At the same time the teaching of Paul was also directed towards structural changes. He fought the enslaving tactics of those Christians who insisted that non-Jews also had to become Jews culturally in order to be saved. His teachings on inner freedom, in spite of social slavery, was his non-violent approach to overthrow the ideological foundations of power-abusive systems.

Religious power abuse today

Our understanding of who Jesus is lies anchored in the language, culture and sub-culture of our own particular world. Patriarchal aspects of western culture, a low view of women and limited value of children (especially females) also had a great influence on early Christianity.

While the gospel points the way to freedom from power

abuse, there are still dysfunctional Christian families, organisations and churches. One reason is the cultural need to fall back on old village relationship patterns mentioned earlier. Another factor is that change is not automatic. The gospel must penetrate a culture and only then can it purify that culture from the inside. Sexual abuse in the church, therefore, means that the gospel has taken insufficient root in the values and patterns of our culture.[5]

Practical steps towards freedom

If the counsellee himself or herself begins to have problems with the abusive church culture, you can try and explain to them how Jesus dealt with that in his time. It is unwise to suggest that they break their church affiliation. Where necessary, you can advise them to seek a temporary 'hiding place' in another church in order to grow strong, before coming to a final decision about where their place is; with inner freedom in a dysfunctional system or with a freedom to leave such a system behind. Counselling about abusive patterns is then needed especially, as those who have left repressive structures are often caught again in another one.

Personal victory over a dysfunctional culture

The many stories I have heard from incest survivors have given me a new respect for human willpower. In some way or another, and without help from others, many of them have miraculously chosen a lifestyle other than the dysfunctional, deformed world of the past. Pastoral workers need to watch out for such personal victories and not assume that an abusive past automatically means there are still many problems. The pastoral worker needs to have faith that the gospel can take root and grow in a culture of abuse. Before that is possible, a personal reformation is needed as part of one's preparation.

Pastoral training for working in the culture of abuse

To become effective in contacting those who live in the culture of the abused, one needs more than training and faith. There is a need for a reformation of one's values about the weak, women, power and serving. In this way, 'professional literature' on missions suddenly becomes very timely. A good way to learn to enter into this new culture is to find a guide, an abuse survivor, to coach you. Let them tell you how they look at the world. Taking some of the cultural patterns which I describe can be a help in asking the right questions! The first task of a missionary after arrival is to discover what God already has done in the hearts of people before his or her arrival. Like pearls, this work of God is waiting to be found.

Hidden pearls in the culture of the abused

In order to test the premise that every culture, including the incest culture, has 'pearls', I would like to invite you to go with me on a discovery tour. This discovery of pearls in the culture of sexual abuse is of considerable therapeutic value. There are treasures to be found in the urge to survive, dysfunctional relationships, traumatic sexualisation, betrayal, powerlessness and stigmatisation! This realisation can give a whole new view to the meaning of one's life.

1. The urge to survive

The fact that you meet a victim also means you are meeting a survivor. By discovering what strengths they developed, you can then use that urge to survive and develop ways to coach, which are linked to such an inner strength. So show admiration for the very fact that they are still alive. This shifts the attention from the past to the present, and to God's work in them now.

The urge to survive can turn into a desire to die. Often I find that abuse survivors have such a strong longing to live a normal and full life, which seems out of reach, that the urge to live is rechannelled in an urge to die. To discover the pearl of life one must thus be prepared to face the issue of suicide squarely. Several factors play a role but I shall mention three:

a) Sexual abuse is emotional murder

A young boy, just about eight years old, sat at the waterside, intently looking at his fishing rod. An older man crouched next to him and offered sweets. The boy smiled and watched his rod again. The older man started to chat, became more and more friendly and stroked him gently. 'At that time my father was often away. I liked his attention'. Then the stroking became sexually stimulating. When he looked into the man's eyes, he froze. 'I have never forgotten how he stared at me, I saw murder in his eyes. I knew he could kill me'. This 'experience of death' is not unusual in abuse survivors. The Bible also links perversion with death.[6] No wonder that the Law called for capital punishment when a sexual abuser was caught.

b) Parental sexual abuse is suicide of parenthood

When parents become sexually involved with children, they change a fundamental role from parent to an illicit lover. After having heard countless incest victims complain about the fact that they always felt like orphans, I sense that they have been right all the time. Parenthood dies; a victim becomes at that moment practically an orphan.

This insight has helped those who wrestle with the biblical instruction to 'honour your father and mother'. They then can find relief in the fact that it is possible for a sexually abused child to have honoured parenthood, before the abuse took place. After that, the parent lost the title, became a stranger, a Mr or Mrs X, an unknown person. It sounds terrible; suicide of parenthood, and it is! Yet paradoxically, this insight also offers a door of hope. The gospel teaches us faith in the 'resurrection of the dead'. It does occasionally happen that survivors are able to restore interpersonal relationships, even the parent/child relationship. However, this is almost as great a miracle as the resurrection of Jesus himself! I have met a few. But as yet they feel unable to step out into the limelight. We desperately need more stories of hope.

If the abuser is a church leader then it can mean that, as far as the victim is concerned, God 'dies' as well, or 'God should be killed as well'. The very fact that we, as pastoral workers, 'represent' God makes it possible for the deep cry of 'Where was God when I called for help?' to be uttered, or their further unbelief in him to be shared. These explosions of agony bring into focus more sharply the distance between the survivor and God. As I have stated before don't, as a helper, try to defend God. He doesn't need a lawyer. He can speak for himself, whenever someone is ready to hear! Just be there and listen. When the time to say at least something has come, I sometimes ask, 'Well, may I believe for you? Is it all right if I talk to God about you, as you can't bring yourself to meet him just yet?' That permission gives you the chance to pray silently or, if possible, to pray a short, direct prayer out loud: 'God, this person doesn't want this kind of life any more, she (or he) wants real life!' Some even need encouragement that they can discover that there is life before death! Such an awareness of 'representing God's mercy' allowed me to respond positively to a person who asked for help recently and said 'I had written off God, but if his people are like you, I'll give him a chance'.

c) Suicide, as a desire to kill the abuser

Many a survivor has told me 'but I feel as if he is still inside me.' The urge to destroy the abuser can thus also turn into self-destruction.

If a suicidal urge remains strong, pastoral volunteers should at least seek advice from a professional helper. I sometimes point out the fact that the abuser was an emotional killer already. 'Would you want him to succeed in your physical death as well? Would it not be a relief for him not to be able to be accused any more?' If it is difficult to see a change of such a death-wish, then the survivor's G.P. or the local mental health authorities are the most obvious channels through which to seek assistance.

Even people who have done well for years can lose hope when change finally is in sight. They are then in danger of 'sinking in sight of the harbour'. By this I mean that because of the help that is now offered, the fighting spirit can ebb away. The survivor suddenly cannot go any further and the danger of suicidal feelings increases. That's why a careful approach is needed, with respect and admiration and a confirmation of the survival techniques they already possess.

2. Dysfunctional relationships

One other pearl is the fact that many incest survivors choose, later in life, to shift from the 'victim role' to the 'helper role' (see Chapter 4). This desire to help others can be transformed into a healthy attitude to life and harbour hope for the future. But there has to be a radical change in dysfunctional relationship patterns. Otherwise their attempt to help becomes merely a repetition of the dysfunctional relationships of the past. This unfortunately happens all too often in counselling, where the abused of the past become abusive helpers today. But instead of stopping people in recovery from dysfunctional relationships from helping, it is better to supervise and coach them into better helping styles.[7] This statement is also based on practical observations; they will seek to help people anyhow, whether we like it or not. A sense of self-respect is very important in the healing process; to be used by God in helping someone else, despite one's own handicap, gives purpose to life.[8]

3. Traumatic sexualisation

The recognition that traumatic sexualisation is not just a warped childhood fantasy has brought about a radical change in secular helping. Formerly there was talk of 'value-free' helping, whereby ethical norms were left out of the picture; everything was cultural, but that's changed. There is now a foundation where secular and pastoral workers can meet, that is, an acceptance of the fact that the normal development of a child is damaged through an untimely exposure to sexual activity by the very persons from whom it should grow away. Abuse survivors can serve as beacons of healthy values in a society where respect for borders, power abuse and sexual norms continue to erode.

4. Betrayal

Incest survivors have a great need for reliability and confidentiality. Their need to control anything that happens to them can be turned into a positive lifestyle. You can respond positively by confirming the need for distrust. If they feel insecure, then work within these limits.

The sensitivity to betrayal can result in an increased capacity of observation. Their 'antennas' are always turned on and the 'radar screen' in a permanent state of readiness. Such an alertness can then act as a spring-board to further growth in the capacity to analyse and observe. It is also true that not everyone is to be trusted! We need the sensitivity to the abuse of power which survivors have. It is a good thermometer in testing whether you are really serving or dominating!

The isolation that can arise through this feeling of betrayal can also be the occasion for a more independent development as an individual. While increasing loneliness is a symptom of modern society, we can teach survivors to turn loneliness into 'alone-ness with God'. This means giving a central place, in the course of counselling, to a biblical form of meditation and personal worship.

If they find at last 'in you' someone trustworthy, then this may tip the scales and they will swallow everything you say or become very intimate. So you need to be on the alert too, and act the fool a bit if you see they are accepting all too easily everything you do, say or even vaguely suggest. Humour can help here, to make them aware that they are taking you too seriously. The ability to achieve 'nearness' needs to be balanced by the ability to maintain 'distance'. This is one of the more difficult aspects in pastoral counselling by volunteers. Professionals get much training in this and know methods with which to maintain a proper balance. The distrust of an abuse survivor can be an excellent training for pastoral volunteers, if they can teach the helpseekers to give frank feedback!

5. *Powerlessness*

The abuser, by definition, uses some form of spiritual, emotional, physical or social power. This easily overwhelms the victim. In the past they experienced how nothing could change the situation. It became learned powerlessness. Any counselling situation has moments when one feels 'stuck'. That is the moment to show another response to powerlessness; creative helplessness. God's answer through the gospel, which gives us power, can break the overpowering sense of weakness. In their weakness, they can learn to say 'But Christ is in me.' The infilling with the power of the Holy Spirit can bring a tremendous lift. It also harbours a danger if the weakness and helplessness is not understood correctly. If they despise it, they are in danger of attempting to have 'a corner on God's power' and run the danger of an inflated ego, out of fear of being 'helpless' again. The Bible teaches through scores of lives about the reality of weakness, needs, and the way God is able through his grace to use people, while being weak.

6. *Stigmatisation*

Feelings of shame because of the abuse, reinforce the feeling of being 'different', 'branded' or stigmatised.

The uniqueness of every person is a positive approach to the feeling of being 'branded' that the survivor has because of past experiences. Instead of allowing them to fade into the background, we can teach them to accept current limitations and talk about their own identity, as they are now; to be proud that they are survivors. The introverts will probably want to do that less obtrusively than others. Positive acceptance of differences can here be a help: 'I still find confrontation difficult'; 'When I was depressed, I started to overeat'.

The need for self-help groups

The positive use of one's past is especially of value in self-help groups. Especially in Scandinavia, a network of incest-support centres have earned great respect. Run by survivors themselves, they provide immediate and free help.

Self-help groups bring together people with the same experience. There is a need for non-abuse based relationships, in order to discover 'normal' life. The church can and should provide such a setting. It does not have a good track-record though, in helping sexually abused persons. The recurrent stress on renewal should be more than a personal renewal: there should be renewal of abusive church systems and abusive pastoral approaches as well.

Notes

1. Jn 1:9; Acts 17:24–28; Col 1:15–17
2. Mark Laaser (1992), Sandra D. Wilson (1990), Harry W. Schaumberg (1992). Charlotte Davis Kasl (1988).
3. Ps 51 seems to me more a personal statement of David of sin from generation to generation, than a theological statement.
4. 1 Cor 6:9–11
5. See Rom 12:1–2, Also: Schreitner, Robert J, *Constructing Local Theologies*, Maryknol, 1985.
6. Prov 7:27
7. Heb 12:12. This is also a validation of abuse survivors helping others, as a part of a support group.
8. 2 Cor 1:4.

CHAPTER EIGHT

THE CHURCH AND THE CULTURE OF ABUSE

Historic failures

The history of religion shows us how religion has both freed people from evil constraints, bringing liberty, but also brought suppression, persecution and death. In some instances it appears that the church which says, 'We see,' has an acute case of blindness to reality. The Enlightenment, as a reaction to religious dogmatism, discovered in the process the child, not as a miniature adult, but as a person-in-development. The New Age movement stresses the need for a holistic view of reality and rebels against the separation of soul and body, something they have observed in many Christian circles. The feminist movement stood up against male domination. They were also the first to raise the issue of the sexual abuse of women and more specific abuse within the family—incest. This shows me again how God at times raises people who consider themselves 'outsiders' to call his children to their senses. The effect of the Enlightenment was a new approach to the place of children in the church. The New Age movement has once again forced us to affirm that the body itself is not evil. Through the feminist insistence, sexual abuse of women has finally received the attention of the church.[1]

Failures of the church regarding child sexual abuse

The church has long been ignorant about child sexual abuse. Many church leaders are still unwilling to listen to the nervous, stumbling attempts of a survivor to share childhood abuse secrets. Abuse is hushed up, offenders quietly reassigned. Can one expect anything of the church now? Abuse survivors, coming out of hiding, have braved the denial, the suspicion, the unbelief. As 'experience specialists' they tell us about the failures of secular as well as religious helpers.[2]

Failures of the secular system regarding child sexual abuse

For a long time, incest and child abuse were denied in the traditional institutions for helping hurting people. Psychoanalytical theories about children's sex fantasies were often used to explain the bizarre stories survivors told. To use historic failure as a basis for rejecting the church as a credible channel for healing, and to promote only secular forms of help, is a biased and unwise conclusion. To be involved in treatment is the best way to become aware of the devastation that sexual abuse causes. If we want churches to change, we should urge them to be involved! But how?

The need for the church to be involved

The fact that abuse survivors *do* seek church-based help is partly because survivors with a Christian culture background find that secular help alone is insufficient for them. But when such survivors ask for pastoral help, they often meet unbelief or are brow-beaten with statements such as, 'You should forgive', 'Repent of your anger', etc. Church leaders often choose to avoid a scandal rather than to take sides with a victim. No wonder that many turn away from such churches. Most of those whom I met continued to have spiritual longings, but were somewhat allergic to any form of organised religion. That can cause problems in therapy, as one survivor once told me:

> When the therapist started to probe my disgust with the church, he found an easy prey. As he encouraged me to turn away from my church, I lost my social network as well. The only thing I had left was the incest-support group. From then on, I met people for the sole reason of being an abuse survivor. My whole life started to

revolve around it. I ended up where I did not want to be, again in a 'special corner'. I desperately wanted to be a normal person.

This story indicates that abuse survivors need culturally sensitive treatment. Recent discussions with secular helpers in the Netherlands indicate that there is a growing willingness to help people within their cultural framework.

The church has always been 'people together'. What resources are there in the fellowship that could be called upon to equip the saints for ministry? What 'experience specialists' are there; the survivors who have faced their past and now can learn to help others? While professional helpers can only be seen by appointment, we need another specialisation as well; caring people who are specialists in giving personal support. We need pastoral workers who understand the burning questions, who allow a voice to be raised to God, who can also deal with the question of the meaningless of life which many experience and who know how to empower survivors in the art of a free and full life.

Whenever I speak about involvement of pastoral volunteers in the field of serious abuse, I meet concern in the eyes of formally trained workers. Their studies have shown how vast the needs are, how many mistakes can be made. Yet the Bible shows us how God wants to equip common believers to be 'priests in this world'. It also gives a comprehensive system of thinking and tested rules of ethical behaviour. Above all, the word gives us the power to share hope and life. The church is also called to help isolated people to learn to relate. While abuse survival support groups can do this as well, they are limited because they centre around a specific need. The church fellowship centres around a Person. Some believers can function as non-formal trained abuse specialists with their own possibilities and limits. To understand each other's possibilities and limits allows psychologists and psychiatrists who are professionals in abuse treatment to take on those cases where others can't go any further.

The need for church-related abuse treatment specialists

Helping survivors means enabling them to learn to live with the shame and pain of sexual abuse. Their needs are often complicated by an additional set of normal problems. They usually consider these problems insignificant until key wounds of the abuse start to heal. This backlog of untreated non-abusive problems then complicates the healing process. Some lasting results of abuse trauma cannot be reversed, such as the decision not to get married. After one is healed, there follows the agony of the realisation that vital chances to choose a life mate, to have a family life and possibly children, may have passed by.

We need specialists to walk along the dark corridors of twisted lives that are in need of emotional and behavioural restructuring. The way that the survivor coped with abuse made sense at the time of the abuse. Naturally they needed to have regular forms of emotional pain killers, and it is easy to understand that they would avoid abusive types. But in the healing process, new patterns have to be learned. Just as not everyone is a good teacher, in the same way not everyone will have the patience and the skill to help people 'untwist'.

Because the needs are complicated, helpers can fall into the trap of simplification. This happens quite naturally through the responses of those we help. Once sexual abuse has been shown as *one* cause of the problems, it soon becomes *the* cause. Just as a sick person on a sinking ship has two problems, we should look beyond the individual need of abuse survivors and face the larger picture as well.

The needs within a need

The need for experiences

Abuse survivors don't have just one problem. Especially in the west, the individualisation, the loss of social glue and the increasing meaningless of life add to their woes. This larger need has been focused on in a recent report by the Dutch Council of Churches. It points to the growing desire of people to experience, to feel *something*. Over the last fifty years

western masses have turned away from church-based help to
any other possible solution. In my country every type of esoteric
method of help is available from a patchwork of eastern
religions to old-fashioned animism and occultism, with a
current price tag of about 600 million guilders (about £225
million) per year.

Abuse survivors face intense emotional needs as they learn to
deal with repressed anger, hatred and the desire to destroy.
Many of them learned to 'be absent' while abuse took place.
That was their way to survive. In time this can become such a
habit that their creation-based gift to worship God the Creator,[3]
gets a new focus. They can sink away through concentration
into emptiness ('stepping into a black hole'), or turn to excitement or materialism. The healing of this escapism can be
fostered by a return to the original creation gift of worship.
This will empower them to stay with it and not to escape into
nothingness or fancy dreams.

Worship of the Almighty is one of the greatest gifts the
Christian church has received and is a healthy platform for a
God-focused experience. Tragically, many churches have
shrivelled the potential to help people to have such experiences. Doctrinal truth, which can be the back-bone for biblical
experiences, too easily has become a hindrance for emotional
expression. In fact, it has robbed God's people of an united
experience to stand in awe before the Almighty in worship.[4]

Church-based abuse-treatment specialists have a rich store of
biblically based worship to receive strength and solace for
themselves as well as for those who seek help.

The need for integration, the holistic emphasis

The Christian emphasis on spiritual (in other words, mental)
facts, and the sometimes open hatred of the physical body as
'the enemy', have brought a vacuum in the experiences of faith.
Yet Christianity is a very physical religion. The Bible talks
about the resurrection of dead bodies! We believe that the
Spirit of God can live in our frail human bodies, thus making
us a 'temple of the Spirit'! Abuse survivors-in-recovery often

learn from New Age-related holistic information about how good the body can be.

Church-based abuse-treatment specialists will need to come to terms with their own understanding of holism and the integration of their spirit, soul and body, through the God of peace.[5] Then they will be able to place what New Age offers to abuse-survivors in a proper context and serve seekers of help with a tested, bible-based framework for experiences in spirit, soul and body.

The limitations of church-based help

The church, as a community of believers seeking action together, cannot do everything. This self-understanding helps to decide when to refer trauma survivors to others. Too often 'difficult cases' become 'difficult people' for us, but the church is all-embracing. We dare not push them away and yet we feel powerless to help.

The answer is, I believe, that each church needs some people who understand and can walk with these survivors. Even when we can't promise healing, we can affirm the validity of the promise that Jesus wants to come into our pain. The Shalom 'hiding place' is then at least a help, even if we don't have the skills to meet survivors at the level of their need.

If mental health specialists are available, and willing to work within the framework of the values of a Christian client, they can provide a meaningful contribution to the healing process. However, if they disregard the survivor's basic values their help might become yet another abusive experience. The same rule must also be applied to situations where a church-based ministry is involved in helping someone who has not yet clarified their own religious values. To insist that they accept our values before help is given is just as abusive.

I believe in the church, but I also know that there are gifts of God to be found in secular settings. God's gracious intervention does not only operate through those who are committed Christians. The experience of a missionary in Asia can serve as an example. Recurrent illness had a crippling effect on his work. The mission doctors were convinced that there were deep psychological aspects to his condition, which they had been unable to touch. The blunt advice he received was to 'shape up or ship out'. Then they gave him the address of a psychiatrist in a nearby city. The psychiatrist listened to the man's story, his shattered dreams, his fears and his sense of failure. After an hour he remarked, 'I am not a Christian, but I do know something of the Bible. It appears to me that you know a God of wrath, of fire. But you don't seem to know the God of love and forgiveness, the One who waits for you and helps you start over again.' The missionary later shared that he felt like Paul, who was blinded on the road to Damascus, but healed when someone prayed for him and the 'scales fell from his eyes.' There and then, this missionary was awakened to the love of God. It was the mirror which the psychiatrist held in front of him which showed a deep cause of internal struggle and which proved later to be directly linked to his healing.

On the other hand, there are also accounts in which individual Christians have been treated by secular helpers in an unethical way. Churches, too, are not all beneficial. Survivors often perceive action-oriented churches as abusive. They seem to heal better in a low-key approach to church life. I am not stating that all aggressively evangelistic churches are, by definition, abrasive. Low-key churches can also be manipulative in a subtle way. The difference is that low-key churches usually allow church members much more freedom and survivors can thus avoid manipulative situations.

A healing atmosphere for an incest survivor

How can a church fellowship provide a healing atmosphere? I see at least four necessary ingredients:

1. Providing healing social structures;
2. Incest survivors who are realistic in their expectations of help and who are willing to work on a self-help programme;
3. Volunteers who support the self-help programme;

4. Accessibility to professionals for help, where necessary, should the other three factors prove insufficient.

1. Providing healing social structures

The church has great abilities to motivate people into action. The need for social structures which promote healing can easily be filled by a church which is sensitive to the special needs of abuse survivors. It must be an approach which is at least as sensitive as when asylum seekers are welcomed.

As the church cannot do everything, some churches might pool resources, and there is the possibility of exchanging pastoral workers. Abuse survivors want privacy. They often find it hard to really 'tell it all' to a person they might meet again many years from now. Specialist structures and centres could be set up with support from different fellowships.

These structures are needed for a survivor in order to learn a new way to relate. The incest culture is, in principle, dysfunctional. Manipulation is normal. A healing social community is therefore one that is anti-manipulative; where there is personal freedom and responsibility; where there is no pressure from the leadership of the fellowship on the survivors to 'do their bit'. Non-commitment is essential. Everything that binds has a reverse effect. This is valid for both a secular group and/or a church.

In principle, I see three circles of involvement in a church which fosters healing:

1. An inner circle

The committed nucleus (the pastor and other officials). These people live for the continued existence of the church, and that is right. Without such a dedicated group, a church will not survive for long.

2. A second circle

In this circle people are active in their free time but in a limited way. This is the secondary leadership level, Bible-study group leaders and Sunday-School workers, for example.

3. The third circle

Here are the ordinary believers who are called to be active in the world and who find support within the church for this task. There is little or no expectation from the other two circles that the people in the outer circle actually do anything for the church, except contributing to the collection! On the contrary, they are encouraged to be active in the world. Often I notice how abuse survivors choose this circle. I have the impression that the other circles create too much pressure of expectations and long-term commitment.

2. A good self-help programme

Incest survivors need to understand their own cultural world. I see immigrants or refugees as an example of this. When they are taken into our church communities we realise it takes time for them to understand and get used to the Dutch culture and church culture. On the other hand, it's mind-expanding for the Dutch believer to learn from them how they experience God. In this way, we can take a look at our own culture through the eyes of the stranger and perhaps identify and acknowledge things which are biblically unacceptable. If we apply this example to the incest culture, we come to the same conclusions. Just as immigrants have to learn in practice, with the assistance of Dutch volunteers, what the Dutch culture is, in the same way I see how important volunteers are in incest counselling. A mutual tolerance is needed, but survivors also need to be encouraged to help themselves.[6]

Breaking out of the incest culture starts with a rejection of what is evil. The danger is that cultural isolation can occur if they can't see what is good in their culture of origin. Incest survivors can observe new values in the helpers and gain new insight into what can be changed in their own lives. This is certainly not the easiest period of their healing. Tremendous anger can break out when they realise what they have missed, and they will need help in dealing with this anger and learning to concentrate on the positive issues.

3. Wise volunteers

Through regular contact between volunteers and incest survivors, the patient-oriented counselling model can be avoided. Volunteers can serve as cultural bridges to smooth the entrance to a church community without pampering the survivor.

In the first talk with an incest survivor I usually tell them about the need of emotional self-defence. They are in control of what is or is not discussed. They can give direction to the conversation. They determine how deeply something is discussed and when to change the subject. They can cancel appointments at the last minute if they are suddenly afraid. Anything that can strengthen their will is good.

Because the will has been broken, we speak of a kind of 'emotional hernia'. Any kind of pressure or force is heavy and hurts, and is therefore harmful. But, as a pastoral worker, you are just as much in control as far as your own life is concerned. You can also direct, determine the boundaries and make a new appointment when *you* can cope with it, not when they want it. Demonstrate a healthy use of the will!

4. Availability of professional help

There will be times when you feel you're getting nowhere. The culture shock, the present reality, are all too much. Or there are stumbling-blocks in the communication and social contact, which are not being solved within the kind of healing atmosphere suggested above. Then don't be afraid of admitting honestly that it's not working and that expert help is needed.

Accept that resources may be limited

These four factors together are necessary for church pastoral help to function properly. The availability of help within a church can be very appealing to incest survivors, who may want to join such a church for that very reason! But if the whole system doesn't function properly, it will cause too great a pressure on the pastoral volunteers, which means that other areas of work are left unattended. In that case, it's better to say to inquirers 'At present, we can't cope with your request. We are prepared to help you find the right professional help to support you in the process. But we'd like to help you in other areas.' But I do advise pastoral workers to make use of the opportunity of sitting in on the counselling sessions with the professionals, if possible, to see what they can learn!

The need for hope

Confused by many conflicting feelings, people in social upheaval need helpers with an understanding of the process of cultural adaptation. That is one of the tasks of development workers and missionaries. As specialists in change they are able to assist the working out of the gospel in a particular culture. Pastoral workers can also learn to do this and, with that knowledge, help incest survivors to inner freedom. Faith that this is possible gives helpers greath strength. That faith can be infectious, as you stand with one foot in the mud, searching for firm ground, and the other foot on the solid rock of faith.

Hope is not a new idea for incest survivors. After all, they have kept going, one way or another. That means they must have had some hope that they could break out of the situation. And they prayed. Sometimes a survivor tells me 'God was there, somehow. Through him I was able to go on; he was my only comfort.' They probably also had hope that through marriage, for example, they would be able to leave the old life behind. But on the other hand, they have been disappointed time and again, even in God. Their prayers were not answered. There was no change. God was far away. That's why hope and despair, faith and disbelief, are almost inseparable in the incest survivor.

As pastoral helpers, we represent the hope that God gives. We can't turn the clock back. What is done, is done. What happened is now history. Neither is it our task to give 'purpose to suffering'. If there is a purpose, then God will have to make it clear! But we can continue to express our faith in a God who, right at the beginning of the Bible, made something new out of chaos and said 'Let there be light!'

Levels of competence in the church

I still passionately believe that it is God's intention for the churches to be like islands of healing in a broken world, and that they will fill the world which such places of health. I believe in the church, because there is something which people can receive in a Christian fellowship that no secular counselling can provide. There are non-religious groups which create a sense of belonging, and teach people with a great variety of personalities to live together in harmony. As such, the church is not unique. What *is* different is the claim that, as believers together, we have the opportunity of experiencing an encounter with Jesus himself. God wants us to have such fellowship together, in order to demonstrate to the evil powers that Jesus is Lord; that there are people who choose to love God unconditionally.[7] To make these encounters possible and keep them from being infiltrated by pseudo-manifestations—religious 'highs' without Christ—we need structures, a platform and quality control.

While the church as a whole can manifest the right kind of help, not everyone has the same gifts or the same level of helping ability. When pastoral counsellors accept these limitations, they can help with a greater freedom, and refer people to others when they know they have reached their own limits. Those who work with what God has given and are relaxed about what they do not have, often become more skilled in the process!

If nothing else, any counsellor with a heart for abused persons can teach them how to avoid further abuse and abusive settings. Then they can look around for the type of helper to suit the specific situation of a counsellee. In addition, a right choice will need to be made about church membership and informal contacts, which will enable a person to re-socialise or learn for the first time how to relate to groups of people.

In order to be able to relate to people, we need to have some insight into who we are. The bad self-concept of an abuse survivor is a hindrance to forming the relationships vital for healing. One of the first tasks of a pastoral counsellor is to help a victim exchange the self-concept of a victim for that of a skilled survivor, as I will discuss in the next chapter.

Notes

1. Imbes and Jonker were the first to raise the Christian perspective in the Netherlands. They describe, *Religion and Incest*, the added burden when incest takes place in an ideologically-charged environment, be it Christian or otherwise. They and others have not been able to show that incest occurs either more or less in Christian circles than other areas of society. But there is evidence of a link between incest and a life in more-closed families and communities. Their samples included also a victim who was not raised as a Christian, but in an ideological/politically-charged climate.
2. Alice Miller, 1990; Imbes and Jonker, 1985.
3. Rom 1:18–23
4. The apostle Paul describes in 2 Cor 12:1–5 how he himself had such an intense experience of which he did not know if it happened outside his body or inside his body. The conclusion is obvious, that this does not matter. I note that Paul says these things in the context of suffering. Thus I conclude that people in suffering can withstand better what happens through worship of the Almighty. This is supported by the reports of martyrs who died seemingly not showing any signs of pain, such as Stephanus in Acts 7:55–60. There are many witnesses in church history who indicate the same.
5. 1 Thess 5:23
6. Gal 6:5
7. Eph 3:10–11

CHAPTER NINE

FROM VICTIMS TO SKILLED SURVIVORS

Deep traumas mark a person, even if they can hide it. Some people who have been in concentration camps show deep emotion when that period of their life is mentioned. Others can talk about it remotely, as if it concerned someone else. One thing is certain; it is important how one perceives the past. Are you still a victim or have you become a survivor? The label we give ourselves influences our identity.

What's in a name?

Let me give some examples to explain the importance of names. I just phoned one of my daughters. She answered the phone with her maiden name. She is happily married. It made me feel good, though, to hear our family name coming back to me through the phone. Names have something to do with identity, they are symbols. Symbols are important in communication. The connotation they hold for us, though, will differ. The flag which makes one person's heart beat faster gives another heartburn! Some words or symbols are so powerful that they influence everything around them. They set the tone. Examples are the Red Cross and the Red Crescent, its Islamic counterpart.

Some of the children in the class of a teacher friend have changed names several times, as mother remarried. One can only wonder what this does to the identity of a child. Changing names has an impact. Changing names indicates a new status, a new relationship. Abram became Abraham. Jacob became Israel. A whole story lies behind these changes.

A change of paradigm

Changing names means changing the way one looks at things, a change of paradigm, a reframing of a concept from a different perspective. An example of paradigm change happened recently in our family. My wife paints watercolours. Once she painted a picture she did not like, so she washed it out. What was left still showed some pretty colours. With a large brush, she played with the paint and quite an unusual picture developed. She decided not to throw it away. Then an art dealer took several of her pictures, including this near-reject. When she went to the art shop, she was utterly amazed at the effect a good frame had made. It had been so beautifully done that she bought her own picture back! This 'reframing of perspective' is called a paradigm change.

Abuse victims also need a paradigm change. The word 'victim' points to abuse in the present tense. 'Survivor' indicates that you went through something in the past. The use of the word 'survivor' rather than 'victim' is a mental change of location. That change of location is the vital first step if we want to leave the past behind.

A paradigm change can take place quickly, for instance, the apostle Paul's instant conversion on the road to Damascus. The persecutor turns into a disciple and asks immediately 'What do you want me to do, Lord?' The radical change of perspective in the mind of Paul still had to be followed by years of change. He needed to relearn what faith was like, through years of isolation, waiting, and learning to express his faith in Antioch. Then he was ready to become the Paul we know from his writings.

The importance of paradigm change in relation to sexual perversion and abuse is obvious when Paul discusses the new status of believers who were once perverts and victims. 'You have been like that, but not any more . . . you are now a temple of the Holy Spirit.' (1 Cor 6:11,19)

Let me tell you about Betsy, who at the beginning had a rather slow change of a major symbol in her life; males. Any man coming close caused her to be alert and tense and no wonder, when you heard what men had done to her. So Betsy had started to believe that all men were brutes and dangerous. Not only her feelings, but also what her mother had told her, had shaped a variety of negative paradigms. Then her female counsellor had introduced the idea that at some stage she would have to learn to relate more positively to men, otherwise the lasting effects of abuse would rob her of much enjoyment of life. Betsy learned coping strategies to prepare her to meet men in a more mature way. She began to relate incidents which showed that the ice was thawing. Then she agreed to allow a male counsellor to take part in her treatment. As I was invited into the room her whole body language showed fear. Yet, in this first encounter, something happened. In an atmosphere of openness, she started to share long-suppressed stories. I became the first male she trusted. While the counselling had slowly awakened Betsy to the fact that not all men are brutes, it was still a shock for her to realise that she could even feel secure with some of them. Thus the paradigm began to change.

Belief systems

Different paradigms together form a belief system. For example, Christianity is not just a way of looking at things, but a whole spectrum of paradigms; the cross, the Bible, the person of Jesus, concepts such as faith, hope, love, etc. These paradigms are closely linked, which means that if you degrade the Bible from a divinely-inspired book to an interesting tale full of misconceptions, the Christian belief system starts to fall apart.

1. The belief systems of the abused

The world of an abuse survivor has been shattered (if it had time to become shaped in the first place). The trusted parent-figure becomes a person who creates confusion, fear, distrust. New ways to cope with the situation become ingrained in a child.

Then there is the constant brainwashing, the input of wrong information into a child by the abuser and often by the environment as well. Mother says 'Don't lie to me about your father.' The pastor says 'You are a bad girl to tell such tales. I know your father; he wouldn't do that.' A new belief system is built, based on lies, false guilt feelings and futile attempts by a powerless child to cope.

Helping abuse survivors means introducing them to another belief system about themselves and about what has happened. Also, practical information needs to be shared about the body and the physiological responses brought about by sexual stimulation. Morality needs to be taught. 'It is not true that all fathers who really love their children do this.' Values of right and wrong need to be taught. For counsellors who work non-directively—letting the client set the stage—this is a change. 'How can I tell them what is good and what is bad?' Religious or not, however, any helper will have some ideas about the ultimate questions of existence, and thoughts about evil, good, life and death. And pastoral counsellors have always given some direction in the counselling. The person who seeks help knows that. The choice of receiving pastoral help automatically has consequences. The victim knows, by the type of pastoral help he seeks, what belief system the counsellor will have.[1]

2. The belief systems of counsellors

It is not only the belief system of the counsellee that is important. We must also look at the beliefs of the counsellor, because this will influence what they hear and see. The idea of Transgenerational Trauma came into focus when some Dutch therapists started to become aware that they were avoiding painful areas in clients and choosing other topics instead. When children of concentration camp survivors came for help to therapists whose parents had faced war traumas, they found that their counsellors bypassed major painful issues. 'Second generation scars' played a role. The same seems to be the case with sexual-abuse victimisation. Decades of refusal by counsellors to believe that there was such a high incidence of sexual abuse can be traced to a similar symptom.

We have already noticed how religious beliefs also play a strong role. To add one more example; what one believes about the existence of evil spirits will influence one's perspective on counsellees' symptoms.

Cross-currents of belief systems

Pastoral counsellors have at least two major belief systems; what the church believes and considers valuable, as well as the fundamental beliefs and values of the culture in which they live.

As we live in both systems, our faith will be influenced by both. No wonder the apostle Paul encourages us to continue the never-ending process of change.[2] It is here that we face the battle of Incarnation on a private level. 'Who is God for me? What do I believe about him?' We can't be good consellors unless we clarify some of the basic tenets of our own faith. Otherwise, the questioning of others will alarm us and raise insecurities which will discourage an open interaction between counsellor and counsellee.

Because our belief systems are so influential on the way we perceive the things around us, we need to find some common ground. This is needed in politics, in culture and in religion. Diversity can only exist if there is also a form of unity. It is the Creator's plan to have diversity, but he also teaches us how the universe, with all its diversity, demonstrates the need for unity.

Creation values and belief systems

As we study mankind and his belief systems, we can find a unity which transcends religious and cultural borders. There is a common development of the human being which gives us the possibility of a similar perspective. Thus the question 'Is incest really bad?' does not even need biblical authority. It has already been answered from an observation of human development.

Incest is an act which is done at the wrong time, by the wrong person, with a wrong motive.

Once, when I gave a seminar on incest for directors of boarding schools in Denmark, I was shown a list of films which schools were allowed to use. One of them was positive about sexual intimacy within a family which included children. Since this film was made, the incest problem had exploded and brought about a paradigm change in public opinion. The resulting laws, which were designed to protect children from incest, carry just about the stiffest penalties in Europe. Paradoxically, the freedom of the media still allowed that film to be screened.

While an over-emphasis on morality can lead to fanaticism and a new inquisition, the line has to be drawn somewhere. One factor in determining when such a line is crossed, comes from our understanding of creation. There are some indisputable rights of human beings. One of them is that the nature of human development demands protection up to a certain point.

The study of creation and the gifts the Creator gave us to be developed and used, can help us in the paradigm change from victim to survivor.

Surviving through creation gifts

Sitting on the edge of a beautiful fountain in a plaza in Rome, we can discuss the great architecture we see. It is a hot day. As you refresh your face in the water, a friend playfully pushes you down. Within 15 seconds, all thoughts about architecture have gone, and when it lasts even longer, panic and violence can erupt. It becomes a battle for survival. This instant change from beauty to a fight for survival is a creation gift. The greater the threat to our existence, the more intense, raw and frantic our responses will be.

The profound threat to the personality posed by abuse creates a basic survival pattern which shows similarities in whatever culture one studies. These universal responses facilitate the design of a pastoral approach on how to share the universal gospel with abuse survivors. A treatment programme will be more effective if it corresponds with the natural responses creation has already put into us. If we can observe that a counsellee has already learned to use these survival gifts, we can then build on that. For instance, pain is a universal phenomenon. How people deal with physical or emotional pain, however, can differ considerably.

Dr Brand, a veteran missionary surgeon and pioneer in the field of leprosy teatment, sees pain as a gift from God. It is a great fact of creation which assures our well-being. But our ability to deal with pain varies. Also, if we concentrate on pain, the sense of pain can increase subjectively, even if there is no pain being inflicted at that moment. A caring dentist once explained this pain-sensitivity to a child. The little girl was trembling with fear in the dentist's chair. Then, as he reached out to her, but before he touched her teeth, she started to cringe with pain. He tried to show her how fear increases the pain-sensitivity. But he also knew that we can increase our ability to deal with pain if we focus on something else. So he pointed to a beautiful picture of butterflies on the ceiling above the dentist's chair, and her attention was sufficiently diverted for the treatment to begin.

There can come a moment though, when the pain and suffering are simply too much. Creation has made provision for that as well. Somehow the alarms are switched off, the body goes cold, and a numbness takes over. In the more serious cases, when the shock or the pain level becomes too intense, a person can faint.

As I hear from survivors how they have coped with their ordeals, I am amazed at the unique use of these survival-gifts; how they developed personalised patterns which allowed them to cope. The human spark to live on, in spite of terrible conditions, is incredible. Take Peter, for instance, who could really tell stories. His fantasy was unlimited. He often used that gift to talk himself out of tight spots with remarkable skill. Truth became rather fluid for him. 'How you put it depends on the circumstances.' The problem was that Peter sometimes did not realise the difference between truth and fantasy. Others would simply conclude he was lying. That hurt him very much.

Through counselling, he discovered how his fantasy had worked for him; when his mother's new husband started to abuse him, fantasies were his only escape. A helpful coping strategy developed. When the abuse had stopped, it seemed the natural thing to carry on using this fantasy in order to be the popular story-teller. It also helped him to be creative in 'slanting' the truth or, as others would call it, lying.

Counselling abuse survivors becomes even more difficult if the abusers have employed refined techniques which also make use of survival gifts. I know of survivors who were manipulated into 'splitting off' from reality, or 'dissociating', in order to make them more compliant survivors and meek as lambs. Albert told me how he could still feel physically the heat of the fire used on his body. It was part of the torture inflicted on him as a child. He developed an imaginary 'ice palace'. This huge building provided him with sufficient room to hide so that he could not be caught. The cold also numbed his feelings and helped him to cope. In time he could remember more of what had happened. Then he realised that his tormentors had planned this 'withdrawal into the cold' in order to have a docile victim for their sordid games. Initially, they would put him into a large cold-storage room before starting the burning torture. Later they skipped that and he created his own 'cold world'. It is hard to believe that people can do such things to children and even more amazing how some of them recover. Even if they don't know it, I believe that there is a gracious God who stands with them in their pain.

Surviving through supernatural gifts

Beatrice could not escape meeting the abuser who had raped her; they both lived in the same small town. There had been no way to prove it. After it had happened, she had walked for hours in the cold night, numbed and feeling dead. Her parents just thought she had made up the story as an excuse for coming home late. They made sure that she did not go to the police. She struggled with her responses.

When we met, I observed that there were moments when, right in the middle of a talk, she would drift away. It was as if she 'evaporated'. After some time she would talk, without actually saying anything. Her problem, she thought, was her inability to move elsewhere. Living in the village was a daily ordeal, especially when she saw the smug face of the rapist. Then I introduced to her the idea of a 'fog', a kind of 'holy indifference', a 'divine ego-trip'. It would make her less sensitive to the situation.

Within her belief system, this became a practical prayer that she could use. I demonstrated how to pray for this and simply asked God to give her this 'fog'. What I meant was a high concentration of the presence of God to enable her to live in the present, and a lessening of the obsession with the rapist and the past. Weeks later she called me to say that it was still working and that she could pray for it whenever she needed it. This calmed her down enough to learn to show anger and demonstrate her freedom to go where she wanted.

Guideposts in the dark

As we try to help survivors with their unique questions and at times impossible situations, there are no standard answers for what one encounters. The only thing you can do is to give a survivor 'guideposts' which will enable them to grope their way, even if it is dark.

I thought about this as I drove back from Iceland's capital city of Reykjavik to Keflavik Airport. I had just heard some tough stories from a survivor, but I had to return home. I was glad that some of the students I left behind had taken an interest in this person and I prayed that they might find a way to help. As I looked outside, I saw the moon-like landscape of Iceland. When fog or winter darkness covered the area, travellers in former times would easily get lost, so little piles of rocks were made as guideposts. I hoped that some of the principles I had shared in the course would likewise help the students find their way.

Let me tell you about Evelyn and Tina, two people who asked for help but did not respond easily to the help offered. Through their stories, I will also point out some guideposts which can show us the next steps, as we grope from one helping principle to another.

Evelyn was, as it were, shaking an angry first at God. Her struggles to leave the past behind, to become a skilled survivor, had failed. She had not suffered abuse in a direct form. Hers was a life in an abusive environment—seeing abuse happen to her older sister. When I met Evelyn she was the mother of three. She had become increasingly depressed. There was obviously a major reason for the lack of security she had experienced as a child. When she was five, her father was taken away. A sympathetic woman kept asking questions about her father, which she did not understand. She wasn't sure if she had answered them right or not, because the woman never talked about it again. She did come back, but all her attention went to Evelyn's older sister. Without any explanation, parents divorced. Mother never remarried. Except for her uncle, there was never another man in the house again.

As there was more peace in the home, Evelyn's emotional stability improved. She fell in love and married. Initially everything went well, except that she realised she was sexually unresponsive. Her husband was very understanding, perhaps that became a part of the problem. He compensated for her lack of response, but never initiated any help for both of them. When they did seek counselling, they did not feel that it helped much. Increasingly, she would have dark moods and became more and more depressive. Through a friend, she heard about the gospel and decided to become a Christian. It didn't do much for her marriage and she had trouble with all the happy smiling faces and the lively singing in church. She kind of liked it, but it often felt as if she were on the outside looking in. A pastoral counsellor and his wife took a special interest in her. They had related stories of people in the church who had also gone through tough times and how they came through. Some of them were quite open and gave 'testimonies' in the church service of how the Lord had helped them. As Evelyn could not break the depression, and as her faith did not bring about any change, she started to question the validity of her faith, and finally wondered if she were a believer at all.

Tina's story emerged after a church service when she asked for help. She was rather nervous and shaking physically as she told her story of being raped not far from her own home, at the age of 15. I was the first one to hear. Later I wondered if it was because her father refused to listen to it and scolded her for being careless. Previously she had been a vivacious girl with many friends. She was very active in the church. She told me how she had felt unable to talk about it to anyone. A grey loneliness had settled over her. Prayer and Bible reading became meaningless. She developed throat problems; she thought this was linked to the fact that the rapist used a nylon stocking as a noose around her neck to force her to comply. How does one respond to something like that as a counsellor?

Evelyn's pastoral counsellors felt insecure because of the lack of progress. They felt they must have failed and suggested she see a secular helper. Evelyn herself objected very strongly to the idea of a secular helper.

Tina's counsellors had received a fair amount of training, but they told me how they, too, struggled to find the right responses. How does one answer such requests for help? What are some guidelines?

The need for hope

What Evelyn teaches us is that positive stories from other survivors do have some effect, but they are not always helpful! Where there is already some hope, positive stories can increase that hope. Where there is a lingering despair, it can easily backfire. The positive stories of others might even affirm a victim in their opinion that they are a permanent failure.

Evelyn kept looking for a solution, for situations and things to change. What she needed to discover was the uniqueness of the gospel of Jesus; that he meets us where we are. He does that in many different ways. He can come through a smile from a stranger on the bus, with the sudden beam of sunlight on a rainy, misty day, in a quiet inner voice which urges a specific action, or as a friend who sits down to sort out the mess you are in.

As long as Evelyn was unable to grasp that hope, her counsellors were her life line to God. In fact, at one time they comforted her with the statement 'Don't try so hard; let us trust God for you.' 'That', she told me later, 'pulled me through many a dark night of despair.'

Hope is that spark of life which cannot be taught; it needs to be caught. It is a spark from a person who has hope, caught by another who has none. Hope can make us burn with new energy. Perhaps one of the greatest gifts a pastoral counsellor has is to introduce to the source of hope, Jesus himself.

However, there is a problem involved in catching hope. The stranger's smile on the bus might arise from the wrong kind of interest. The quiet inner voice might be an echo of one's own desires and not from God. The friend who sits down to help us sort out problems might be programmed with standard answers.

How do we know that the hope we are hanging on to is the right hope? God knew that there was a need for standards, for words with clear meaning, to make communication between him and us possible. The tool he used for that was the word of God. Through the many stories in the Bible, both good and bad, words such as love, faith and hope become not only wonderful concepts, but their content, their quality, is also clarified. This allows survivors to come to their own conclusions; they can go directly to the source of these concepts through reading the word.

The power of the word of God

Because abuse survivors grew up with warped values of good and evil, they will need to find ways to rediscover the basis of Christian values and learn to make choices accordingly.

Anyone who works with abuse survivors will need to help them to develop their own life. A Christian pastoral counsellor has the benefit of values which are clearly described in the word of God. This even allows a counsellor to be humble and to admit his or her own inability to keep certain standards. In attempting to be a role model, our task is rather to model hope than to be giants who can show what we have achieved through faith.

Both these girls were confused about themselves, and had confused emotions. Tina at one time felt so dirty that she badly wanted a 'clean sexual experience' and nearly seduced a good friend in order to get one. Evelyn had considered divorce several times, hoping that perhaps she would cope better alone. Yet the power of the word of God gave them both an anchor and provided an 'institutional shelter' which allowed them to go through infantile periods without doing things which were against their own principles.

The power of the cross

Every person has his or her own struggles. In some form or another, we have all suffered verbal, emotional or physical abuse. That is why Jesus came, allowing himself to be abused. The message of Jesus has been recorded in both Old and New Testaments. The Bible uses many metaphors—pictures, parables, biographies—to explain the human predicament of pain and suffering. The ultimate symbol of abuse is the cross. We often make the story less brutal than it actually was, in the same way that Evelyn's parents did not want to believe her ugly story. The crucifixion is actually an event which closely resembles a rape! Jesus surely knows what it means to be brutally and shamefully violated.

There are pains and problems which the Bible does not mention. It is not a textbook on all vital questions of life today, and pastoral counselling cannot provide all the answers. But the Bible speaks about a God who is alive and who understands the uniqueness of the pain. Thus he doesn't just come to us, but asks to be invited, to be allowed to come in and share with us. That coming of Jesus breaks the loneliness of the suffering that others cannot understand. Such a perspective creates a healing climate which invigorates the natural self-help capabilities of people. The hope which grows—through the reading of the word and the story of Jesus—empowers counsellees to start working on painful realities with the tutorial help of skilful mental-health counsellors.

The power of skilful helpers

Evelyn was still victimised by her past. Somehow she needed a breakthrough. However much other people could do, a change had to take place somehere inside Evelyn's own belief system. Many factors finally brought about this turning-point. In the first place there were her faithful counsellors. When Evelyn one day blurted out her agony, her unbelief, her sense of being forgotten by God, they took the position of temporary parents and believed God for her, when she was on the point of giving up. As she later explained, 'It was as if I became a child again, who could trust parents to take responsibilities for some huge questions I couldn't handle.' Such a temporary 'take-over' can be necessary and can be a reason why a person should sometimes seek temporary institutional help. Evelyn was fortunate to have committed counsellors who were not only able to talk with her, but also opened up their house to her. She realised that she needed to grow up. It became a battle: to be dependent or to be responsible.

A major paradigm change in her understanding of maturity came when she heard me speak about 'Peace and Reality'. It was a sermon based on Psalm 131, in which King David expresses very poetically his own secret of being a successful ruler. The peace of God that he experienced, like being a baby on his mother's lap, enabled him to face reality. In order to have a right view of himself, of others and of his plans for the future, David needed an inner rest in God. I spoke about the denial of reality as one way of dealing with pain—how, in my pastoral experience, I have seen that often people first need to experience the peace of God before they can face reality or remember ugly events they have suppressed. The sermon was short, to allow enough time for the Communion service. Evelyn and others came forward, not just to receive the Communion, but for a time of blessing, of receiving a 'gift of peace' from God. Later, she shared how this service became a turning point, how she started to see new realities. 'I was always looking for a solution to my problems, for a key which would change my moods, help me to see the sunshine, give me a lively tone in my voice again. I searched for a solution, for "it", until I realised that the good news of Jesus was different: that God comes to us where we are, even if situations are tough. I started to understand that the suffering of Jesus was not only his story, but an historic metaphor which gives meaning to my life. It is a picture of what we as humans can suffer—and he understands. The Shalom of God has helped me to come alive.'

Evelyn's period of maturing followed the main stages in human development: infancy (the temporary absence of responsibilities); childhood, in which she learned basic life skills; puberty and its rebellion, wanting to be child and wanting to be adult. Then followed adolescence: her uneasy steps to go back to her apartment, alone, with a sense of faith that adulthood would follow.

These stages were equally important for the development of her religious life: the security of the institutional setting of religion; then the freedom provided by open discussions with her counsellors to evaluate critically the values of her faith; and the transcendent experiences, the mystical elements of a young mature person who surrenders to her faith.[3]

On reflection, it appeared that Evelyn's tension-filled youth lacked basic security and deprived her of the ability to give and receive unconditional love. She never became secure enough to challenge her mother's principles, to develop a healthy criticism and a value system of her own. The counselling and support she received was like a re-parenting process. This allowed her not only an experience of basic security, but also the opportunity for the profound spiritual questioning she needed to go through, as an 'emotional teenager'. This in time helped her to make some very mature decisions about her personal relationship with God.

The power of the gift of peace

Evelyn had the privilege of patient counsellors who did not give up. When they were at a loss to know what to do, they just did what they felt was best. Only later did they discover how many of their steps had been guided by God. In a way, Evelyn became a teacher for them, so they are now more conscious of what they are doing than before. As I got to know these people, they also demonstrated a quality which probably provided the basis for their effectiveness. They were people who had the gift of peace.

Tina too, saw a 'door of hope' opened. She asked her counsellors to have a concentrated time of prayer and blessing. When they did, Tina became aware of a manifestation of the presence of the God of peace. She was advised to take time for that, to rest in it. Tina could not help but feel the immense difference between the peace of that moment and the chaos of the past. This automatically made her shift the focus away from Jesus, to her pain. When the counsellors noticed this, they encouraged her to get up from her knees. It is better to first learn to move back into the peace of God when painful memories come to the surface. Only when you know how to choose peace is it wise to let these memories come.

At another time, during counselling and prayer, Tina again realised: I am not alone, the Lord is here. Then she felt strong enough to look reality straight in the face. She relived the occasion of the rape. For the first time she could grieve about it, giving freedom to her agony and pain. She left that day 'tons lighter'. A few days later she shared that she also had a rather bland feeling, not numb, but a kind of indifference. It took her some time to understand that the peace of God had slowed down her intuitive, very sensitive and fearful reactions. She was no longer so tense. In another time of prayer, she once again relived the rape, but this time she saw it in front of her, as on a TV screen. Then she felt strong enough to have the picture enlarged. She automatically used her hands to protect her neck and doubled up, groaning in pain. As she was helped to have a 'stereo-experience' of the Presence and the pain, she relaxed. It was then that a lid was removed from even deeper hurts which, as we understood later, were from her early childhood. We did not have to go into detail. She had waves of pain, nausea and shame, without any pictures or memories, just feelings. We continued to bless her and she was encouraged NOT to form pictures, not to give these feelings a face, but just to wait and see if any pictures presented themselves. She had none, and we did not probe further. Tina reported later on a new level of inner tranquillity and that some unrelated memories had surfaced, which she was able to check with family members. They were accurate. She learned to deal with that as well. Somehow she had hoped that these vague feelings had only been fantasies. It was painful to have to accept them as real.

While two of the pastoral team were professionals, the non-professional pastoral worker was at that time the most sensitive in leading this young woman to the God of peace. Naturally, it took time to see the effects of this peace. She had learned a principle in facing pain, but needed a time of re-parenting as well. We had thought she had been quite a well-adjusted young woman before the rape, only to discover that the rape opened up other issues she originally thought she could handle. Now old hurts came back in full force; an emotionally absent father, a bossy mother and a brother who often beat her.

God's peace touches deep hurts

Tina's encounter with the peace of God also helped her to deal with the constant neck pains. Research on the memory indicates that it is not clear where memory is located. We do know that deep traumas often show a direct link to certain parts of the body. The body remembers events, touch, smell. Is this the reason why Jesus was so physical in his approach? When he spoke about the kingdom of God, he shared more than words; he also manifested the power of God. Nearly 70 per cent of what we read about Jesus' actions includes a physical touch. Somehow the reality of God's power became evident as a result. The Bible does make clear the need to commit our bodies to the

Lord and to expect a physical touch from him.[4] Such experiences can include a deep silence, during which it is hard just to sit, and when kneeling or lying down (as in Psalm 23) seem to be more comfortable and reverent. Then there is the other end of the spectrum. I have seen how through a simple, Jesus-centred prayer, the peace of God brought about a release from deep tension, the release becoming visible through involuntary muscle movements. The effect of such experiences seems to be that somehow, in these moments, deep emotions are also touched—emotions which a person had no other way of expressing and which could not be reached by words. At times it was an overwhelming silence and supernatural peace, at times a glow of life, at times a deep heartfelt sorrow with an equally deep physical effect, and at times an awareness of surges of physical strength, like being charged with electricity.

This 'blessing' approach has proved helpful in those situations when one can't communicate properly (with children, across cultural barriers, or in the case of such deep traumas that they are, for the present, beyond sharing). When the God of peace touches the body, a whole new insight emerges into what has happened; a paradigm change. We can say 'A new era has begun; I am a new creation.'[5] 'I am different; I am a temple of the Holy Spirit;[6] the Lord lives in me!'

God's peace and inexplicable fear

Both Evelyn and Tina told us of times when waves of inexplicable fear would come over them. I have observed that this can also happen after an experience with the peace of God. First there is the sense of safety, followed by waves of fear.

I was puzzled by this until the feedback I received started to make sense. Some people described it as follows; the experience of God's peace took them back to the awareness of peace they experienced *before* the first deep trauma. They then felt as if they were back in time, just before the moment that 'it' would happen. As one person expressed it; 'It was as if I was six again. If I wanted to grow up, I had to face what happened to me at that time or stay stuck'. Sudden surges of memory, 'shadows of the past', are felt as real. To relive it gives a person the opportunity of responding to the abuse in new ways. The ugly feelings of helplessness are overcome by a new awareness of anger and the power to say 'no' to the pictures and to choose another scenario. This is how the weak become strong!

Psychotherapists who have read my notes often indicate that many of my approaches are well known to them. They too help people to relive the past, or as some do, create through hypnosis, a 'peaceful place inside', as a refuge when emotions rage. The difference which I see is that in a 'Powerful Peace' approach, we do not have to use mind-power to bring a person into a hypnotic state. We also don't have to delve painfully into the past. As pastoral counsellors, we have the benefit of very powerful metaphors from the Christian heritage to draw from. Not by yielding to the instructions of a hypnotist,[7] but by responding to the word of God, there can come a manifestation of the presence of Jesus,[8] who gives peace as a free gift. Powerful metaphors are available to transform this biblical truth into a personal reality, such as 'the green pastures' of Psalm 23, the 'wings of God' of Psalm 91, God as a dove, covering us with his wings. Then, when they are aware of that Presence, they can learn to use that 'inner safe place' which Christ gives as a starting point. It is that peace which allows a survivor to face realities, as they come up by themselves, without digging. This gives full control to the seekers of help, and pastoral volunteers don't have to engage in 'playing psychiatrist', digging up past events.

These examples, and my explanation, naturally beg the question 'Can anyone actually help others to have such a manifestation of Jesus?' Is there anything we can do to help a person to experience this powerful peace? How does one receive as well as share it? In the next chapter I will try to deal with these questions.

Notes

1. In thirty years of pastoral ministry, I have found many reasons why people sought help from me. Not all of them were acceptable to me! Some thought they knew what I would say, and wanted to use my opinion or insight for what they did not dare to say themselves. Others were sure I was going to reject them and that is what they needed at that time. Then there were those who considered themselves hopeless and were sure that even I could not help them. It is here where I believe pastoral ministries are more difficult than psychological counselling. As pastoral helpers, we cannot keep a neutral stand; there are issues of morality which need to be faced. How to do this, without becoming abusive, is even a greater problem. I have found help in the example and the words of Jesus about being a servant and having a truly biblical servant heart. In this we are servants of the Lord and his truth first, not just people pleasers (Gal 1:10).
2. Rom 12:1–2
3. Gerald W. Hughes in *God of Surprises*, p11, refers to these phases in the work of Von Hugel, *The Mystical Element in Religion*.
4. Thess 5:23; 1 Cor 6:13; 2 Cor 7:1
5. Cf. 2 Cor 5:17
6. Cf 1 Cor 6:19
7. As I have stated before, secular helpers need to understand that many Christians are concerned about the use of hypnotic power, even if it does yield positive results. For many it is a 'grey' area, easily linked to the occult world. Not because the hypnotist is seen as 'active in the demonic', but because yielding to the mental powers of others can open a gate to unseen powers, of which neither the therapist nor the client is aware. If a therapist suggests such an approach to Christians, he can expect a rather strong resistance.
8. Mt 18:19,20

CHAPTER TEN

POWERFUL PEACE

My personal encounter with Powerful Peace

In one of the villages in north east Thailand I witnessed how a caring family attempted to bring 'inner tranquillity' back to a man who had miraculously escaped death in a car accident. The 'Sukwan Ceremony'[1] is a way in which relatives express their love and current for a victim of severe trauma or a serious illness. Everything these rural Thai do is linked to the fear of evil spiritual forces and their effects. Therefore the appeasement of these spirits is also involved. The aim, however, is to achieve an inner rest for a victim. It is done at home. No 'professional outsiders', such as a Buddhist priest or a spirit doctor, are needed. Because of the involvement of the spirit world, most Thai Christians refused to be involved in such ceremonies.[2] We keenly felt a need for something similar, which would exclude the demon-appeasement, while maintaining the care and concern. The answer to our search evolved more in practice than that we actually planned it.

As a part of my pastoral work I often did family counselling. The paper-thin walls of the village houses, made of leaves and bamboo, do not allow much privacy! Thus marriage quarrels were easily heard by others. When I would come to give counsel, the neighbours too, would listen in. Naturally pastoral prayer would take place as well. Then, afterwards, non-Christian villagers would give me comments on what they heard. When they started to ask for prayer as well, I asked if they wanted to become Christians. Their answer usually would be 'No, but it feels so good when you pray'. This made me worried. My Reformed background would prefer them to feel that they were sinners, and then they could meet God through my prayers. I wondered if I was missing something in my presentation. Then I read how Jesus blessed people, how the disciples were sent out to bless, just like him and that we too are 'royal priests', called to bless. That blessing is sharing the life of Christ in us, through word and/or deed. Thus my prayer made them aware of God's Shalom, his goodness, as a possible starting point for personal faith in Christ.[3] In this way I learned to look at what God already was doing in people who did not (yet) confess their faith in him. In time I learned to become more deliberate in my choice to bless, to search for the right people.[4] Returning to the Netherlands, with different pastoral settings, I lost sight of this 'blessing' aspect and the powerful effect this can have for a time. Then it happened that I myself came in touch with the meaning of 'the God of peace, working in our spirit, soul and body' as a part of his desire to clean us, to make us holy.[5] As hidden traumas of World War II surfaced, I was able to deal with them, empowered by the peace of God. The psychologist Erickson once noted that such personal changes not only influence the type of work you do as a therapist, it is also as if people receive an invisible wire. Suddenly they are on your doorstep with a need for the same changes. This is what happened to me as well, as I discovered the secret world of early sexual abuse. In the process I also refocused on deliberately choosing to bless, to share Shalom, the gracious peace of God. In time this developed into a ministry which I call 'Powerful Peace'.

What kind of peace are we looking for?

Inner tranquillity or 'peace' is, as we have seen before, one of the universal values which all human beings share. Thai Christians did not want 'rest' by appeasing spirits or demons. In the western world we need likewise to question what the source of our peace is. Many new cultures—through waves of non-western immigrants and the import of Hinduistic ideas—are importing a great variety of values. Understanding each others' values better is at least one step towards racial harmony. Western cultures should not deny their Christian roots. Thus, from a cultural point of view, we need to ask ourselves what there is in Christianity that can help us to find answers in our search for peace. Those who confess to being personal Christians need even more to use the resources which faith in Christ offers. We can turn to the great missionary Paul, to see how he works out his ministry of peace in a time of religious conflicts and the introduction of Christian faith.

How did the Apostle Paul present peace?

As I have noted before, the apostle Paul brings the peace concept in at least two different forms:

—prefaced by the concept of grace. Both words are his signature, his *ex libris*, the mark of his handwriting. We find this in every opening of his pastoral letters.
—wedged in between two other concepts, righteousness and joy through the Holy Spirit.

This way of presenting 'peace' is important, as the one word is influenced by the others. Grace refers to God's promises. He has decided *not* to treat us according to our deeds, but according to his grace, which comes to us, through Jesus. The promise-(or covenant) based peace comes first. Happiness is a mood, which can follow.

A major reason why people seek peace is in order to be happy. The Bible shows us a somewhat different road; faithfulness is more important than happiness. When I saw that, it suddenly became clear to me why so many seek peace and so few seem to find it. It is difficult to give an adequate statement of what 'happiness' is. It is a word which changes like money. There is an inflation or a devaluation. It's market value is not stable. Faithfulness on the other hand, can be measured. There are agreements which we can make and promises to keep. Attention to faithfulness will allow someone to say 'I kept my word', even if he is not happy in the process. Yet there is satisfaction. Happiness is a mood, to be compared with music. Faithfulness is then the music instrument; the sound it produces, for a short while, is happiness. Joy is different from happiness, since it is, in the biblical context, linked to a relationship. Paul presents joy as something which follows righteousness and peace. In other words, if you seek peace, it will be hard to find. Peace is a by-product of something else; of relating to a gracious God, who loves us unconditionally. God, the Creator, desires a personal relationship with us. Because of the Fall, and the way sin came in the world, we all are like cut flowers, beautiful, but dying. Thus God created another way for restoration. Jesus came to bridge the gap between Creator and creation. This bridging can be seen like linking up different electricity systems, where one needs a transformer. Jesus became that transformer, being both God and man. Because he comes to live in us, his peace is there, even if we do not always experience it. Peace is not 'it', but 'him'!

Grace and peace for survivors

A life in the 'culture of the abused' results in an abnormal moral development and a confused world of values, guilt feelings and shame. There has to be a whole new calibration of values. They grew up with conditional love; if you do this, you are a nice girl. Or they were silently rewarded with things or with some form of kindness, after they cooperated. Grace says, 'We love you unconditionally.'

Peace as a gift and as fruit

I see two sources of this peace that Jesus gives; peace as a gift and peace as fruit. The gift is received free. We do not have to do anything but to accept it. Believers and non-believers alike are invited to come to Jesus to receive that free gift, without any requirement to do something first, to change our behaviour. Jesus just gives it. In troubled situations, without even praying, suddenly a calmness can come. An awareness of the Presence can shift the attention to new solutions. This peace, or Christ-at-work, can also be noticed in evangelism. When our Maranatha prayer is answered and there is a manifestation of God's peace, non-believers are able to listen to the gospel without the threat of damnation or judgement. It allows them to consider quietly the claims of Jesus on their life.

Peace as fruit is dependent on a personal relationship with Jesus. To be allowed to have such a relationship is grace as well, a sign of God's unconditional love. Peace as a result of this relationship is one of the gems of the gospel. It is a promise for abuse survivors who know mentally that they are not guilty, nor bad, but feel emotionally so responsible, dirty and tainted. The promise that God works in us and changes us is like a magnet. It can pull us forward towards the future, rather than allow the abuse experienced in the past to remain the central focus of our life.

Introducing survivors to peace

How can we 'aim at peace', as the writer to the Hebrews[6] encourages us? One way which I have found helpful when survivors looked for this peace is linked to a special gift which there is in creation. Every human being has the gift of high concentration, an ability to focus intensely on one thing at the expense of something else. To earn money for my missionary training I worked in a bakery. Once, early in the morning, the baker said: 'Teo, are you in love?' I was shocked. How did he know? I was busy putting dough in the tins. First I had to take a lump of dough, pull it out, fold it and place it in a baking tin. I looked at him as he grinned and pointed at the dough; 'You have been pulling and pushing that piece of dough for over ten minutes . . . ' I was 'highly concentrated' on something else and he was right!

This gift of concentration is an ability to make choices about how intensely and to what degree we want to be absorbed in a topic or a person. This gift originates, I believe, in God's desire that we give him all the attention we would like to give to concentrate on him and share our love with him.

A child who faces overwhelming emotions of mortal danger, can, as an escape, use this gift of concentration and thus start to feel as if they are somewhere else. This eventually becomes a habit, a set pattern which psychologists call 'dissociation'. It is one way of 'creating peace'.

This ability to create peace, to escape reality, can be a good starting point to introduce Shalom-peace, the reality of God's peace, as a blanket in which they can wrap themselves, as a guard which makes the painful realities fade away, as Jesus 'fades in'. Somewhere deep inside, as the 'holy of holies' of our temple, we can become so filled with the presence of God that there is a detachment from the painful realities and a resulting increased attachment to the Lord. This gives a spiritual 'hiding place' in the midst of the ugly realities.

A Christ-centred gospel as an anchor for religious experience

Religious experiences can be very captivating and even enslaving. It is possible to get addicted to religious experiences. Not without reason, Karl Marx observed that religion functions as the opium of the people. Out of fear of excesses, church leaders tend to be cautious about too much attention on religious experience. To present 'Powerful Peace' as an escape route from reality is exactly *not* what I propose. How can we promote the reality of 'rest in God', of 'hiding in God's presence' and yet stay fully alert in this world? The following topics can serve as markers on a slippery slope of subjective experiences. When we know how to stay within these markers the ride can indeed by awesome. If we do not, church history is full of deadly lessons about those who took subjective experience as their guide. Working in a ministry where emotions are important, I have found help in the following approaches:

1. The basic question of the counsellee and the basic question of God are not always the same.

A counsellee will come with a specific need. The temptation is then that the present need becomes the focus. As pastoral workers we are not only client-directed, we also turn together to God. Pastoral care always starts with this basic premise, 'in the name of the Father, Son and Holy Spirit'. In order to gain perspective, we need light. Asking for the presence of God as a starting point places help seekers and helpers in the same humble position.

2. Start with worship or a worshipful attitude.

Deliberately-chosen worship can enable us to 'tune into the Holy', to worship God for whom he is. High concentration on the Lord ('fix then your eyes on Jesus', says the writer to the Hebrews) can help us to focus away from the things around for a time. A good place to start is to take any of the names of God to meditate on and to show our appreciation for that part of his nature or character. This is especially helpful in a time of spiritual darkness, where God seems the most distant One in the universe.[7]

3. Worship God for what he has already done in us.

From the worship of one of the names of God, we can turn to what that name means for us today. It is possible to meditate on God's faithfulness in general, even if at this moment, it does not seem to make sense. Then one can turn to the moments that we observed his faithfulness in our own lives, and at least thank him for that.[8]

4. Realise that there are 'stereo-feelings'.

We all face moments when more than one emotion is active, we can be sad and angry, or grieve and be happy. The peace of God can be manifested very clearly at one moment, while at the

202 FROM SHAME TO PEACE

same time we hurt deeply because of a tragedy. I deliberately use the word manifestation, because that is what Jesus promised what he would do, if we would join in prayer. How we express that manifestation is culturally influenced. Some will dance, others turn silent.

5. Learn to focus solidly on the peace of God alone, in spite of serious needs of ourselves or those around.

Many people are addicted in some way or another, as addiction often functions as a painkiller; it turns the attention away from a problem. There are the disgusting addictions such as open drug abuse, alcoholism, open sensuality. There are also very 'nice' addictions, such as hidden sex addictions, workaholism and materialism. To meet the God of peace will mean to step into the light of God and face reality. This is often too tough. Thus I encourage first a time of seeking only the peace of God, unrelated to the needs around.[9] This can be done by making an agreement that when a painful memory comes up, we will stop praying for a time. Then focus on Jesus again and rest in Him. This can be done practically by choosing times of silence, to allow a person to kneel, or to be as 'cool as a cat' in a bundle on a couch and give them time; to be 'just there'. The aim is to learn to focus away from pain, before it can deliberately be called to the surface by the seekers of help, when they want this. This gives them a high sense of control, which is vital for their self-protection.

This control issue can also be encouraged when survivors choose to attend a church service. Often I see how they like to sit against a wall, with no-one behind them, and not too far away the door! I have often encourged survivors-in-a-healing-process to monitor the level of tension inside and to keep it at a safe level. If it becomes too high, it may be better to slip out quietly and have a walk alone. Often I encourage them to plan in advance how long they will stay, so that when they leave, they do not have a sense of failure that they could not sit through the whole service, but rather a sense of accomplishment.

Small group meetings are often a problem. They like the

company but they do not like the closeness and especially the often-inquisitive evangelical questioning. If we encourage them to go to such small group meetings, it is wise for them to take a friend along who understands and deflects attention where necessary.

6. When emotional pains are faced, do not rush.

The experience of peace and the experience of pain allow a person to slip back into an earlier emotional age. By this time they can learn that the peace of God can protect heart and mind. Going back to an earlier emotional age also shows itself at times in the way that the voice sounds and in vocabulary. Slow down your speed of talking to them during these moments.

7. The 'silver box' metaphor.

I have been in situations where it was impossible even to believe that a person ever could be 'healed' of a memory. A mother saw her child brutally killed while others held her back. The eyes of the child, the screams, are so alive. How can she ever live in the present?

Some atrocities cannot be 'healed', they need to be 'put in a silver box and locked up. Then the key is given to Jesus'. This metaphor has helped me to come to terms with some things which are othewise too hard to face. A believer in Jesus has the benefit of some of these powerful metaphors like Psalms 23, 91 and 131. They can ask him to stand in between them and the past, so they can live in the present!

8. Abuse ministries demand a good grasp of biblical theology.

Facing the complex emotions of abuse survivors, I had an increasing need to become more theologically precise. Major questions such as 'Where is God when people suffer?' must be faced. The reality of sin and the biblical teaching on forgiveness, revenge, punishment and restoration must be worked through.

9. Learn to live with pain and anger.

The best way I have found to avoid 'religion as a painkiller' is the understanding that in this world, we will suffer. Even if our social, emotional, physical and spiritual wellbeing could be 'perfect', we still cannot escape pain. When we focus away from our pain, there is still the pain of Jesus, who invites us to an intimate relationship and asks us to suffer with him. He wants to share his pain with us. Hence my conclusion; pain will always be with us.

It is possible to escape painful realities in the world and in the heart of God if we do not face our anger at the unrighteousness we see. One psychiatrist shared how he noticed that churches where anger was taboo, there was very little social awareness or spiritual fervour. Anger is a beautiful motor for action.

Variations in responses to God's peace

While God has promised to manifest himself, the experience of that manifestation is not the same for everybody. Genetic differences influence the development of our personality, including how we respond outwardly to the peace of God. Then there is the impact of culture on the way our personality is expressed. Scientists have debated long about these 'nurture or culture' aspects. The feminist movement has tried to promote equal treatment by minimising these genetic, nature-based differences. For a time it was even politically unacceptable to talk about such genetic effects on personality and performance. In recent years we have become more aware of the effect of hormones on the development of a male foetus. There is also a difference later in life based on the hormonal mixture we have. Males tend, at a younger age, to have more male than female hormones. The reverse is the case for women. The male hormone has been associated with more aggressive behaviour. When men become older, their production of male hormones diminishes, and they tend to become less agressive. As women become older, their female hormone also declines, resulting in a greater amount of male hormones, and more aggression becomes visible.[10] This mixture of hormones is not the same for everybody. Thus variations among both males and females can be considerable. This means that some men just do not 'feel' much, if they compare themselves with women. This can cause confusion, guilt feelings and even a decline of spiritual interest, as they never seem to make the grade. My question is; who actually determines what the standard is? Is this not another form of the imposition upon men of what is currently in vogue in female culture? The peace of God is not a feeling, but a Person, whose presence has an effect on our personality. This effect can differ, some males being like a Caribbean steel drum and some women like a harp, each of them with a different need from the player to produce a response.

Responding with spirit, soul and body

Through worship, the peace of God can become an experience for our total being, in spirit, soul and body. I believe that God had an educational purpose in speaking about these three manifestations of our one personality.

It is my understanding that our spirit is that part of our total being which is unique, timeless, and irrespective of age, gender or culture. While the spirit is unique, there is also a sameness, an equality.[11] It originated from the Creator, but because of the fall of Adam and Eve there is not an automatic intimate relationship. There is life, but as in cut flowers, death is already at work. Anyone who received the gift of life 'from above' (Jn 3:3), has a special equality; to be born from above, to have the same loving God as the source of life today. Our being can be compared with a triangle. Through worship, we activate our spirit-side to turn to the Almighty, but automatically this involves the other two sides.

The soul is that part of the triangle which is very much related to culture, gender and age. There are differences in expression between African and western souls. I believe this is the part where we worship God in great diversity. Worshipping God with a soul-focus means expressing gratitude for who we are because of him.[12] We can thank God for our age, gender and culture and the fact that, because of this, we can worship him in our own special way. If our spirit is the focus of worship then the character of God is central; if our soul is the focus then what God can do in and through us is central.

The body is the third part of the triangle. It enables the invisible qualities of the spirit and the soul to become visible. But it has also a function of its own. For instance, memory is very much linked to the body. Teachers know this and let pupils listen, look and do things, in order to learn something new. These memories can also be spontaneous. For instance, when we meet a person who has caused us great trouble, our stomachs can respond with tension before we know who is there. A touch, a smell, a sound can instantly recall an event. Our body influences our emotions, just as our emotions or our mind can influence our physical condition. A relaxed person can, because of a situation or a habit in which the body language becomes 'tight' again, start to feel anxious. It is the stress experience in the body which influences the emotions to follow suit. This is one reason why it is important what we do with the body.[13]

The worship of God with our bodies also implies using non-verbal expressions. Thus the Bible describes dance, rhythm, clapping, kneeling, and lifting of hands as fully authentic expressions of worship.

The combination of spirit, soul and body is like the three sides of the triangle, each having their own place; together they form more than each side alone. Our being is not restricted to one part; we need all three to express ourselves fully. That is why I believe the resurrection of our bodies is so important. We know that we need a new body in order to belong to God's people, fully and without hindrance, in a new era when there will be a new heaven and a new earth.

When response to God's peace is impaired through abuse

Through such an integrated act of worship in spirit, soul and body we meet the Living One. It is then that God's life can touch us more effectively and deeply than before. Meeting Christ, our Peace, enables us to register this peace with our spirit, soul and body. It is especially this registration, this awareness of the peace in soul and body, which has been impaired in abuse survivors. If we can help them to open up and become aware of God's peace in these two areas they recover from the abuse much faster.

As I have observed this happening, I have wondered what was going on. I have the impression that it works as follows: trauma survivors carry painful memories in their bodies. As they get in touch with the Shalom, the manifested presence of Jesus, their bodies can also experience the touch of peace. A new memory is recorded on that part of the body; I am a temple of the Holy Spirit. Christ *in* me. The locked-up tension can be released. At times, this happens in ways we are not (or no longer) used to in church. One can go to a therapist and see how tense muscles become released with shaking and involuntary body movements. To have this happen in church is fairly unusual and often not appreciated. Because such releases of tension are also happening in some non-Christian therapy groups or in New Age gatherings, they become suspect, based on the premise that similar experiences must have a similar cause.

Another road towards physical relaxation—that of eastern meditation techniques—has also spoiled the market for true, Christian mystical experiences. We are afraid of such things, so we stay away from them.

The fact is that such non-Christian approaches to an experience of peace are the result of the absence of clear biblical teaching on how to receive Christ, our peace, and the effects of that peace in spirit, soul and body. Dry orthodox religion has made many a seeker look for greener pastures elsewhere, so we should not blame New-Agers for trying to be missionaries of their faith. Rather we should ask ourselves how it was possible that the church did not develop a better theology of experiencing God.

Cultural variations of peace experiences

In different denominations there are different cultures. I suggest that before you try to introduce new forms of worship, or other ways of experiencing the Holy One, you first look for avenues your church already offers in experiencing the God of peace. In one denomination, this can be through times of silent, communal prayer, whereby we direct our spirit and soul to God. Also, the act of standing together as a congregation and reciting the Apostles' Creed can be an act of faith when it is done not just out of habit, but out of a conscious decision; I am going to stand, I want to be active in doing this. In another setting, the Communion service or the Mass gives ample opportunity to experience the Presence, or one can go for private confession and receive a personal blessing.

Peace experiences in the culture of the abused

I have found that attention to the body can be very helpful for trauma survivors when praying for peace. As stated before, the whole area of 'experiences' is often faced with suspicion. Abuse survivors are usually persons of great sensitivity. Any 'experience'-oriented meeting can drive them up the wall. There are also people who need religious experiences constantly, in order to suppress their pain. Then it becomes a religious addiction.

Coaching a survivor to an awareness of the Holy One demands great sensitivity. The suggestions earlier in this chapter, of markers on the 'slippery slope' of experiences, can prepare a helper to be fully in control of his or her life and allow full control to the survivor who wants to meet the presence of God and is hungry and thirsty for righteousness, peace and joy. These markers aim at keeping a Christ-centered gospel, focused on the suffering of Jesus on the cross, the resurrection and his suffering now today with us and with a broken world.

Peace for the body

As sexual abuse is the abuse of power involving the body of a victim, the body also needs special attention. The apostle Paul speaks about this in different scriptures.[14] Worship can now include the body, with thanksgiving for the peace of God which is already at work and which can be observed in those parts of the body which are already relaxed. Then mention the parts that are still tense and ask for more relaxation in those parts too.

This worship route—first the spirit, then the soul, before we deal with physical relaxation—is important, especially for those people who have experience of meditation techniques or other forms of relaxation which they now reject as 'rest coming from a wrong source'. They have understood that these approaches, far from being innocent, were abusive and rooted in a non-biblical philosophy. While they can accept objective biblical theology about peace, the subjective experience of peace seems to create fear. Their allergy to what they previously experienced hinders their enjoyment of what God has for them now. We need to respect such fears and encourage them to grow more in an objective understanding of peace theology. On the other hand, we should be careful that these novices, converts from occult groups, New Age or other meditative streams, do not set the standard for our own experiences.

The apostle Paul encountered a similar problem with new converts from spirit worship, in his letter to the Romans. The issue there was meat, sacrificed in the heathen temple to demons, spiritual entities which were evil. The meat people ate was bought from sacrifices. That money would go to the temple. Or people would be invited to meals with friends, where the meat was dedicated to a god. Novices ('those weak in faith') were upset when they saw mature believers eat meat like that, without any reserve. Paul then counsels that we should adapt our behaviour, without accepting their premise. A similar situation arises when people are bothered by drinking alcohol. When converts from, for instance, Hinduism or the New Age enter our churches, one would do well to affirm the validity of their feelings of fear, and to explain that what we do—and how we test the quality of what we do—is based on objective theology.

One way to do this testing was suggested by John Wimber, the founder of the Vineyard movement. He told students at Fuller Theological Seminary how he often gets calls from people who report that yet another famous musician has turned to Jesus. His standard reply would be 'Introduce them to me seven years from now, after they have matured some.' I am afraid that a too-hasty public appearance of those who have been in politics, arts, show business, the occult, New Age, could give them a prominence which they try to translate into leadership in the church. I have observed especially how converts from New Age have become very allergic to experiences, as they have seen how 'soulish' it all can be. They also caused quite a few problems through their immaturity. Their past experience and current insight is not an adequate standard for the church of today. I prefer an emphasis on regular reflection on objective theology, stressing the priority of first directing one's spirit, then the soul, before we turn our bodies to God in worship. This gives us a permanent quality control, not unlike the automatic computer-virus check programme which I have currently on my computer hard disk. Through a total turning of the Lord, with spirit and soul as well as our bodies, and in that order, we can trust that, as we seek him, he will not give stones for bread. After all, it is this peace of God which is designed to protect us from a wrong focus.[15] To turn to God as a whole being encourages the wholeness of our personality.[16]

Touched by peace

When a survivor asks for prayer, for a time of blessing, there are various ways to respond. We as royal priests receive our spiritual authority from God to bless, to share Shalom. There are various methods and denominational cultures. There are also bad experiences in the past, which the survivor has not worked through. How we pray (with or without laying on of hands, sitting, kneeling, 'curling up' or any other way) depends fully on the person who asks for such help. Remember, control is the key. If any specific approach is suggested, it should be said in such a way that they can say 'No' without feeling embarrassed. This can be done by giving at least three options from which they can choose, one of which is to do nothing special at all. Whatever you do, avoid standing behind a person while praying. The need to control the situation involves also the need to watch, if they wish, the people who are blessing them.

Spontaneous experiences

There are times, usually in the even more private setting of a therapeutic appointment, when the peaceful environment and the empowering of the Holy Spirit equips the survivor to face some ugly realities. This has sometimes brought about a spontaneous reliving of painful episodes. It is then that we, as counsellors, are there to facilitate the working through of these memories. This is done by expressing our own calmness and by allowing them to express the depths of their feelings if they wish. The deeper the experience of peace and empowering, the more intense the emotional reactions can be. When flood gates of hidden pent-up emotions, such as aggression and fear of death, are opened up, it is easy to be shocked. Not only counsellors, but also counsellees can suddenly 'freeze up' under these events and try to stop it.

With an outburst of aggression, some counsellors, who recognise that demonic forces can be at work among us, will decide too quickly that this must be demonic. Sexually violated people have been treated unrighteously and have a right to be angry. What they need to learn is how to respond in a biblical way.[17] We can only learn to be angry *without* sin by coming to the Lord, as angry as we are, *with* sin. Then God can clean the sin out, and we can be angry without sinning. This brings us back to an old Reformation principle; we don't have to clean up the sin in order to meet God. We go as sinners to him. He does the cleaning after we come.

Fear is another emotion which often occurs when emotional

release takes place. This can have a variety of causes. For some, it is the overwhelming reality of the helplessness of the abusive moments which brings back this emotion. For others it is a sense that they had died: their bodies started to feel cold (due to high tension?). Escape via 'dissociation', escaping from the body, can give the impression of looking at oneself, as a corpse. The relationship between sexual abuse and death is even clearer as we see that it is violence, sexually expressed. One has only to remember how war, killing and rape have been associated with each other since the beginning of human history.

Both anger and fear of death can be an opening for evil forces to infiltrate.[18] If that has happened, an encounter with the God of peace can cause quite a conflict and at times, intense emotional expression. If these emotions are so intense, and louder than is right for a particular situation, then 'crying into a pillow' can drown much of the excessive volume.[19]

Planning for a peace encounter

I prefer not to 'dig up' past information. When it comes spontaneously it is time to deal with it. Yet there are moments when a survivor desires that we help them to 'walk back into time', through a peaceful presence of God, to be equipped to face past realities and to see what the Lord would allow them to remember. If we have come together to an agreement that such an 'archaeological expedition' is right, we want to be sure that we have Jesus as a tour guide! We would not want to destroy anything! In some 'healing of memories' methods, one is encouraged to 'imagine Jesus to come into the situation'. The problem I have here is the word 'imagine'. We can not just order God around, and use an image of him to deal with problems. We need Jesus himself, not his image. No pastoral prayer can just 'make that happen'. When there is a manifestation of the Lord and this is translated into a mental picture, we have quite a different story. Then we do not relate to an image *we* create, helped if necessary by the counsellor, but to an image *he* makes.

When we have agreement on seeking God's presence and seeing if this results in 'going back' in time, we encourage the person to seek a body position which is most comfortable for them at that moment, an easy chair, kneeling down or curling up under a cover, on a couch. Exercising Psalm 23 in this way can have great impact.

What happens next varies greatly. Some people just come to an inner tranquillity, others sense at once how relaxation also lowers the inner resistance against remembering. This could result in an automatic response being learned; when there is peace, you will remember painful events. We aim at the opposite; an ability to remember, with a level of pain which can be carried, without any need to deny or to find painkillers.

From the start it is agreed that we will seek first a time of rest in God, without a focus on painful memories. In this way a firm foundation is laid for experiences; the reality of the peace of God. Then, when painful memories come up, 'stereo-feeling' can occur—two distinct different realities at the same time—to be afraid and yet to be confident; the Lord is here, I can manage.

The focus on this peace of God is also important, to prevent memories running away with us. This is why I don't stress the need for factual truth, but rather aim at symbolic truth. Instead of having to test every memory with the 'can this be true?' question, I start out with the assumption that many images and feelings can be symbolic, an expression of something else, for which we have no words.

When the peace of God touches our bodies, it is understandable that the tension lowers in the muscles, thus the blood flows more easily. A tense body can in this way come to a release. This can cause observable results, such as various sensations in the skin, muscle twitching or a flush of warmth. To me this physical relaxation is a helpful by-product of something else; a person is directing spirit, soul and body towards the God of peace. I believe that this can be helpful, because the body of a survivor of early sexual abuse has registered so many feelings and facts for which there were no words or understanding. A new experience of peace can be the beginning of a sense of wholeness, with the ultimate result that the body has new memories which override the old ones. It seems that Paul encouraged such a physical awareness of God's presence in a city where sensual expriences were very important.[20] I do not want to over-emphasise physical experiences, but merely point to the possibility of them and to possible effects of the God of peace at work, in our bodies, even to the point where old memories fade out as new ones become a safe and peaceful reality.

From death to life

The power of Jesus over death, the reality of death as the last enemy and how to respond to that enemy are vital issues in abuse counselling. Most survivors have faced suicidal thoughts at one time or another. An experience of the presence of God and the resulting peace in spirit, soul and body, can bring reality back again. Death is not a friend who quietly waits, a final escape from abuse. It still is our enemy.[21] Where there once was a choice to die, there now needs to come a choice to live. Giving in to suicidal thoughts is also allowing the abuser the ultimate victory. Their deadly act of destruction is accepted and turned into self-destruction.

The message of hope which abuse survivors need to hear and see in us is that 'there is life before death'! As a missionary, I know how quickly we can take the messages that worked in our culture and share them 'elsewhere'. This is one reason why I have taken a long time to speak about the principles behind Powerful Peace ministry. The 'how' is closely linked to culture. In the next chapter I will be more specific about how this can be applied in western culture among people who have traditional Christian values. Readers who face different situations are encouraged to keep this in mind when I explain how I have learned to work with these concepts. I accept readily that it is a cultural attempt to see the word of God 'incarnate' in a specific culture, the hidden people of the abused.

One of the reasons behind the destructive urges of abuse

survivors is the intense sense of shame. How to leave shame behind and come to peace is the topic of the next chapter.

Notes

1. S.J. Tambiah, 1970.
2. Missionary Jim Gustafson, working in north east Thailand, has, since we left Thailand, together with Thai co-workers such as Banphot Weehchekama, developed a Christian form of this custom. It is quite controversial for at least two reasons. Many Thai believers and western missionaries reject it on spiritual grounds. It is too close to the Thai spirit world from which the new believers came, with all the dangers of syncretism. This problem can be seen as a parallel with the problems the believers in Rome had with meat sacrificed to the idols (Rom 14,15) or the matter of hairstyle in 1 Cor 11. Others, especially some of the more educated Thai, told me that they did not want the church to become a 'cultural zoo', with old customs ruling church life. Adaptation of old customs and syncretism often go hand in hand, as we can see with our Christmas tree, Easter Bunny, wedding customs etc. In time, it seems to start to carry less of the original 'biblical foreign load', as it becomes a matter of 'culture influenced by the gospel' and where needed, cleansed from occult aspects.
3. Rom 2:4; Lk 5:8; Jer 5:24
4. Mt 10:11
5. Cf. 1 Thess 5:23
6. Heb 12:14
7. Is 50:10,11
8. Ps. 103;1–3
9. Phil 4:6–9
10. Anne Moir and David Jessel, (1989) Carol R. Hartman (1993).
11. Gal 3:28
12. Col 3:1–4
13. 1 Cor 6:18
14. 1 Thess 5:23; 2 Cor 7:1, 1 Cor 6:13
15. Phil 4:1–8
16. Rom 12;1,2; 1 Thess 5:23
17. Eph 4:26
18. Gen 4:7, Heb 2:14,15
19. There are Christian psychiatrists who work with intense emotions through allowing the deep scream of buried horror to come out. One of them, Dr Chris Andrews FFRACS, MRCPsych, London, introduces to some of his clients the ideas of Dr Arthur Janov, who uses the term 'Primal Scream'. Dr Andrews suggests using a

pillow, in which people can let go of such a scream. He also encourages charismatic clients to stand up in worship and really 'let go forcefully in tongues' as an excellent way of setting oneself free from earlier repression.

20. 1 Cor 6:11,19
21. 1 Cor 15:26

CHAPTER ELEVEN

FROM SHAME TO PEACE

In Chapter Four I discussed at some length the tremendous impact of shame on the survivor of sexual abuse. The more I meet this effect of shame, the more I observe the devastating effect of shame. As I have been searching for answers I have found that an experience of the peace of God can go deeper than all what we try to say, it can touch spirit soul *and* body all at once.[1] But how do we get there?

The rest in God

The writer to the Hebrews invites believers to enter 'the rest in God' and links this directly to the idea that the word of God is like a sharp sword separating bone and marrow. More and more, I wonder if this has a literal meaning as well; the peace of God, becoming a physical reality, can even touch bone-marrow.[2] Over a period of time our prayer teams discovered how necessary such specific prayer was, and began to expect cleansing negative experiences of the body through a new experience, the rest in God.[3]

To encourage an experience can easily be misunderstood as if we can manipulate God. That is the paradox. God urges us to 'enter into the rest' and then gives it to us as a gracious gift. It is God who decides when and how to *manifest* himself. Any idea that we just can 'dial him up' should be avoided. God is God and we created beings are different. Yet God has promised to be with us. How we experience that presence is also linked to our culture. Cultures vary in the way people communicate and how they receive communications. Communication is more than using words and one important aspect of communication is the various forms of symbolism which we can use. Some African Christians will start to swing in his presence, while northern Europeans tend to become silent. This response is a symbol of an inner reality and both are valid.

Symbolic communication is essential when we work with different cultures. It is an indirect form of speech. A movement with a hand, or a story or parables, are examples of symbolic communication. The advantage of symbolic communication, be it a movement of a hand, or a parable, is the fact that the listener can receive only that meaning from it which can be understood. The listener hears and observes, but can only respond to that which fits into their world of ideas. Thus Jesus shared the truth of the kingdom in parables. The religious leaders, who set more on their power position than on servanthood, could not follow what Jesus was saying. Their attitude prevented them from grasping the truth. Likewise, the apostle John on Patmos was looking far into the future, including our own times. There were things beyond his practical understanding, so he received it in symbolic language and was thus able to express these future realities.

Understanding symbolic language is helpful when we work in the culture of the abused. Words such as 'father'; body-language (like hugging); the concepts such as 'forgiving is essential for spiritual growth'; all have a special meaning to survivors of early sexual abuse. Also, certain forms of prayer can carry a different meaning for the survivor than that intended by the people who pray. To 'lay on hands' might be a custom in some churches, but for abuse survivors the physical touch alone can give the shivers! When that happens they cannot even listen anymore.

Symbolic communication of Powerful Peace concepts

'So, I am not crazy?', is one of the frequent remarks which I get, when I explain the culture of the abused. Suddenly survivors recognize themselves. Even the use of culture is a symbol, an explanation model. The persistent desire to understand oneself is a major reason why people seek help. 'Why am I doing this?' In the years that I have worked with abuse survivors, I have developed a variety of explanatory models. Some of them need to be mentioned now.

The difference between emotional and chronological age

We can all recall times when we responded childishly. Our behaviour was not on the level of our chronological age. This can be a 'younger' response, but also a child can turn into a parent, to take care of the infantile needs of their parents. The lower emotional age can be shown in the following picture. The core of the personality has not grown equally everywhere to fill the expected chronological age. There were growth blockages. For early victims of sexual abuse these include the sexual traumas, the betrayal by events. Also, a dysfunctional family life can create a chronic trauma; one cannot just point to one event. While the outward appearance continues to change, the inner self stays immature in those areas (A). This causes a pressure through creating a vacuum (B). One has to perform in a way which is not in harmony with inner realities. Thus an incest survivor marries, emotionally ready for everything except sexual activity. In that area she is still a child. Children are not interested in active sex, they seek more cuddling or intimate friendship. By willpower they chose to be sexually active, but it does not come naturally. The outer layer (C) becomes wooden. To stand the pressure, inner counter pressure needs to be developed, to keep the outside from collapsing (D). Thus immature areas often show up through lack of flexibility. An accident, childbirth or other major life event can create a sudden surge of pressure which breaks the outer shell. One gets a breakdown and now responds outwardly (more easily) at a lower emotional age.

The peace of God can fill the vacuum between the emotional age and the chronological age. This reduces the inner pressure and relaxes the hardened outside shell. The peace of God can

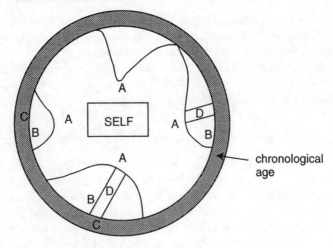

A. immature areas
B. pressure due to absence of maturity
   inability to respond as a mature person
C. lack of flexibility
D. inner-counter pressure

Chronological and emotional age

also envelop the trauma in such a way, that it becomes isolated. For that I use the metaphor of the silver box, in the previous chapter. I often use the example of the white blood cells which envelop a bacteria and by doing so, kill the bacteria and die themselves as well. This again is a good metaphor to explain something about the death of Christ for us!

In this picture, there are several growth blockages at different emotional ages.

The wounded child within

The metaphor of the wounded child has been quite well developed in secular counselling. The apostle Paul spoke about our need to grow up, to become mature. He also uses a figure of speech of talking to himself, an inner dialogue, where he argues with himself.[4] We also find this in the Psalms.[5] To consider this 'child-inside' as a true part of oneself can be a help in taking pastoral care of one's own soul. The inner dialogue can become a trialogue, in which God becomes the third partner in the discussion. The importance of recognising this immature self is seen when it becomes evident how communication with these sides of our personalities needs a care which fits them. I was sitting in a bus from Los Angeles Airport to my host in Simi Valley when a lady next to me heard my Dutch accent and asked if she could join me. She was a Dutch immigrant to the USA. When she found out that I was a pastor, she started to beam and told me about her recently found personal faith. Then, becoming rather personal, she started to share, in Dutch, about her abusive youth. I just listened. After some time she looked at me with amazement. 'Now I can talk about it, I just could not explain what I felt to the pastor, in English. Is it because it happened in Dutch, that I needed to talk about it in my own language?'

A negative emotional age

Once we accept the picture language of a lower emotional age, we can expand this to a negative emotional age. Let me explain. The apostle Paul speaks about a life direction towards life or towards death.[6] It is possible to be emotionally immature and then to grow up in a negative direction, to become mature in evil. We see this when teenagers, still emotionally children, are caught in a crime and put in jail. Soon they come out, much more mature, learning quickly how not to be caught. I talked to a young man who told me that he felt like an old man, ready to die. 'I have had everything.' He was suicidal and hard to stop. He had grown up so negatively. This metaphor of a negative emotional age can explain what happens when people decide to change life direction. When Angela chose to turn to God for help, to turn away from her death pre-occupation, there was still a way to go before she was mature. Her choice was right but to

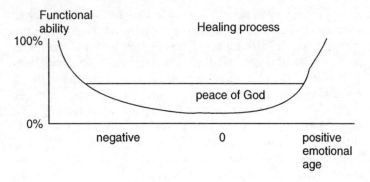

work it out took time. Then she observed something strange. It seemed as if her ability to function in the home decreased. She felt that she was becoming more and more like a little girl. I used the following graph to explain to her in picture language, what seemed to be the case:

The vertical axis is the performance indicator. The horizontal axis displays the emotional age. The zero point is the indicator where a negative emotional age becomes positive. The 'reverse bell-curve', is the pattern of performance. The more Angela grew up, the closer she came to zero point! The peace of God became a cushion to help her not to sink too deeply.

Angela had to accept that she was living in two realities; she was a mature woman and a child at the same time. In time Angela grew up. One day I called her to change an appointment. She responded with laughter. 'I just read a story to my little inside girl and put her to bed. So now I am on my way to the bedroom to surprise my husband with the mature woman I am!' Angela had the benefit of a very understanding husband, who had learned to use this child-within concept to show him when to respond to his wife as a little girl and when to see her as a grown woman.

Our life as a house

One can see a life, with the various time periods, as a house. Then the peace of God can be invited to come into the bedroom of the parents, the nursery, the playroom, and so on. This picture language gives also the opportunity to express which people are 'resident' in us. As many survivors of sexual abuse still feel that the abuser is 'still inside me', a 'house-cleaning ceremony' can show a way out.

The 'anger and sadness' processing factor

One day I was praying with a very disturbed young man. He was severely blocked in his emotions, yet everything seemed to indicate that he was ready to burst. His condition became clear to me through a picture. Two containers were ready to burst, on one was written 'anger', the other 'sadness'. I recognised how there was a link between the two and a pressure meter on maximum, while the flow meter was on zero. It graphically expressed my observations; he was ready to explode. My natural reaction was to turn off the gas which was burning under the containers. Then I realized there were at least three gas streams to deal with: one coming from a wounded ego, which needed to be brought to the cross of Jesus; one coming from hell, that had to closed off; and one coming from the heart of God. He too, was angry and sad with the situations this young man faced. To prevent bursting, there was an exhaust pipe which emptied in three different lakes: one of mercy ministries; one of worship; and one of creativity. Then I realized also God's answer for this young man. After dealing with the wrong fire, he still had a need to express his emotions. I knew by experience what a motivator anger and sadness can be in mercy ministry. Worship allows us to get in touch also with the anger and sadness of God, as I described in my understanding of a theology of suffering. Creativity too can be a tremendous outlet for those who have been hurting. Our true personality often only shows up when the outer shell is cracked.

The peace of God is the operator who controls the factory, monitors the levels of emotions and selects the source of our anger and sadness. Thus we can become sad and angry, without sinning.[7]

Prayer as a part of a survivor's recovery programme

Many people will need first insight and instruction about how to pray for themselves. Thus praying together will probably precede individual prayerful attention for healing of body memories. But how to do this without causing embarrassment? After all many of us cannot easily discuss our very private feelings or private physical experiences. It causes shame and blocks us up. Then there are feelings and events which we registered somehow as a child, but for which we did not have words at that time. Whatever the reason may be, in such situations it is possible to bless and wait silently, as there is an inner dialogue. For some who can discuss these issues with a trusted person, this can be followed by a silent prayer together to commit this to the Lord.[8]

Praying together

Praying together fosters safety in different ways. There is the need for theological safety. We can watch each other and be alert that what happens is biblically right. There is also the need for social safety, through the use of teams. Then there is the need for emotional safety.

Theological safety

The more I am involved in this rather intense type of involvement with sexual-abuse survivors, the more I sense a need to pray in a way which is doctrinally correct; to reaffirm the basic truths of the word which apply to a situation; to worship the Lord for who he is; and to focus on the reality of Jesus as helper. When we accept that 'blessing' is a part of the task of believers, as a royal priesthood, we also should remember who we represent. We speak to the eternal one, in the name of Jesus. The priests in Old Testament times had some very strict rules. Using 'strange fire', rather than the sacred flame, resulted in instant death. This awe for the Living God makes one careful and observant and is, as such, the beginning of true wisdom.[9] It also helps us to avoid presumption. God is at work. He is God;

we are co-workers, yes, but co-workers who should know their place.

As most sexual-abuse survivors have a pervasive sense of guilt, I have observed that our word choices need to be very sensitive. It will be needed to avoid the idea that they need 'cleansing' in the sense that they are guilty. (The responsibility and the guilt is always with the one who abused their power and position of trust.)

Even prayer can strengthen the wrong view of the body and what it did, if our perspective is negative. Worship of God as creator, reaffirming a positive body image, quoting Scripture during prayer[11] which supports this all, can work together to achieve that purpose. At the same time, the reality of what the body had to do can stand out in strong contrast with what we pray. Again, affirmation of innocence can be a help. If abuse survivors were older at the time it happened, and now feel they had some responsibility, a stress on general forgiveness first and the grace of God might be needed. I encourage people not to confess any sins specifically until they are more used to the grace and peace of God. They will need this to filter their observations and thoughts about it.[10]

Social safety

In my practice we often work with mixed teams of male and female, and the survivor can indicate who should take the lead in the process. Another reason for team-work is the fact that working with danger on a long-term basis can make one careless. An acquaintance of ours worked as a high-voltage electricity specialist. He never did this alone. His first mistake would be his last. There was always someone watching every step he took, and he also watched the other one when it was his turn! Routine pastoral involvement with the Holy One can likewise make us careless and we can profane the name of God. Ananias and Sapphira discovered that deadly truth and so will we, perhaps not by dropping dead when we confess a greater commitment than is actually the case, but profaning the name can still have a deadly effect in spirit, soul and body. This is why I strongly encourage people involved in 'power ministries' not to work alone, and to keep an eye on each other. To touch God, the Holy One, is more dangerous than touching 10,000 volts!

Emotional safety

Abuse of pastoral power, particular pastoral methods or use of emotional expressions which do not fit the culture or the personal preference can all become barriers for other times of prayer-ministry. A sensitive counsellor will become aware of a survivor's special needs before a prayer time. Some negative feelings are rooted in a hidden past and only surface because we touch them. The survivors could not have told us before that they would feel like that.

The very use of the word 'power', in Powerful Peace, should warn us that power abuse can occur. For instance a friendly suggestion to kneel, without any relaxed way for the survivor to respond negatively or to suggest something else, can become abusive to the survivor. Some pastoral methods, such as laying on of hands are normal practice in some denominations, but very unusual or frowned upon by others. Also, a person may have some very negative attitudes towards them because of what they saw happen to others or to themselves. There are emotional expressions which happen as a result of released tension. A fear of looking a fool can hold a survivor back from expressing deep emotions. The setting in which this type of prayer happens is also important.

The power of symbolism

Language in itself is an accepted way of exchanging sound symbols. We have non-verbal communication too; some emotions which we express are universal, such as joy and grief, others are different in various cultures. Some people would rather use indirect speech, such as a parable, others use objects to give a name to something and then the object becomes the symbol for something else, such as a flag of a nation. The body is universally the most frequent source of symbols. Thus it is not strange that there is meaning linked to certain body-parts, for those who survived sexual abuse. Symbols can get a new meaning. A flag can be burned, when hatred between nations arises. A hand as a symbol of beating a child, can become a hand of blessing.

Believing the body

The physical experiences of a survivor also need a reformation. This can be done through prayer, to redefine their ugly meaning, to 'make them holy', through prayer and blessing.[11] We need to look in more detail at such a physical involvement by lay-counsellors in the assistance we give to abuse survivors.

Secular counselling of sexual abuse survivors in the Netherlands has, until recently, concentrated on verbal forms of communication. New forms, such as art therapy, body movements, drama and dance, have been added to the helping repertoire. Some secular abuse counsellors have started to include physiotherapy and touch, deliberately aimed at the needs of healing past trauma, in their programme. They report that people who seem not to respond to verbal counselling alone do better if there is a physical touch as a part of the whole counselling process. Several of my students who are physiotherapists have informed me how deep emotions can surface through touch, especially of the spine.

I have seen the same happen in a pastoral and ritual form, when we touched someone. Done carefully and wisely, it can have amazing effects.

Naturally, cultural and individual norms play an important role here. Dr Anne Terruwe, who I mentioned earlier, noted that male patients needed more verbal touch, but that female patients definitely needed physical touch if deprivation neuroses were going to be healed. Her approach demands a great ability to show empathy and is very time-consuming. The idea of 'a touch of God' through prayer might be a help here. Pastoral volunteers working as a team can pray the Maranatha prayer and expect a manifestation of the peace of God. Exactly how to experience

God is a problem for many a seeker of help. Often you will need to point to a slight perception change; the inner coldness they know can change into a peaceful inner-silence, in which, together, we focus our attention on who God is and meditate on him. Once the counsellee realises a shift in perception, in the silence I often see something amazing happen; they start to listen to their own body. That then also can quickly cause problems; the minute a body relaxes it can actually release more suppressed information. The following story might explain this. An older single missionary suffered the worst thing she ever could imagine. During a local feast, she was raped by a half-drunk policeman. It shattered all her assumptions of God and his protection for which she had prayed so fervently. Her emotional collapse resulted in an early furlough. When her personnel director asked me to become involved we made a series of appointments. At some time she realized how highly strung her body was and she wanted us to pray for that. As my co-worker laid hands on her and prayed for peace, she sank deeper in the couch, leaning backwards. A quiet smile indicated that she seemed to have a good time. Then she opened her eyes in panic, crawled into the arms of my (female) co-worker, and sobbed incoherently. We just sat there, sometimes silent, sometimes encouraging. Finally she faced me and said, 'I just remembered what happened to me when I was ten. I have always pushed this far away, and never discussed it with anyone. A man your age, Teo, raped me'. It was clear that the emotional collapse on the mission field was not just because of this one terrible incident, but also because of the hidden trauma which she never was able to deal with. In time something else became clear. As she learned to listen to her body and stopped the denial, something changed in her personal faith life. As a very effective missionary she had seen scores of churches established in a long and fruitful career. There was only one problem; it was hard for her to have faith for anything for herself. Now her faith for herself started to bloom. She suddenly dared to have desires and took initiatives of which she had not dreamt before.

I have seen this parallel between denial and unbelief in

different other counselling situations. Perhaps we need to spend less time in trying to convince people of spiritual truths and allow them first to become free from the denial of their own realities!

Realities of touching

What happens when such a touch takes place? Is it because the touch directs the attention to that part of the body and thus creates an awareness of a need? Is there something more to touch, as the woman who touched the clothing of Jesus and Jesus felt power going out of him?[12] Was there more to the fact that Peter helped a lame person stand? Did the touch do something as well?[13] When Jesus instructs us to lay hands on the sick,[14] does this include an idea of a non-verbal communication as well as sharing power from God? We read that Paul prayed first, then layed hands on, with the aim to heal.[15] What does it mean when Jesus promises, that 'you will receive power when the Holy Spirit comes upon you'?[16] The answers to these questions will probably also determine how you pray today.

It is not only our insight into what these scriptures mean that will determine our style of prayer. There are also cultural matters which we should respect. In Asia there is no way that a man can touch a woman. In prayer, at a distance, we have at times symbolically directed only our hands in a blessing form towards the woman for whom we prayed. Yet, in that culture, the manifestation of the presence of Jesus sometimes had just the same effect as if we had touched. The locked-up tension in the body would be released for a time and some involuntary muscle movements would take place, as if an invisible hand was loosening them up. I have seen the same with sexual-abuse survivors, who became scared of this and needed an explanation of what was happening. Once they understood and allowed the peace of God to relax the body, it would at times even be too amusing for themselves, how their body started to act up. My explanation keeps it down to earth. I see at least two possibilities why some people have physical reactions during prayer.

Just as a memory can give you the shivers, when the peace of God touches the emotions I can see how that could create physical responses. The opposite can just be as true. When there is a deep physical relaxation because of the peace of God the blood will flow better and stiff muscles (which otherwise need loosening up through massage) let go of locked-up tensions. This can then trigger emotional responses similar to the ones which caused the tension.

Specific physical prayer

The pervasive shame as a result of sexual abuse needs to be removed. Thus we see that abuse survivors often have a sense of pervasive dirt on them, which can't be washed away.[17]

Wherever people pray to God and present their bodies to God in simple prayer, without others involved, that is wonderful. My experience is that many abuse survivors, and according Dr Anna Terruwe also many others, *do* need something more: they need actual physical touch.

Start with the positive experiences they know

As I stated before, we need to avoid the negative image of a person's own body becoming the focus of our prayers. It is better to start with affirming a positive perspective on the body, through worship of the Creator. After this, it is usually not a problem in western culture then to pray for some of the parts either in a general and sometimes in a more specific way.

This can be made practical by spending first time on finding out when they do feel relaxed in their bodies, where they notice peace. For some this is quite hard. It is then helpful to ask them where they feel various emotions such as anger, sadness. Many males indicate that anger makes their shoulders stiffen, while many women respond with a tight feeling in their stomach. I then explain that it is possible to feel angry about unrighteousness and yet to have the peace of God as well; thus 'stereo feelings'. This is needed to expand their emotional awareness; in some parts of my body I have stress, in others I am relaxed.

This positive start helps them to face the painful realities of what their body might be telling them.

The hands

Children have often been forced to use their hands to satisfy the abuser sexually. These hands then carry a shadow, a smell, which no amount of washing will remove. To commit these hands to the Lord, to claim the power of the blood of Jesus, is one way to communicate to that part of a person's experience. The apostle Paul too, speaks about the need to realise the function of holy hands in worship.[18]

The eyes

Survivors often have been told how seductive they were. They were often told that a certain look would 'set the abuser off' and they were then punished by having to satisfy the emotions they caused in the abuser. The child, unaware of what that look is, learns to fear the eyes. It can also be that as adults, they again see lust in the eyes of those around them. How does one respond now? To pray for healing for the eyes is one way to deal with this problem. If we agree that this should be done, I lay hands on the eyes and bless them in Jesus' name. I also tell them that they are allowed to be angry, and if necessary to shoot fire! Just as a sense of humour helps in the normal encounters between men and women, I also encourage survivors to develop more humorous responses. One phrase which I let them say to themselves quietly when someone admires their body is 'I am like a flower garden; it's all right to look at the flowers but just don't touch them.' There are also times when I have to convince them that it is not bad to be beautiful; that it is quite all right to agree with someone and thank them for a positive remark to that effect, as long as it's polite.

The head

Tension can cause muscles in the head to tighten up and thus reduce the flow of blood. To pray specifically for Shalom on the head and to share the peace of God there can result in a greater relaxation, a better circulation and a greater sense of well-being.

The neck

In the Bible, the neck is a symbol of a person's will. To bless the will can often be symbolised by blessing the neck.

The jaws

Persons with locked-up anger sometimes have very high stress on the jaws. I have seen people who received a blessing on these jaws relax and lose that stress. Some who were in treatment because of headaches caused by wrong jaw position could discontinue this. They were healed.

The back

There seem to be so many emotions locked up in the back. While body language is not the same in all cultures, it helps to become aware that in western culture 'being burdened' can show up in a stooped back. Locked-up anger can have an effect on the lower back, causing lower-back pain. Bitterness can also create tension in the upper part of the back. Sadness as well as a fear can influence the breathing muscles. To bless the spine and ask for Shalom there can have some remarkable results.

The nose

At one time I felt led to pray for a lady's nose. She agreed that she had very little sense of smell, so it seemed to her a good idea. As I prayed, she suddenly pushed my hand away. 'It's dirty, it stinks.' Now I just had washed them, so I knew that was not true. I gently suggested that she might have a smell-memory. Then she started to feel sick, as she remembered how she was fored to participate in oral sex as a child. The lady herself realized what was happening and suggested prayer for her mouth and throat too. She understood then why she had always felt a tension in her throat.

The feet

It is amazing how children battle with their feet, as they walk along with an abuser. It is as if they won't obey. I have often found that, through praying for the feet and blessing them, the Shalom of God can touch deep emotions. Possibly this also happened during the foot-washing of the disciples. We do not have foot-washing sessions that often. To take time and bless a person's feet could constitute dry-cleaning!

The skin

It is not hard to imagine why we need sometimes to pray for a new memory for the skin. It is our largest organ and a main receptor of sexual impulses during abuse. Often, years later, abused persons can still feel these hands all over them. A prayer for peace on the skin can then be beneficial. The realization that I am a temple of the Holy Spirit and God by his grace has decided to live within me—thus with my skin too, and not just 'somewhere up there'—can give a new awareness of wholeness and cleansing.

The whole body

The Holy Spirit has 'good manners'. I believe that there are many parts of the body which need a touch from the Lord, but we do not have to mention them. There are times when, after prayer for head and feet, we can include the request, 'And now, Lord, please bless everything in between as well.'

Once I helped an abused six-year-old girl. In the years following we had contact now and then, as she needed some support in working out her healing. When she turned twelve she noticed the reaction of males to her changing body. This became extremely problematical, as she tried to hide herself in loose clothing. She asked her mother if I could pray for her once more. I was aware of her childlike faith and realized I had to help her somehow within the scope of that request. Pondering how to respond, I found the key in pointing out to her that feet are very sensitive to emotions. I asked if she could demonstrate this to us. As vivacious as she was, she did so, and very expressively too. Then I explained the foot-washing of Jesus and asked her if I could bless her feet and ask God to help her with her feelings. She agreed and I knelt down, somewhat at a distance, lightly touching her feet. It then became visible that the peace of God was touching her. We were silent for a time, letting her have her own experience. Then I prayed for her eyes and told her how she could make them shoot fire if people were impolite. Her back, used to bending, seemed to straighten out at the same time! Some days later her mother called and told me that upon coming home, the girl had put on her tightest T-shirt and gone out to play. I have observed how also others, both boys and girls, with similar problems have found peace with their bodies in some way or another, through a combination of humour, common sense and wise prayer.

Stepping aside

In this approach of helping through blessing, the stress on teamwork seems self-evident. To be present when God affirms his promise and manifests his presence continues to be something awesome for me, something to remember for a long time. Again there is a need for caution; a person who is present at such a moment can also easily become part of that memory. This could foster an emotional bonding which is unhealthy. To have more than one person present lessens this danger. Another danger is that the skilled helper gets too much attention. By reaffirming the message of the cross and resurrection we attempt to keep the attention on the Healer and not on us. Despite all attempts to be careful, deep emotional experiences can turn the attention too much to helpers. Those are the moments when a literal stepping aside will be needed. This can help a counsellee to experience him even better alone. Something similar happened to my wife and I when our first baby was born. When, after the first clean-up, we held that little miracle in our arms, we were filled with awe and gratitude. Then the midwife excused herself for a minute, and left us alone. She felt that she should not be a part of this. In a similar way we, too, can sometimes excuse ourselves and literally or figuratively (through keeping a sufficiently long period of silence) leave a counsellee alone. Thus we help them to preserve that unique moment. Deep spiritual satisfaction, joy or pain, can sometimes only be experienced in full when we are alone with God.

Praying alone

As a rule, sexual abuse survivors have often struggled in silence before. To be encouraged to pray alone can simply mean sinking once again into a silent despair. Or they revert to eastern meditation forms they learned previously, where emptiness is the centre of attention. Through biblical teaching they may know that individual believers are assured of God's presence.[19] But we surely do not always sense that this is the case. Joint prayer can change that.[20] Still, we always must keep in mind that growing up towards maturity[21] demands individual facing of loneliness and turning loneliness into aloneness with God.

Victims who are changing into survivors need to be coached to see themselves not as patients, but as specialists in surviving, with themselves in the leading role. There is a real danger that too much attention is given to what others do to help. This can be balanced by helping survivors to find new ways of self-help, which they can use on their own, to 'bless themselves'. To pray alone, even in a group, is possible, if we allow times of silence. Survivors can also be equipped and empowered to go home and work details out on their own.

One creative way of planning an individual self-care programme is the 'Esther Programme'. Once struggling to encourage a severely abused woman to gain a new view on her body, the word 'Esther' came into my mind. This idea developed in a practical approach to encourage a sense of physical well-being of both women as well as men. It has shown a positive effect on persons who feel intense disgust at their own body. It is based on the book of Esther in the Bible. This is a unique portion of biblical canon, as it actually does not mention God, or even prayer, at all. The closest we come to a religious expression is a call to fast, when Esther plans to go uninvited to King Xerxes, with the danger of being sentenced to death. But the absence of overt religious content does not mean that the Unnamed One is not there. On each page one can see the hand of God, protecting and guiding his people. The book of Esther was very popular among the Jews who were deported from Israel. This might be the reason that more copies of this book have been found than of any other Bible book.[22] It describes the life of a simple Jewish girl, who is taken into a very oppressive system: a potential wife for the absolute monarch, the king. When King Xerxes faced a defiant wife, he chose, or rather was forced, to get rid of her. Xerxes wanted another queen. He had enough concubines in his harem, but he desired something else; someone who knew how to relate to him as a ruler, a queen, not just a female body. So his servants set out to select girls to receive a training to be 'more than a female body'. It was in such a dysfunctional atmosphere that Esther was chosen as one of the potential candidates. Esther was a sheltered, shy, simple Jewish alien, an orphan raised by an uncle. The story tells us how she was transformed into a woman who knew to use her power. At the same time she was able to avoid slipping over the cultural precipice which had made the previous queen fall out of grace. To achieve this, Esther was given time to develop her personality and her sense of worth. It involved the bathing, perfumes, clothing and preparation for a private party with the king.

The following practical steps of the 'Esther Programme' have become for many a similar adventure, resulting in a new appreciation of the body as a house of God, a temple, where body care became a wordless prayer. In this way the pollution by abusers, who related so negatively to the body of their victims, was washed off. Self-respect became a part of their body language.

Such a physical reframing of the victim's self-image is needed, as abusers are known to be on the look-out for new targets and body language can often give them tell-tale signs that a person has already been a prey. I hope that you also can appreciate the humour in this 'Esther Programme'. The full force of this project might only really become evident when you choose to read this particular portion to someone else!

The Esther Programme

Esther was bathed, perfumed, dressed and made ready for a party with the King. These four events triggered the following suggestions which have developed in the course of time, and through feed-back from those who applied it.

Abuse survivors often feel uneasy in the bathroom. Apparently more than half of the early sexual abuse in the west seems to start in the bathroom. So no wonder that some keep checking the lock of the door and/or race in and out of a shower quickly. When I introduce this programme, I ask survivors to check for themselves how well they can handle this first test. If it creates too much stress, they should drop the programme.

Bathing

Test programme: for two weeks, twice a day, spend ten minutes under the shower, or in a bubble bath (the issue is to feel one's skin). Use body lotion after the shower, to prevent dry skin and itching. Initially the time can be shorter, but it should soon increase to ten minutes. If the tension becomes too high and after two weeks this showering is still not pleasant, drop the programme. There are other things you might want to work on first, such as physical exercises. After two weeks of doing this once or twice a day, I have often received reports from abuse and rape survivors that these two weeks alone have made a terrific impact on their self-awareness. Also, those who had lost the sense of feeling in their skin and who mutilated themselves just to have a sense of pain were helped by slowly waking up to the feeling of water. The idea of rinsing off what others had done to them is also a help.

Some of the responses I received taught me how deeply shame is linked to the skin. One lady told me how she felt so relaxed she just wanted to lie down. As no-one was at home at that time, she dried herself and crawled into bed. At once she felt how much skin she had. Her first reaction was to get up again and dress. Then she decided that this was a good chance to learn to be more free with her body. Perhaps this was God's way of giving her a chance to see a change in her sex life, as she disliked her husband stroking her body. 'For a moment I was in deep panic, waves of shame reeled through my body. I concentrated on the music which I had put on while taking a bath and finally I calmed down. I never knew I had so much shame in me. After a while I fell into a deep sleep'. Others, who were seemingly used to nudity in the presence of their husbands, had similar shame reactions and thus realised how controlled their love-life still was, trying to keep all emotions in line.

Perfuming

Perfume (for men a lotion or aftershave) is like a positive signal (it smells good). It has one problem; after a few seconds, you don't smell it yourself any more, while others do! Perfume also carries a kind of warning. If someone comes close enough to smell the perfume you are wearing, it helps that person to check the closeness of relationship. The smell is like a kind of underwear. As such it might be good to ask yourself who gave it to you and, above all, do you really like it? If not, push it aside.

After putting aside all that does not suit you, the next step is hard for some; go to a perfume shop and keep smelling and choosing, until the right smell shows up. There is one condition; don't look at the price. Just remember that the psychiatrist is more expensive!

Once the first perfume has become part of the normal body smell, go back a second time and buy one for special occasions. Then, if one is married, one can decide if a third type is needed as well. Many abuse survivors have sexual-adjustment problems. The result is that the caring partner often holds back, waits for a signal and becomes passive. I know from many women that this is precisely what they do not want. So the third smell might be a subtle way of saying, 'We might, or we might not, but try it . . . '

Clothing

With the perfume issue settled, a new project starts; to choose one special outfit. I have discovered that many women, especially those who have been abused, buy nice clothing and then don't dare to wear it; or they look longingly at it, but cannot make a choice. They sense it is just not right for them. It would call too much attention to the body. Male survivors often respond with slovenliness (and get away with it better). Often only after much prodding by a partner can they bring themselves to the extravagance of buying something new. ('Why a new sweater? Is this one not good enough?')

Make a list of what one normal outfit would cost and multiply it by four! Then start saving for *one* outfit at that price. This is way beyond the norm, so it takes time to save. The key issue to this part of the Esther project is to keep it a secret. Just put some money aside quietly each month. Also buy some fashion magazines to study the clothing in the price range for which you are saving. This becomes quite self-educating. It also takes time to develop one's taste in this range. That is not a problem for most of us, as it will take quite some time to save the necessary funds secretly! For most of us this project could last many months. Once the money is in, go to the special boutiques where they sell more expensive clothing and browse around. Let the assistants advise you; they will smell your money and treat you royally. After six weeks of choosing (not fewer), take a good friend along who will not impose her or his views of what is nice upon you; just someone to laugh with and to encourage you. Then make your choice within six weeks at the most.

The party

Once the money for the new outfit is in, there are at least six weeks in which to save a bit more for the Grand Finale, the party. If you are single, invite friends to the party and then be the talk of the evening. If married, a different approach is suggested. Most of the reports I get are from women who have been able to carry this programme through to the end. Few men have done it, so I will report now in the female gender.

Book a weekend in a hotel secretly. Let someone into the secret and ask them to help watch the children, if there are any. When your husband comes home, have his and your suitcases ready. Just let him get back into the car, or a waiting taxi, for a surprise trip. Then let him wait in the hotel bar while you dress up alone. Then when you come down, you will see the amazement, perhaps even the worried look. Then it is important to say the right first words, 'Shalom, it's all paid for . . . '

This self-care creates an atmosphere in which one was not just praying, but in which spirit, soul and body become more harmonious elements—a prayer in themselves. It is not a self-care programme for others, but more for themselves to enable them to be at home in their own body. From the humour (and the common sense), we still should get back to the reality that working the area of 'experiences', can cause problems as well.

Addicted to 'experiences'?

Excitement is a normal part of human experience. The moment we say 'normal', someone will ask, 'But who sets the norms?' I agree that what is normal is also cultural; think again about believers in Africa swinging for the Lord and Nordic Christians who have a much quieter response. That is a matter of culture. There is a rather more basic norm, which I believe is universal and that is excitement, either for excitement's sake, or an excitement as a part of being related to creation, to the Creator. The awe of the beauty of creation, the awe of a couple deeply in love with each other. The awe of standing before a Holy God.

With all the good things which there are in life, something can go astray. We can become 'nature freaks' for the thrill only; we can fall in love with sexual experiences, not focused on a person, but on the act; it is possible to seek a 'feeling of presence', rather than the Lord. Dr A.B. Simpson, the founder of a world-wide mission, The Christian and Missionary Alliance, was a man with a passion for people and their salvation. He also introduced prayer for physical healing in a traditional reformed setting in the U.S.A. in the latter half of last century. He was also a poet and wrote a song which still speaks to us today, 'Once I sought the blessing, now I seek the Lord'. This frank statement says it all; immature responses to a manifestation of the presence of God can make people look for more. That is the potential beginning of any excitement addiction which we can develop. What gave a certain level of excitement before is soon no longer enough. More intense thrills need to be experienced. Religious addictions can vary of a craving for 'solemn' occasions, of melancholic presentation of the suffering of Jesus, to the highs of ecstatic expressions of religious experiences in large meetings.

In one meeting where I spoke, someone asked for a prayer of blessing. He had introduced himself to me before, as a Christian psychotherapist. As we prayed for him, at the altar of a Lutheran Church, he suddenly seemed to become drunk. Gently rocking back and forth, he stayed in a state of awe. This lasted for over half an hour. Then he left quietly. The next week he was back and asked 'more of the same'. I could smell the alcohol and suggested that we talk a bit. Then he told how he left the week before in a cloud of peace. It enveloped him for several days. He took some days off to enjoy nature and be alone. Then he had to come back to town, met some of his old friends and suddenly became depressed. I asked him more about his faith. I found then that he was deeply involved in eastern mysticism, looking for various religious thrills. We talked about blessing and what it had cost Jesus to bring us blessing. When I discussed the cross, he pulled back. I asked God for mercy, then he left. Later I heard that his search for thrills ruined him completely both in his work as well as in his personal life.

A wrong presentation of powerful peace, with a stress on the experiences rather than the Lord, can also cause problems. This is why I stress, as I explained earlier in greater detail, a personal discipline to be exercised before any 'blessing' takes place: first we turn our spirits to God, then our souls and finally our bodies. When we do this with others, as believers together, we can have their non-condemning critical evaluation. Sin did come in the world and still has effect among us. I believe that if we approach God in this way, in humility and keeping the right order in our worship of spirit, soul and then our body, not insisting on any experiences, that he will not give us 'stones for bread'.

The need of 'seeking God together', and how the fellowship of believers in a church can bring healing is the main theme of the next chapter.

Notes

1. 1 Thess. 5:23
2. Heb 4:1–13
3. 2 Cor 7:1
4. Rom 7:24, 25
5. Ps 42:11 is only one example of many.
6. 2 Cor 7:10
7. Eph 4:26
8. Rom 12:1,2
9. Prov 1:7
10. Heb. 10:22
11. 2 Cor 7:10; 1 Thess 5:23
12. Lk 8:46
13. Acts 3:7
14. Mk 16:18
15. Acts 28:8
16. Acts 1:8
17. 2 Cor 7:1
18. 1 Tim 2:8
19. Mt 28:20
20. Mt 18:19,20
21. Eph. 4:13
22. *New Bible Commentary*, Inter Varsity Press, Leicester, 1970

CHAPTER TWELVE

POWERFUL PEACE THROUGH THE CHURCH

I started this book with the needs of victims and survivors. We have seen how destructive early sexual abuse is for the development of relationships resulting in a great stress on individualism. In my approach, I first see a need for individual help, but more is needed. The New Testament stresses the 'together' aspect of believers, the church.

Discussions about church life among survivors is often a depressing experience. To suggest that peace can flow in such a setting demands some faith then! Yet, as victims turn into survivors, they need to learn to relate to others, not as victims and ultimately not as survivors either. Their self-image needs to look beyond survival; to be people with a future, unfettered by the past.

The church does not exist solely because of the need of people, it is a part of God's plan to bring salvation to mankind. He decided to use people to achieve this plan. Broken and hurt themselves, they still could be used by God for others.[1]

The most amazing aspect of the church is probably that God himself decided to join in this venture of the community of believers. This is expressed in the pastoral opening phrase 'In the Name of the Father, Son and Holy Spirit.' It affirms our awareness that there is an Other One. Even angels are involved, usually unseen, as we minister.[2] God has decided to let the church be a platform for his grace. This speaks about the whole life of the Church, not only pastoral counselling. It also includes the positive place of the sermon, the fellowship, and a smaller 'kinship' group where believers are more known personally. Then there is the communal action into the needs of society and together with other groups in society. Participating in the life of the church is healing in itself, yet here also is a problem for survivors. Their ability to relate has been damaged. The specific type of church fellowship can also be a problem if it does not match the needs of those who grew up in a culture of the abused.

Matching needs and supply

My experience is that the lack of peace and understanding often is due to a mismatch of needs and supply between survivors and the church members as well as church leadership. Different perceptions of what is expected by a church can also cause a problem for someone entering into a church fellowship. Clarification of what the needs are and what a fellowship can offer will prevent at least some of the disappointments.

The following picture might clarify this better:

survivor needs/supply	church fellowship needs/supply
social	social
emotional	emotional
cognitive	cognitive
miracle	miracle
commitment	commitment
growth	growth

The social needs can be something practical like, 'Can you help me find a house?' or 'Can you come and help clean the church?' The emotional needs can involve the need for time, to be able to tell your story, the need to be believed *or* the expectation that you will join in with glorious praise, even while you are depressed. The cognitive needs can be a desire to have a better understanding what power-abuse can do *or* the desire of church leadership that you attend 'basic faith classes'.

The miracle needs can be a prayer of a survivor, to be freed instantly from the effects of a life in the culture of the abused. But also some churches believe that this is the best way to help abuse survivors. Then survivors would hope for a sense of commitment from the church, especially when they are 'low'; the church members would like to see regular participation and often translate 'lows' as 'lack of commitment'. Then finally, both sides can expect that growth should be the result of participation in church life and often show disappointment when things go wrong.

A mismatch of expectations can make things only worse, such as a cognitive expectation of a survivor, who is not ready to meet the commitment expectation of the church.

Survivor-friendly churches

What is needed for a church to be a healing fellowship in which an abuse survivor can find his or her own way, with some help from the church? I believe it includes at least the following elements:

1. A practical view on suffering.
2. Avoidance of inflation of the gospel.
3. The development of structures which liberate.

A practical view on suffering

One fundamental need which will help us to liberate abuse survivors is a practical, balanced, biblical view on suffering. It should be practical, because it needs to speak to their daily struggles. It should be balanced, because there are paradoxes we should not try to resolve; God is almighty, God is good and innocent people suffer. The Bible helps us to develop a personal view, but it must also be translated into a common view for a congregation. It should be biblical and that is only possible as we interact with many others who have applied the word in their situation of suffering.

There is something very private about suffering and likewise something very private about the healing process. A right atmosphere empowers an abuse survivor to walk away from the past, without suppressing the memories or ignoring the consequences. Survivors who still suffer from the long-term consequences of sexual abuse can be shown the hardships we all face at some time and how, in spite of this, we go on, even if a situation goes from bad to worse. The aim should be to help a suffering person become aware of God's probing question, 'Do you love me anyhow?'

Avoidance of inflation of the gospel

In an effort to 'sell' the gospel, claims are sometimes made of what Jesus can do for us if we believe in him, claims which go beyond God's clear statements. An evangelist can glibly make all types of promises, while pastoral workers will face the results later on in disappointed believers.

A church which liberates does not promise anything except the assured presence of Jesus in our suffering. With that one promise, faith is strengthened, people can then cope and yield their lives to God. Then in that attitude of inner tranquillity and rest, miracles can happen, unexpected solutions arise and what we did not dare to hope for can happen. The knowledge of Christ in me is the only solid rock of hope. A church which promises more than Jesus alone will present an inflated gospel and create deeply disappointed church members.

On the other hand the message about Jesus, with a focus on his death and Resurrection, prepares people for the reality of pain and suffering. This happened to Pastor Sing from Dong Hua Chi village in north-east Thailand. He was once a witch-doctor as well as a gunsmith. Through powers which we in the west cannot understand (and which we therefore term trans-rational), he was able to touch hot iron with his bare hands without burning his fingers. When he became a Christian, he had to use tongs, otherwise his hands burned like anyone else! Finally he stopped making guns and went to the Maranatha Bible School, a unique four-year pastoral training for leprosy patients. Upon his return, he became a village pastor. One day, as he was cutting wood, his axe slipped out of his hand. It hit his leg but did not hurt him at all. His automatic thought was, 'The force is still with me.' Just a short time later, the same thing happened again. A sharp cut produced a stinging pain. As he nursed his wounds, he breathed a prayer to Jesus. Then he felt Jesus was saying, 'I protected you the first time, but you honoured the force of the past . . . !' Later, when he was ill, he told me 'I have decided I would rather be ill with Jesus than be healed by the occult forces of the past.' That viewpoint liberated him from his past and made him a truly new man. Such a change of perspective does not come about in one day. Nor does it happen only through hearing and reading the gospel. The way in which the gospel is brought, and even the church structures, are important in order to come to such a perspective or paradigm change.

The same message is true for survivors. Life is not fair. It is tough to grow up in a culture of abuse. Some cultural traits, like survival mechanisms, escapism and 'pain killer use' have carved deep ingrained patterns. It takes time to change. Some aspects might need more than a lifetime!

Church structures that liberate

The long-term effects of early sexual abuse have much to do with the development of the personality during the period of abuse. While a new perspective on life—a paradigm change such as hope—can come about instantly, the change from deeply-ingrained patterns takes time. For that there are no quick cures. As I described before, a vital factor which can speed up the healing process is a paradigm shift, from a self-image of a victim to a survivor perspective.

Church structures can help to foster this positive image, by responding to them as survivors and not keeping them as victims. Thus the helping process should avoid the idea that they are passive patients in need of surgical help, but people who have won many a battle and with some help, can achieve even a much greater freedom.

A church which places Jesus Christ in the centre, and not the problems, does not have to deny the problems. It rather stresses the right focus; 'Yes, it was terrible, you were a victim, but now, the incarnation is still at work; Christ comes in us, you can do it. His power is there to enable you'.

From the abuse of power to servanthood

Any form of organisation includes decision-making and thus, power. The church, as an organisation, has often used that power for less-than-spiritual aims. We need to stress a repentance from abuse of power to the power to serve, in the development of structures.

Religious groups need to develop structures as well, otherwise it will be difficult to manage a fellowship. The New Testament does speak about the need for church order. How such structures develop depends on the culture. The only way the various New Testament rules on the church forms seem to make sense, is when we see that there is unity in its purpose, but difference in its cultural expressions.

Missions often made the mistake of thinking that the same forms will also mean the same content. This resulted in a cultural imperialism which forced foreign models on believers in different cultures. Outward form became the all-important issue. Such structures enslave.

Missionaries working in the culture of the abused, should show understanding of the fear which abuse survivors have, of suffering power abuse and manipulation. Abuse survivors often feel very keenly how a church or a church leader can be manipulative. Their aversion to this easily causes conflicts, or they quietly withdraw. If leaders want to learn to avoid any appearance of evil, such survivors can be excellent teachers. They can serve as barometers for the type of pressure which there can be exerted by leadership. If these allergic reactions irritate church leadership, it might be wiser to advise a survivor to find a temporary shelter church.

Wise protection

If our ministry involves working with such emotionally-loaded issues as sexual abuse, the formal structures can be a great help in protecting the survivors and their coaches in the art of living. For instance, I urge that counsellors work in teams. This has been a safeguard against both misunderstanding and compromising situations.

The use of old and new symbolism

There are often times that one lacks the words to express what needs to be said. Yet emotions push on, ranging from bounding joy to mute grief. Non-verbal forms of communication are then needed. Certain symbolic actions allow a depth of expression beyond words. When Yahweh decided to reveal himself to Israel, he used the intricate symbolism of the Tabernacle, the worship centre of the Jews, and many rituals which carried deep meaning and produced a sense of awe of the Holy One of Israel.

From a pastoral counselling point of view, such a use of non-verbal or non-structured language is also very important. It comes in various forms. There are sacraments and certain rituals which help us realize that we have historic roots. Then there is also the need to make room for new impulses of the Spirit for today, through charismatic gifts and modern artistic expression.

Sacraments

A traditional view of a sacrament is that it is 'the outward symbol of an inward grace'. I stress the perspective of Christ as the sacrament; he who comes into our suffering, the God who is here and near. Sacraments help us in our search to experience God. One powerful element of a sacrament is its symbolism. Its message, without words, can reach deep emotions which words alone cannot touch. Sacraments are not just empty rituals, but living parables with a powerful non-verbal communication of the gospel, and can be important tools for abuse treatment.

Most church traditions have an historic focus on one or more of the sacraments. Reformed Christians concentrate on two: baptism and Holy Communion. Roman Catholic believers have a wider view. As a counsellor, I try to find out what the church tradition of a counsellee offers, through the use of sacraments, which could be useful in the healing process. In addition to sacraments, certain rituals have been developed in church traditions, which have a special communicative function, such as the laying on of hands, anointing with oil, etcetera.

Incest survivors often feel that their experience has tainted them with death. Death as an escape is also a possibility which lingers in their minds. In such situations, a theology of baptism as a sacramental burial service of the old life can be a powerful metaphor for reframing the inclination towards death into a positive reality; I died with Christ and now live through him! If, in a counsellee's theology, baptism carries the reformed stress on the covenant of God, we can help them to draw hope from that. The fact that the name of God was proclaimed in baptism can become a source of gratitude. Some have expressed their belief that this application of the name, this blessing, somehow protected something beautiful inside which could not be tainted by abuse—that the life of God was stronger than the powers of death; 'Before I knew him, his grace and peace was shared with me. He touched me and no one can outdo what he did for me. No abuse can erase his gracious act'.

Adult baptism has a different perspective, as it allows the survivor to go consciously through this ceremony as a closing ritual, a ceremony which symbolically expresses the closure of an era. By accepting that one has been buried with Christ and now lives by resurrection power, a symbolic way has been found to accept a new identity. Rather than waiting until the abuse has been worked through, it is possible to proclaim, 'I am not the same person any more. I am still suffering under the consequences of what happened to me, but I am a different person.' Care needs to be taken that this powerful symbolism is not used by the survivor in order to avoid facing reality, i.e. by closing the door on the past prematurely. If you suspect this is the case, then the ongoing process of renewal needs to be stressed.

The use of Holy Communion in counselling also deserves careful attention. I have found it helpful to prepare a counsellee for Communion as part of the treatment programme. From a pastoral point of view, I find the Lutheran understanding of Holy Communion more effective than Calvinist reasoning. Calvinism stresses the commemoration of a great event 2000 years ago and especially the objective fact of what Christ did for us then. Lutheran theology, while also affirming this objective reality, speaks also about experiencing the presence of God through the elements of bread and wine. For me, it was in a formal, highly liturgical setting that I became aware of that reality in this form.

Rituals

Rituals are cultural tools to aid us in situations which can be emotionally highly charged, such as a royal event, a wedding ceremony or death rites. How churches respond to, for instance, bereavement differs in various cultures. Some cultures will expect a 'stiff upper lip' response, a refusal to show grief, pain or disappointment. Others become emotionally very expressive, such as people in the Middle East.

There are times when a counsellor is speechless, like the friends of Job. Tragically, modern culture hardly enables us to sit in silence for seven days with a sufferer, like they did. However, I regularly meet Protestants who go to a Roman Catholic retreat centre, just to find a place of silence in the presence of God.

The pressure to act in some way, when we are actually bereft of words, continues to be intense. It is here that new rituals can give us ways to deal with the unspeakable. Thus I have found it helpful to develop new ritual forms of communicating the gospel, such as a special rite to help parents work through the grief of spontaneous or deliberate abortion. Also, the sharing of the peace of God and my own understanding of 'Powerful Peace' for abuse survivors can be seen in the light of a creative use of our freedom to develop new rituals.

Faith can be expressed in many different ways, but it must

always be in one cultural form or another. To respect culture and to have a servant's heart is the key of understanding the problem which the apostle Paul dealt with in Corinth, when there was a controversy about the ritual head covering of women during worship.[3] The incarnation of the gospel in a specific culture allows for the design of new rituals, especially for their communicative value. Thus the depth of the gospel is shared in ways which words cannot express as well.

Rituals are there, to use, when we need them. Some parents just do it automatically, not realising the significance of what they do, by giving a tape with children's songs of worship. The fearful child falls asleep listening. I also know of children who are old enough to read a written prayer given by a counsellor to be used after a frightening situation, such as a nightmare. Adults too, can go through a period of stress and could benefit from such carefully written prayers. Many believers do this already anyhow, as they turn to the Psalms of David.

Liturgies

Liturgies are rituals used in worshipping the Lord. Historically, written liturgies had an important function in allowing uniformity and quality control. The early church knew that the 'incarnation of the Gospel', takes time. Because of slow communication, supervision and quality control were not easy. With reading and writing as a skill of the very fortunate few, methods had to be developed to make sure that the quality of the presentation of the gospel was right. Pastoral leaders with limited training were expected to hear confession, to celebrate Mass, to baptise, marry and bury the believers. A fixed framework (liturgies) was developed to make supervision more feasible. It also prevented some people from putting in their own words and meaning.

Pastoral use of liturgies

A family which was deeply shocked by the regular abuse of their four-year-old son in a day-care centre received help in such a way. Using a simple prepared liturgy, the minister was able to lead a family gathering (including uncles and aunts, but of course without the child) through a period of grief, anger and need for encouragement.

Charismata

Charismata—grace gifts, or grace expressions—are special abilities which God gives to equip believers for the task to which he calls them. In a sense, they are the expression of God's power at work through a human co-worker. They foster a sense of awe due to the fact that a pure and almighty God wants to work with and through people who have been stained by sin. These gifts of the Spirit continue to belong to God, even when we have received the grace to use them. This divine ownership needs to be stressed in order to maintain a healthy perspective on spiritual realities and plain humility.

Structured and non-structured prayer

Structured prayers, such as the Lord's Prayer, are reflecting objective biblical concepts.[4] Then there is the 'heart-cry' such as we read of in the prophets, as well as from Jesus or Paul. The New Testament also introduces the concept of non-structured forms of prayer. From a pastoral point of view, such forms of prayer—when we no longer know what to say or do—are a way of releasing intense frustration as well as a source of faith-building.[5] The apostle Paul speaks of at least two forms of such prayer: 'groaning in the Spirit'[6] and 'praying in tongues'.[7] These two forms can be with or without audible sounds. These two non-structured forms of prayer were vital in Paul's ministry. He is frank about his frustrations, his nervousness at times and even his despair.[8] Cornered, not knowing what to do or how to pray, the Holy Spirit comes to his aid with 'groaning'. As it is the Spirit's groaning, it appears to be an expression of the pain and suffering of God, with and for us, in our situation.

We do not find much written about 'groaning in the Spirit', although most believers have experienced times when one deep groan is the only way to express in prayer all they want to say to

God. Paul states that in this way the Spirit actually groans through us and intercedes for us.

The apostle Paul also speaks about 'praying with the spirit', or 'praying in tongues'. He uses here the phrase 'my spirit' to mean something different from 'my understanding'.

The nature and purpose of tongues can best be understood, if we view it from the perspective of worship.[9] The Bible calls us to meet the Holy One ourselves. In Old Testament times, this was only possible in an indirect way. Now, because of Jesus, a new and personal road to meet God has been opened. Seeing the Invisible, worship can take on new dimensions. The speechlessness which this can produce creates a problem for a heart which nevertheless desires to express something, somehow. The use of the spiritual gift of praying in tongues is then one way to deal with that dilemma of silent awe and a burning desire to respond.

Speaking in tongues seems to me best explained as 'the ability to utter sounds to the Lord which do not have meaning for the speaker'. If one received this gift from God, then there is the ability to 'make sounds to God'. It is here where divine initiative and personal initiative meet each other. I can decide to pray in tongues, but the only sounds I can think about are those which God places in my mind by inspiration through the Holy Spirit. Thus there is a perfect partnership. I make the sounds which he provides. This ability to concentrate on the Lord, not having to think in meaningful sentences but having free flow of expression, is something very therapeutic.

Initial experience of tongues can release such a wave of feelings, worship and praise that they are not only unstructured, but also somewhat 'uncontrolled'. This can then create the impression that one is drunk.[10] But there is no indication that these gifts are only to be used while one is ecstatic. The very opposite is reflected in Paul's testimony about his use of tongues. He stresses the need of an attitude of reverence, order and decency.[11]

It is not by chance, I believe, that Paul teaches the Corinthian church about the practical use of this prayer language. It is also closely related to our topic of sexual abuse. The city of Corinth was known for its ugly abusive practices and sexual perversions. A temple dedicated to Aphrodite had hundreds of cult prostitutes. If a woman wanted to study, the only possible reason she would do this was to become a temple prostitute. Decent women did not study. Men who wanted to relate socially, to discuss business, science, philosophy or religion, would go to an educated temple prostitute. After an unsuccessful mission to Athens, Paul jumps right into that sordid culture. We can read between the lines that certain patterns did not change that easily, as Paul gives the fatherly advice that it is not a good idea for believers to go to a prostitute. Bluntly referring to their past, when some of them were child molesters, he suggests that they should reframe their self-image into that of a temple of the Holy Spirit and behave accordingly.[12] The idea of a temple introduces the aspect of private, internal worship. I have found that this stress on worship is pivotal in pastoral counselling of abuse.

The need for tongues has not been fully understood and has, tragically, become an issue of theological controversy. If we look at tongues from a pastoral viewpoint, it might provide greater acceptance as a gift with a positive function in pastoral care. A prayer language can be of use in the coaching of sexual-abuse victims in becoming survivors. Anyone hearing the sordid tales of a person who was abused as a child, or seeing the blank stare, the dead eyes of an abused child, will know something of that inner rage about the evil which destroys. To 'groan' or pray in tongues can help to ensure that, in processing the information we receive, we keep a Christ-centered attitude.

Praying in tongues is only one of the tools which God can give, just as he decides what is needed.[13] To discover this need, we receive guidance through the words in Psalm 37:4 which says, 'Delight yourself in the Lord and he will give you the desires of your heart.'

Of course, this has to do with an honest request to God from a heart full of worship. We could even go so far as to say that, if we worship the Lord, inappropriate desires will evaporate.

Psychotherapeutic counselling often focuses on rational thinking and a release of emotions. Some therapists are also very able to show warmth to those who suffer. Pastoral counselling adds another dimension; God who comes into our pain, is in touch, through the pastoral counsellor with the needs which he meets. Then, there is also the extra promise that he will reveal himself personally.

Secular helpers have pointed out the need for emotional expression, where northern European cultures often have suppressed healthy expressions of emotions in church. It is often very hard for Christians to dare to be expressive about anger, pain and the need for revenge. Praying in tongues, or groaning in the Spirit, will help to keep a Christ-centered focus. People within a Christian culture who are hesitant to be expressive about their feelings can thus learn to do so in these liturgical forms of free, unstructured prayer.

Abuse survivors, in agony or confusion, can find relief through 'groaning' or a 'prayer language'. They can express what cannot be said (groaning) or for which there are no words (tongues). I have, as a counsellor, also received much help at times, through the (often silent) use of such unstructured prayer. I wish for every other counsellor the same.[14] I also know of others who work very effectively without it. Paul tells us that God gives what he deems necessary.[15] As I consider the revival of the private use of this prayer-language around the world, it appears to me that God has decided that many more people need that gift as a tool in ministry today.

Gifts of healing

Sexual violation involves the whole personality. While traditional pastoral counselling tends to concentrate on the spiritual and emotional aspects, I believe it does not pay enough attention to the actual physical effects of sexual abuse. The apostle Paul already noticed this direct link between sexual abuse and what it did to a person's body and self-perception. While he speaks specifically about the offender, he also refers to the effect on the survivor, as sex makes two become one.[16] The impact of an abuser on the abused leaves a lasting imprint. Thus sexual sin not only affects the abuser but also those who are 'sinned against'.[17] Elsewhere, Paul stresses the need for a work of the Holy Spirit in every expression of our personality; spirit, soul and body.[18]

There are different gifts of healing and different ceremonial forms of ministering healing, such as laying on of hands, anointing with oil, or allowing a resting in the Spirit (a deep inner tranquillity, whereby a counsellee is allowed a time of prolonged Christ-centered silence in a physically relaxed position at times so forceful that there is an inability to remain standing). Then there is the form of praying for the empowering of the Holy Spirit or to receive an infusion of health through a touch from God; a new awareness that the kingdom of God is not just words, but power. Whatever form of prayer we use, it needs to be shaped culturally into a form which is acceptable to the church fellowship. In a traditional church I encourage a person to kneel or sit down when I see that there is such an 'overwhelming tranquillity'. I would rather not have them fall down in a way which is unacceptable in such an environment, while quite acceptable in some charismatic churches.

Abuse survivors have a forceful need to be in control. A careful pastoral approach which enables the counsellee to stay in control is thus called for. If any emotional or physical expression of faith takes place, then let this be done by choice and under the control of the abuse survivor!

All these different gifts, abilities and insights play a vital role in translating into the culture of a counsellee a knowledge of who God really is and how to approach him. A pastoral worker with a gift of helping people in spiritual areas will approach an issue differently from the one who is skilled in emotional healing. Others have faith for physical healing, irrespective of the sprritual or emotional condition of a person.

Pastor Sikiti, a former Buddhist abbot, had to leave that priesthood because he was diagnosed as having leprosy. He found Christ and eventually became a pastor. He developed a gift of exhortation and was able to minister in a confrontational way that I saw very few other Thai achieve without impairing relationships. Before prayer for healing, he would dig into possible reasons. Pastor Singh, on the other hand, was a quiet man of grace who hardly ever asked probing questions, but just prayed for people and for the mercy of God. Both were used by God. It would have been easy for them to criticise each other, but they did not.

The charismatic gift of healing is more than sharing physical well-being. It is also a God-given skill to help people acquire a new perspective of life; to learn to live, to have hope for the future, to break away from a past orientation. The gospel has a strong element of future orientation as expressed in the second meaning of Maranatha, the confession of faith, 'The Lord will come back!' Such a future orientation can help a survivor to move away from a preoccupation with past tragedies to a life of hope and service. It does not deny the need of revenge nor of the need to be angry. It channels revenge and anger in a positive direction.[19]

Gifts of discernment

a) Discerning first what is good and what is God

Discernment of spirits needs to be exercised in the context of fellowships of believers. The Bible talks about the need of believers (plural) to hear what God is saying.[20] Care needs to be taken that 'discerners' are tested as well. One can easily find that a person who is very committed to a certain point of view and an individualist will accept responsibility to warn the body of Christ against what is going wrong. One Thai church leader caused great consternation when he suspected an adulterous relationship and simply made a pronouncement without checking back.

The number of sex offenders among Christian leaders indicates that we gravely lack the gift of discernment in our midst. It appears to me that one needs to be both sensitive to spiritual realities, as well as mature in personality and faith, in order to use this sensitivity in a correct way.

I must admit that since I work with abuse survivors and have been faced with some serious blind spots about those with whom I worked at times, I am now more non-condemning, critical and observant of addictive patterns. If one does not believe that sexual abuse can happen among us, it will be difficult to see the gift of discernment at work.

b) Discerning evil realities

One Jew said to me, 'After Auschwitz, one must believe in the devil, but I admit I have a hard time to believe in God'. When an abuse survivor reviews her or his life, some say the same. They faced the reality of evil. Undoubtedly there are evil forces at work. Jesus gave them a name according to their job description: a lying spirit, an unclean spirit or a dumb spirit. We can do the same when facing the demonic involved in child sexual abuse, such as a perverse spirit, a sensual spirit, a lying spirit and a spirit of death. As our discernment can be faulty, we need team work and caution.

Deliverance ministries

The Roman Catholic church has a long record of trying to deal with the demonic, which we do well to evaluate. They assign special priests to the issue of the demonic. Teaching pastoral volunteers has made me cautious in introducing this issue. Especially in western culture, which is so rooted in individualism, there is a danger of an individualistic reaction upon reading Mark 16 about casting out demons. These gifts are given to the church. Not every believer should be involved pastorally with such demonic issues.

Facing the demonic in Asia, I found the following rule very helpful; *Do not consider anything demonic, unless the Lord, in some way or other, shows you.*

I admit that such a statement is rather subjective. Yet, if the Lord wants us to be involved on that level, we had better be inwardly sure about what we are doing. If not, it helps to wait. God is able to communicate with us. Often I have found that it was the wisdom of God *not* to show me. The people involved were not ready, or I was not the right one to get involved. Without their own awareness of an evil presence, any help will be short-lived. Our faith in the possibility of freedom can encourage others. There remains a personal responsibility, a personal choice, to achieve lasting freedom of an infiltration of an evil presence. To say it briefly: there is no deliverance, unless there is self-deliverance as well.

If you sense a revelation about something evil and have insight and understanding about what is going on, check with others. If they confirm your impression, ask yourself if you should be the person to follow up on this. If so, never do it alone, and do not do it without the support and approval of leaders of your fellowship.

Two things any believer can do when uncertain. First, turn on the light of the presence of Jesus and focus on him. Secondly, encourage the faith of the one who is troubled and pray for empowering through the Holy Spirit. This enables a survivor to rise up in revolt against any foreign powers which rule their life. Deliverance will be particularly effective as a result of this internal resistance movement. The accent is then not on the counsellor or the ministry of deliverance, but on the survivor, who shakes off the darkness through the power of Christ in them.

The issue of the demonic is a study in itself. As I describe my Powerful Peace approach, I attempt to show how an emphasis on the presence of Jesus and the power of the Holy Spirit, presented in a peaceful way, is often as effective as traditional approaches such as helper-initiated casting out demons, like a policeman arresting a thief. This empowering approach enables the house owner to use his own authority to scare the intruder away. Then we do not have to wait for the police to come to help, but we use our own authority in Christ.[21]

In addition, I find that a low-key approach to a deliverance ministry gives counsellors the opportunity to wait and see if certain manifestations which look demonic (such as very strong expressions of anger) are truly demonic or a very intense pent-up personal anger. I have witnessed situations in which counsellors attempted to evict an evil presence, where ultimately it became apparent that only intense personal feelings were involved.[22]

As the whole deliverance ministry was 'off limits' for a time in Protestant circles, we will probably need more time to learn how to deal with it. Mistakes are made in any area of ministry. I am comforted by the thought that the Lord God has a lot of 'translation' angels. He knows what we really desire for the counsellee. He hears the intent of our prayers.

Amputation or cleansing from evil?

Helping the survivor of evil infiltrations might turn into the amputation of part of the personality, rather than a deliverance from something evil. This happened to Caroline who, as a young woman, joined a Christian youth organisation. She did well and now, 25 years later, is still very active. She asked me for some help. I had been puzzled by her personality, as she was one of those people who could enter the room and you would never notice she was there. A sense of greyness enveloped her. She had also assumed a quiet background role. In our talks, the following story emerged: when she was a young woman, eager and active in Christian ministry, she developed some sexual problems. The counsellor involved discerned evil, unclean powers at work in her and led her in a prayer of deliverance. She was very relieved, and the problems were dealt with, but she also lost a sense of sexual identity. She declined several offers of marriage and is still single today. In our talk, it became clear that she had been very rigorous in the refusal of evil, so together with the unacceptable behaviour and the 'spiritual influence' which had been dealt with, her sexuality had also been amputated. When she realised the tragedy, she cried out to God for restoration of her femininity. The next startling thing was that she developed the old problems again. Now she needed to take a different stand. With some help, she was able to thank God for her sexuality yet refuse the unacceptable behaviour. This opened up a whole new life. She became feminine and attractive again, yet aware of her age and the lost chances. She grieved about the lack of a family life and that she was too old ever to give birth to a child.

As she wept quietly, my mind wandered to the scripture in which Jesus refers to people who cannot have children because of what people have done to them.[23] Uninformed or non-discerning counsellors can, while they mean to do well, instead be a source of much pain. Rather than coaching a counsellee towards holiness,[24] they use forceful language and authority to amputate part of the personality such as sexuality, a healthy pride, or the need to be angry.

There is a verse which speaks about amputating a part of oneself, but not of a counsellor doing the amputation. This is a personal decision by someone who struggles with a salvation-threatening problem:

> If your right eye causes you to sin, gouge it out and throw it away. It is better to lose a part of your body than for your whole body to be thrown into hell. And if your right hand causes you to sin, cut it off and throw it away. It is better to lose a part of your body than for your whole body to be thrown into hell. (Mt 5:29–30)

The meaning of this scripture became clearer to me when an active church member with a difficult marriage once approached me with the startling statement, 'I never knew that adultery could be so beautiful.' He then related how he was having a wonderful but adulterous relationship. He felt so fulfilled, yet at the same time saw the misery he was causing his wife, his children and the church. Based on this scripture, I challenged him to be 'mercifully cruel' by breaking off that relationship and saving himself.

One woman shared with me her increasing urge to abuse children sexually. She had a job in which she worked with small children and there were many unsupervised moments. I urged her to be radical in her choices and not only to seek professional help, but also to seek another job until she was in better control of herself. She did so and felt relieved not to have to be so careful with her emotions. That enabled her to work on her problem.

In both situations, it was the counsellee who had to be radical; to amputate what they really wanted to do, to choose to limit themselves—for their own sakes as well as those for whom they were responsible—and finally, to preserve their own relationship with God.

Prophetic insight

Prophecy is the ability to apply the word of God to the past, the present or the future. It is God's heart expressed through humans, about people, nations, situations or a variety of issues. It sounds so foreign and far away to some, yet I have observed that many believers who never think that they are prophetically sensitive have had impulses and inspiration to do things or to say things with a meaning way beyond what they did or said. Intuition is important in helping others. Prophetic insight goes one step further; it is not just a hunch, but a divinely-inspired idea, parable, or action to take. Recently I worked with a lady who had a rather hard time accepting her own body. I tried to suggest to her to start small, to use a small part of her body for 'healthy pride'. As an example I used her eyebrows. Only later did I hear how she was shocked by that suggestion, as that was literally the only part of her body to which she could look with a smile.

The first incest case I met with in one of the Nordic countries was revealed simply through a divinely-given insight. As the person quietly wept before the Lord, I just 'saw' what had happened and was able to lead her gently along a path of facing reality. I never mentioned abuse to her, but finally asked her, 'Who was it . . . ?' Sharing what she had never told anyone was the beginning of her healing process. The silence was broken.

Likewise, in Thailand, where male counsellors have an even greater limitation when dealing with female survivors, this 'guided insight' can sometimes be the only way to help. Some years ago, during a time of teaching at a Youth With A Mission base in Asia, I was asked to help a very troubled young woman. When she came with her two counsellors, all she could do was sob. As I waited upon the Lord for insight, I had a picture of a field with flowers. Then a big foot came and trampled the flowers in the mud, one by one. As I started to share this, the sobbing increased. Then I simply asked her, 'Who was it?' 'My father,' she whispered. I knew enough and left her with the two lady counsellors. With them she shared the details of her ordeal of sexual abuse by her father. An hour later I was called back in and was able to encourage and bless her. A year later I heard how she had progressed. It was only then that I learned that the phrase 'to trample a flower' was the way her dialect would describe a rape! She knew I could not possibly know this. That realisation gave her a new understanding of the God who is there. 'He knows me,' she repeated later over and over again, 'how he knows me!' I like to use parables in counselling, as they often seem to touch deep areas without having to spell out the details.

A prophetic gift can be misused, through lack of wisdom as to how, when and by whom it should be shared. There is also always the danger that a personal opinion can be mistaken for inspiration. But there is always the possibility of checking it out. As a friend of mine often says, we all prophesy in part, but some of us prophesy more in part than others! Again the place to test such prophetic expression is within a fellowship of believers. For readers with a charismatic background, I would like to give an extra suggestion. In charismatic expressive churches where 'all church members contribute something'[25] this can lead some church members to take the liberty of speaking to survivors in a rather unwise way. I advise survivors in a charismatic church culture systematically to refuse such approaches and to refer these people to their counsellor. If a thought or a scripture is truly from God, then it will still be the case next week! It all can wait and be tested.

Like praying in tongues, a prophetic gift can be received as a gift and developed. Also the creative ability to speak in picture language is something one can learn, even if one would never dare to say that such pictures were inspired. After all, God does what he wants, he can inspire us, if we are ready to acknowledge it as inspiration or just believe that we have a creative mind.

The absolution

To proclaim the vicarious death of Christ 2000 years ago, and to share the reality of forgiveness is another powerful concept which the church needs to reaffirm. This concept is often under-developed in both evangelical and charismatic theology. When we consider creating an atmosphere in which abusers could come forward to confess, I wonder if we need a return to the confessional booth. The anonymity might be a beginning, where grace is proclaimed and courage imparted to seek help face-to-face as part of the process of repenting.

I have asked trusted counsellors from other churches to come along as strangers, unknown to the congregation, when I give a seminar on sexuality. Their only task is to listen and to share the way of forgiveness. It has been amazing to see how people have responded. A most touching moment occurred when a seventy-year-old lady was finally able to break a secret she had carried around like a heavy weight for the whole of her life. Her smile was something I will never forget. Confession and the sharing of Christ's forgiveness needs a new emphasis in the Protestant Church.

The blessing

In Christian tradition, during every church service, a blessing is pronounced on the congregation. It is an echo from the days of Moses, where he affirmed God's presence and the resulting Shalom in the lives of those who surrendered to God. This blessing of the whole congregation will give extra support to the blessing in a counselling setting, where a pastoral team works with the approval of the church. With their prayer support, counselling will be so much more effective.

Sharing the blessing in the community

Through secularisation, many people lost touch first with the church. Then, as the process went on, individualism and fragmentation meant they lost touch with the community around them as well. The church was and is a strong force for social life. While other voices have clamoured for new social structures to replace the churches, this does not seem to have happened.

As secularisation has taken its toll socially, a liberating church should be looking outward. Its place is in the world. This means there is not only a need for church-based programmes but also community programmes. I realise that most churches have not even begun to think about abuse in their midst and what they should do about it, so to talk about communal programmes regarding sexual abuse is perhaps one bridge too far but they could think about it.

One could also look at it from another perspective. The number of pastoral workers who understand the needs of the abused and can share help is still very limited. Perhaps before a local church turns its attention inside, there needs to be a wider view. This could be achieved by inviting people from other churches to join in studies, seminars, courses and in developing programmes. At the same time, local mental health officials will be more than willing to share any material which has already been prepared through official channels.

The application of Powerful Peace in a church counselling programme is reinforced by secular insights, as we will see in the next chapter when we have to discuss the tragedy and the nightmare of many a pastor: there are abusers in my church, help, what do I do now?

Notes

1. Heb 12:12
2. Heb 1:14
3. Michael Green (1982).
4. 1 Cor 14:13–19
5. 1 Cor 14:14
6. Rom 8:26
7. 1 Cor 14:1–18
8. 2 Cor 213; 11:24–28; Phil 2:27
9. 1 Cor 14:17
10. Acts 2
11. 1 Cor 12 and 14
12. 1 Cor 6
13. Phil 4:19; 1 Cor 12:11
14. I am only quoting Paul's strong suggestion in 1 Cor 14:5. This cannot be understood as a 'must', see 1 Cor 7:7 for a similar expression about celibacy.
15. 1 Cor 12:11
16. 1 Cor 6:18–19
17. 1 Cor 6:18
18. 1 Thess 5:23–24
19. Rom 12:19–21
20. Rev 2:7, 11, 29; 3:6, 13, 22

21. There are many books about the demonic. The best one I have yet come across was written by Mark I. Bubeck, *The Adversary: The Christian Versus Demon Activity*, Moody Press, Chicago, 1975. Bubeck is a conservative evangelical from the Moody Bible Institute in Chicago, yet he also covers this issue in a way which is very appealing to charismatic believers.
22. In such situations it is good to realise that 'Satan never takes a vacation' and that anger is an opening. The Lord warned Cain against the opening when he was angry and when the demonic forces which could play a role were ready to attack him. See especially Gen 4:7 in the New English Bible.
23. Mt 19:12
24. 1 Cor 7:1
25. 1 Cor 14:26

CHAPTER THIRTEEN

'PLEASE GOD, NOT IN THE CHURCH . . . '

Over the years, I had counselled a variety of persons who had been abused by Norwegian church workers. As they all were adults, I had left it to them what to do about it. I also kept quiet, because people might have been able to track down such victims if they traced my travels. Then, in 1989, *Vartland*, the Christian newspaper in Norway, published a series of articles about the many missionary children who were sexually abused while they were in boarding schools with the abuser being a missionary. Public response was, predictably, one of shock. Yet, people thought, it must have been an anomaly, something extraordinary. With that in mind and with fourteen years of regular visits to Norway, I was more free to write about my experiences, without mentioning individuals. I can understand the disbelief of many when, in spring 1990, *Vartland* published a series of articles about my work with sexual abuse survivors in Norway, among them sixty who had been abused by church workers in their youth. My stories brought a painful truth even closer to home.

What to do about sexual abuse in the church

After the shock and some very strong responses for and against publishing such stories, the discussion died down until recently, when the discussion has flared up again, showing that sexual abuse by Christian leaders is still going on. Now discussions are taking place on what to do about prevention and what to do when 'it' happens in a church.

If we accept that there is a risk, then the attention shifts to prevention and early detection of problems. The practical questions surrounding sexual abuse are many. The following principles which lie behind my responses were developed from practical situations.

Principle 1: two sets of laws apply

Working from a Christian perspective, we face two sets of values; those which arise from our understanding of the word of God, and those which are built into the laws of the land.

For example, an official church worker has molested a child. He or she asks for forgiveness. The decision on how to respond to this is based on biblical principles, yet there are also the laws of the land. The person can be forgiven, but the consequences of their behaviour, including legal action, have to be faced. The least a church leader should do is to consult a professional mental health worker or the social services in the area, to seek advice on current legal practice. While the laws are increasingly strict, the application can in reality be modified in favour of the survivor. For instance, if the abuser is a member of the child's household, the child could be removed from the home. But there is the recognised risk that an abuse survivor can be abused again in a foster family or children's home. The other option is to remove the abuser rather than the victim. Wise application of the power of the law is to help in ensuring that abusers get effective treatment. It even creates the possibility of keeping a family together while the abuser is under treatment.[1]

Principle 2: interaction and co-operation with specialists

As sexual abuse is more than a transgression of biblical principles, pastoral workers need to relate to the social institutions in their area. According to Bolten et al, abusers are often very manipulative and difficult to help. A team approach is needed to break through their resistance and wake them up to the reality of their own pain, before they can even start to sense the pain they have caused in others.[2] The co-operation of pastoral workers and secular mental health workers may raise questions in strict evangelical communities. I have found that secular helpers sometimes have negative attitudes to Christian values. But if we take time to listen to them, we might understand more readily why they feel as they do. As I have found ways of relating to them, another world has opened up for both parties. The following understandings have helped me to arrive at this point:

1) Theology tends to follow sociological developments. For instance, Martin Luther's protest did not evolve in a sociological vacuum. There were circumstances which made him just one voice among others which instigated the Reformation. We, like Martin Luther, are children of our time, thus current social developments and the lessons learned in the social sciences have something to say to pastoral workers. As I have shown in earlier chapters, both the secular helping systems (social work, psychiatry, psychology, etc.) and the church have been blind to the issue of incest. A major task of theology is to apply the word of God to the specific situations in which people live. It takes time for the church to respond to changes in social awareness. The secular institutions responded to the issue of incest before the church did. There is no need to feel guilty about being 'later'. God works through those who believe as well as through those who deny his existence. Factual truth is still truth, whoever observes it first.

2) Western countries are rapidly changing into multi-ethnic societies. Each culture brings along some of its peculiarities which seem odd to others. Discussions with secular helpers are easier if you state that you accept–as a basis for your talks—that Christianity be viewed as a culture with specific values. Just as Muslims can claim respect for their values, so can evangelical Christians!

For example:

Adult abuse survivors have often suppressed reality for so

long that to open up is a major shift of reality in their lives. The long-term consequences of abuse, also long denied, are blatantly and brutally obvious. Such seriously wounded church members, especially those who are suicidal, need a variety of specialised help, of which pastoral care should be one. This help is most effective if it is given within the culture of the believer.[3]

Professional health workers can be asked to work within the culture of a client, irrespective of their personal beliefs. Some admit that they cannot do this due to lack of experience or because of a personal negative bias to the Christian faith. In that case, they should be able to help you find an alternative. If there are professionals of the same (Christian) culture who can offer help, there is already a natural bridge for the trust which is needed.

This relationship with professionals is also necessary because some survivors will, in the course of the healing process, have such intense experiences that temporary medication or hospital admission might be needed.

Principle 3: responding in the opposite spirit

Parents have a great impact in forming the value system of the child. By sharing positive values, we can 'inoculate' a child against an infection with the culture of the abused and avoid the long-term consequences.

Youth With A Mission, the international and interdenominational youth organisation with which I have worked in various forms for nearly 20 years, stresses one value in particular which is vital for this inoculation process: to respond in the 'opposite spirit'. The idea is that greed is countered by liberal sharing, hatred by love, criticism by respect, etc. Responding in the opposite spirit to the culture of the abused involves attention to survival systems, dysfunctional relationships, traumatic sexualisation, betrayal, helplessness and stigmatisation:

a) The survival systems can involve 'out of body' experiences, pathological forms of escape from pain and disappointment.

Responding in the opposite spirit would mean giving extra attention to being 'here and now', to enjoying one's body.

For example: Teaching about sexual values should be as normal in the church as it is in the Bible. The reality of sin should be presented and an awareness created that female and male care-givers can abuse chidren sexually. But this does not mean that males or females should stop having wise, open, warm contact with children. Positive, clean affection is a wonderful gift which any church worker can give to a child. Many a Sunday School teacher has thus had valuable input to a child.

Teaching about a biblical response to suffering helps people to face reality, rather than escapism. Also worship can help us to keep the right focus on Jesus.

b) Dysfunctional relationship patterns can be easily exposed through a church life where servanthood, respect and freedom in personal responsibilities are normal.

For example: Churches constantly need people to 'do something'. The way in which people are recruited can be respectful or manipulative. Life in the city makes long-term commitments difficult. We can accept this cultural reality, or force people to go on with a task by using guilt feelings. If not, they resign in spite of protests, and feel guilty anyhow. We can place people as the most important reason for the existence of the church, or we can insist on 'programmes'. One church, tired of pushing people into Sunday School tasks, simply cancelled having Sunday School at all, making it a point of discussion whether there should be any Sunday School in the future.

c) Traumatic sexualisation can start early before anyone 'touches' a child. The way the topic is approached in Sunday School or in regular church services sets the tone. Then, when sexual abuse takes place, the official response to this can immediately be traumatising. Sexuality can in this way easily become tainted. Such responses are reactionary. We need to choose to have responses on a different level.

For example: Pastoral counselling of parents to have an atmosphere of 'sexual peace' in the home goes a long way to teach a child non-abusive values. Peacefulness of physical expressions of warmth includes for instance, the freedom for

274 FROM SHAME TO PEACE

a child *not* to kiss, to sit on someone's lap, or to be physically involved in any other way with anyone unless it wishes.

d) Betrayal of trust in a church setting has an added poison to it: it will easily reflect on God himself and suggest that he is not trustworthy. To respond in the opposite spirit can be done through consistency of church values on confidentiality and on believing the child, when it comes with a complaint. This does not mean that a child's complaint immediately means that someone is guilty, but at least that from the child's perspective, there is a problem. A careful, wise and loving behaviour, which is consistent and observable by co-workers, is in time the best character defence, if this is ever needed.

For example: If a child does get molested in a church which has set out to be non-abusive in every way, it will be traumatic, but not involve a general distrust of adults or of the church. There will be less confusion when he or she knows that what happened was terribly wrong and the person who did it is evil.

e) The issue of powerlessness of survivors surfaces time and again, when they meet manipulative persons or suspect a manipulative motive. Abusers are, by definition, manipulative and untrustworthy. Long-term exposure to an abusive atmosphere can infect survivors in such a way that they become abusive themselves, or they develop an allergic reaction to any form of authority and translate normal expectations into the belief that 'this is manipulation'.

For example: Teaching people how to reject manipulation, as a life principle, is a helpful way to make them shy away from abusers! When such a distaste for manipulation becomes a deeply-rooted value, it will affirm the process of learning how not to become like their abusers.

To respond in the opposite spirit of abuse of power, we can empower children psychologically, socially, physically and spiritually.

For example:

Psychological empowering comes when we show that we take the child seriously, that we listen and treat them as a valid person. To show respect for the will of adults and child alike, to teach them the power of the will, as well as the consequences of decisions, is also a helpful inoculation against an abuse infection.

Social empowering takes place when we teach a child to be responsible and to face the consequences of its choices. Not just by rebuking them afterwards, or saying 'I told you so', but by sitting down and discussing the consequences of choices and to plan together how these consequences could be dealt with.

Physical empowering happens when a child learns early in life that there are personal rights, including those about physical boundaries. A sense of helplessness is normal for a child in a world where most people are bigger, and where emotions and new experiences can be overpowering. Information on how and where they can find protection against undue force, and from whom, is as vital as how to stand up against powerful forces themselves.

Spiritual empowering comes through the realisation that a child, too, can make spiritual choices and can have at quite a young age biblical insight of who God is. If, on the other hand, God is seen as the one who will do what we ask when we pray, then the question will be, 'Where was God when this happened?' How to deal with disappointments in prayer should be a part of church teaching.

Reality about life as it is now should also take away unrealistic ideas about personal power. Natural disasters strike, unexpected events force us to change plans, others get better chances than we do. How to deal with the fact that life is not fair and how to maintain a personal vitality in spite of adversities can be placed in a biblical context; when I am powerless, God is mighty. Also, identification with the millions of other powerless persons can be a positive effect of facing our own powerlessness.

f) Stigmatisation, the feeling of being different, is already a problem for many children from a Christian culture, living in a secular world. Sexual abuse can only increase the sense of alienation. This can be countered by sharing the uniqueness of each individual. The loneliness of stigmatisation is countered by introducing the idea of a positive 'alone-ness'.

For example: We can demonstrate, explain and witness how silence, privacy and aloneness can be something very beautiful.

Stories of others who were marked by pain and tragedies can become guideposts for a child, signs of hope that disaster can be channelled into a positive outcome.

Principle 4: abusers are sinners and responsible persons

The whole abuse issue has brought the question of morality back to secular counselling. At least pastoral workers and secular workers can agree on a definition of the sin of sexual abuse; to abuse power, through sexual means. Incest then, is one step further, as it also is a betrayal of trust. Care-givers commit 'a relationship suicide', they kill parenthood, being a blood relative, or their position of being a teacher, pastor, counsellor etc.

Pastors should not complain when sinners, including abusers, come to church! Some of them are there or will come, in hope of help.[4] Others, because the church provides an opportunity to seduce children.[5] Then a third group might start out good, but end up bad.[6]

The abuser, as an adult, is responsible for the havoc caused, even if one can understand how they grew into abusers. They should have sought help; and surely, if they were believers in Christ the Saviour, they should have known that they needed help.

Stephen Arterburn and Jack Felton describe in *Toxic Faith* how sexual abuse by Christians can often be just one of the many other addictions which are part of their lives, including religious addiction. The book also provides a goldmine of suggestions on how to help people who are bound to religious addictions, but affirm that it is a tough road towards freedom. Their insights also are applicable to abusers in a Christian culture.[7] We will have to understand abusers in order to treat them.

Christians often confuse spiritual forgiveness with absolving a person from the legal consequences of their behaviour. Church leaders in particular should give careful consideration to this issue. Clergy involved in abusive behaviour are transferred to other positions after they promise never to do it again and then continue their abusive practices. The absence of corrective and preventive measures by church leaders now means that the church is facing liability claims which, according to some, amount to hundreds of millions of dollars.

The gender of abusers

Since I started to work on this book three years ago, one more sexual taboo has been shattered; we know now that women are also abusers and at a much higher percentage than was previously thought. As I have stated before, statistics only reflect what people admit. As many more male and female victims of female abuse come forward, the actual percentage of known female abusers can only increase. The feminist charge that sexual abuse happens as a result of male-dominated society, needs to be re-studied.[8] A report from research by David Finkelhor, Linda Meyer and Ruth Mathews gives us an update on the latest insights on abusers.[9] Finkelhor notes five types of male abusers:

Male abusers

Type 1: the sexually pre-occupied:
Twenty-six per cent of abusive fathers studied by Finkelhor had a 'clear and conscious (often obsessive) sexual interest in their daughters', some of them right from the birth of the child.

Type 2: adolescent regressives:
Thirty-three per cent became sexually interested in their daughter when she ended puberty. They became fixated on the physical changes. 'The father-adult in me shut down, I was like a kid again.'

Type 3: instrumental self-gratifiers:
Twenty per cent indicated that they had fantasies about others while abusing the child, such as their own wife or the daughter grown up. They used the child as a thing.

Type 4: emotionally-dependent:

Just over ten per cent were emotionally needy and depressed persons seeking comfort from their child and looked more for their own needs than for the daughter's real or imagined sexual qualities.

Type 5: angry retaliations:

About ten per cent of the men were more likely to have criminal histories of assault and rape. They abused out of anger or retaliation for the mother not giving them enough attention.

Finkelhor also found that over 50 per cent of the abusers developed interest slowly. Better teaching on sexuality might break the abuse cycle. Of the male abusers, 50 per cent were abused by their fathers and 44 per cent by their mothers. While the effect of care-taker incest is quite severe, it seems that incest by a father affects a child even more.

Female abusers:

Abuse by females is only now becoming clearer. I also meet this in counselling. They are coming forward to ask for help. Ruth Mathews found the following four types:

Type 1: the teacher-lover

Usually an older woman who has sex with a younger adolescent.

Type 2: the experimenter exploiter

Usually girls from strict backgrounds who are trying to find out what sex is. This can happen during baby-sitting etc. They are often terrified of sex.

Type 3: the pre-disposed abusers

Because of previous history of abuse themselves. 'I was treated as an animal; I did not realize that my children were human beings.'

Type 4: the male-coerced women

They have to do this, because men forced them to do it. Only five per cent were, according to Mathews, true female paedophiles. Many of those she interviewed had received no nurture while growing up and were often abused themselves by multiple abusers. 'They linked caring for children with sex.'

Frequent abusers

A review of available literature shows that sexual abuse does not just happen. It is a part of a broader pattern of behaviour. It is not easy to become a regular abuser. One first has to:

1. Overcome internal inhibitions against abuse.
2. Overcome obstacles to committing abuse (time, place, prevention of discovery).
3. Overcome resistance on the part of the child.

These factors indicate that there must be quite a strong motivation present for committing sexual abuse before it actually happens.

Incidental abusers

There is also the phenomenon of 'incidental incest', usually a one-time indiscretion. Although some consider this relatively unimportant, I have found it quite frequently in Christian circles. It differs from regular incest in that:

1. The offender is shocked himself/herself.
2. The internal inhibitions worked, but protested insufficiently or too late.
3. There is unplanned action.
4. The victim is taken by surprise.
5. It was molestation rather than full penetration.

Incidental incest can, however, cause devastation. It depends on various factors: the personality of the victim; the level of trust which is broken; the abuser's fear of his or her own behaviour, which can create a sense of rejection towards the victim; and the unwillingness or inability to discuss it, to deal with it, to restore trust.

Principle 5: abusers need professional help

In this book I advocate the involvement of lay counsellors to coach survivors, where they need this, on their road towards recovery. Abusers are in a different position. As they are very clever at manipulation, a pastor might previously have been taken into confidence by an abuser, as a precaution to assure a benign approach should abuse be discovered. This happened to George, who tried to shake himself loose from a church worker who had molested him for several years. He finally developed courage to talk to the pastor. His molester saw it coming and went to the pastor before George, casually asking if 'anything strange' had happened between them, as George had been complaining about the pastor, something like 'crossing his sexual borders'. The pastor was upset, and when George finally saw him he did not believe the boy. Because of the level of manipulation, previous relationships and habitual blind spots, it seems to me advisable to seek specialised help from outside the congregation, even when there is the pastoral capacity available to deal with the problem.

A loving but firm fellowship, plus outside counsellors can provide a combination of support, social control, and the grace and peace of God, to empower an abuser to change. The abuser needs input towards that goal from two sides. Abusers do have spiritual needs, but also they have developed an abusive life-style which must change. Their will needs to be challenged and personal pain, as well as their addictions to kill the pain (at times related to the abuse they themselves suffered), needs to be faced. As abusers can be so deceitful, pastoral workers often do believe their sincere expressions. Perhaps they are sincere, but how do you know that there is no longer a danger of recurrence? A successful cancer operation is not a guarantee that there will be no cancer in future. In the same way, confession and amputation of evil is no guarantee that the abusive character is changed.

When an abuser asks for help

Pastor Andrew called me in some distress. In a few words he explained the situation. One of his deacons had confessed to an incestuous relationship and asked for help. It had been going on for several years. Did I have any suggestions? His voice manifested the shock and anger. How could this have gone on so long? I informed him that it was right to feel the way he did, but that the deacon probably would expect something else. The deacon would have to understand that although the years of silence were finally broken for him and gave a relief from the stress of the hidden secret, the people around were just starting with their stress! How could I answer him? New models for helping abuse survivors have only been developed in recent years, while current research has not yet yielded much on effective treatment approaches for abusers. To work with the abusers is not a very popular task.[10]

I promised to call him back soon and sat down to write out a list of questions, because the first thing Andrew needed to do was get the facts and write them down.

What had motivated the confession?

Did the deacon really come voluntarily or was he cornered and going to be found out anyhow?

It makes a tremendous difference whether an abuser comes forward to confess because of inner conviction or through outside pressure. Only in cases where there is an inner conviction about the havoc created is there hope that pastoral workers can contribute much. Often, however, there are many selfish reasons for confessing, as pressure builds up around an abuser. A wife might find out belatedly, and threaten exposure and divorce unless he seek help. In other cases, the abuser might suspect that the victim has talked and that it is only a matter of time before he will be confronted with what he did anyhow. I know of cases where the abuser saw it coming and hoped that a 'voluntary' statement would make the consequences easier. There are many reasons for a counsellor to be initially suspicious. This seems tough and unloving. But abusers are not helped by soft measures. Suspicion is justified for the following reasons:

1. In order to practice incest, there has to be a lot of lying and manipulation. An incestuous lifestyle only imprints these patterns more deeply. An older pastor told me once that lying and sensual, unclean spirits are twins; when you find one, look for the other one too.
2. The worst abusers can look like angels. Through consistent denial of abusive tendencies and acts, a dark side of the personality—like that of the moon—can develop. In time, the contrast between the proper, public life and the darker side of abuse can become so marked and painful that total denial becomes a habit, whereby one side of the personality seems to bear no relationship to the other.
3. They are used to brain-washing their victims. So be alert for constant misrepresentation of a situation by abusers. They might try to exercise mind control over you as well. By partially admitting the correctness of what a victim said, but insisting that the victim(s) made up the rest of the story, a seed of doubt is cast on the victim's testimony. Remember, the price of admitting that one is an abuser is very high.

Has the confessor denied guilt later?

Did the deacon later deny confessing his guilt?

Even a self-initiated confession, such as Andrew faced, can have some strange twists. The deacon might become aware of the price of his confession and decide that it is too high. He could turn around and simply say that he never confessed to this and that the pastor was just making it up in order to remove him from office. Some old hurts might be dragged up as well. He might move away, leave the church and thereby leave the pastor and church members with many question marks. This alone is sufficient reason to listen to a voluntary confession without comment, and then immediately seek out another church leader and let the abuser repeat his story.

If the deacon's daughter had come with the story and her father denied it, there would have been a different problem to deal with. There are abusers who put up a careful safety net which protects them, if they become exposed. This can be done by creating an atmosphere of, 'You can't trust this child'. Slander, giving orders and then denying it was ever said will create, in time, a cloud of doubts around a child. The child can even start to doubt their own, accurate, observations, because of this devious entrapment.

Now what can an accused person do, who *is* innocent? From a pastoral point of view, I would make clear to the accused abuser that in order to be believed, there are some things one always can do; to accept a thorough and honest check-up of their emotional and spiritual health. After all, such an accusation, even if false, will cause the accused deep distress. In this distress they can show that their trust is in God. When abuse takes place it is normally a part of an abusive life style. If they are innocent, there is the possibility of positive character witnesses. Those who can affirm that over time, there was no sign of abuse of power or any other sign of an abusive life style, nor addictive behaviour or signs of a dysfunctional family system. Someone who is open, has friends who know him, will be believed more quickly than others who lack such witnesses. Yet it is not true that we can recognise every abuser easily. Pastoral leaders will do well to seek the advice of professionals in such situations. If the case goes beyond the capacity of pastoral leaders, one should involve outside professional help immediately.[11]

Because abusers are skilled manipulators it is wise to not counsel an abuser alone. Two or more people are less easily fooled by potentially slippery statements than one. If the accused is innocent, the experience of Mt 18:19–20 is still possible, even in the trauma of such a situation, as all those involved seek righteousness, peace and joy through the Holy Spirit.

If the abuser cannot deny the charges, what else do you need to know?

Answers by the abuser on questions such as 'When?' 'What?' 'Where?' 'How?' are helpful to establish the seriousness and the extent of the abuse (from improper touch to full penetration), the use of physical violence, whether rewards were given, the kind of blackmail used to keep a victim in line, etc.

Does the abuser attempt to make the situation look less serious than it appears to you?

True conviction will help an abuser to accept overreaction by the environment. So do not be too careful in how you respond to them. If he is rather touchy, then I doubt the sincerity of this confession. Then even confession can be at least partly manipulative.

Were there other victims?

From Andrew's story, this did not seem to be the case. But be on your guard. Incestors can have more than one victim and will treat some more violently than others. Keep asking questions to probe for facts.

What does the Social Office advise?

Andrew did not know any pastoral counsellors who had dealt effectively with sex-offenders. As the church in general has just started to work with abuse survivors, the field of dealing with sex-offenders is rather unknown. Because they can be so manipulative, I advise the involvement of a therapist who understands Christian culture, if he or she is not a Christian, or someone who does not belong to the same denomination. To change the life style of a sex-offender, who by definition is a sex-addict, takes much skill. It is no easier than getting free from heroin! A whole change of perspective has to take place.

Direct action to prevent sexual abuse in the church

Sexual abuse is not an incidental lapse of morality, but a pattern of deceit, secrecy and a host of other personality problems. Pastor Andrew was not prepared. It is not sufficient to pray more often and fervently that such things will not happen. Disaster can strike us and evil people can infiltrate any community, including the church. How do we prepare? The Bible speaks about 'quality control' and the need for clear, open, caution, which protects the victims and does not spare the leadership if it is failing.

Quality control in leadership choices

If you study the advice of the apostle Paul in selecting church leaders, you will notice his insistence on an evaluation of personal and family life. The fact that hidden sexual abuse addiction is often coupled with a more obvious and 'culturally acceptable' addiction (such as being a workaholic or overeating) could be a warning signal. We should also realise that in Paul's day, community life was stronger than we experience it now. So there were fewer secrets. Yet even Paul admits that it takes time before the sins of some people become evident (1 Tim 5:24). If a person is going to be involved in working with children, pointed questions should be asked. It would also be good to know if the person shows any secrecy or is open about who he or she is. What about family life and stress?

Quality control in the preaching and teaching

The culture of the abused does not just happen. It is a deep, long-standing pattern. Preventative teaching on the previously-mentioned aspects of the culture of the abused should not only be done by parents, but by the church as well. A regular review of these topics, and an awareness that 'enslaving systems' never really die this side of heaven, will make us cautious.

Quality control in the church ministry programmes

Quality control also means making practical plans which limit the possibilities of sexual abuse, such as team work, the way in which children are monitored for sudden changes of behaviour, intense friendships between some adults and children. A sanctified suspicion on the part of mature leaders about those who work with our children and young people is of vital importance in selecting the best for the new generation.

Direct action in response to sexual abuse in the church

The apostle Paul also gives clear examples of dealing with public moral failure. The shock and the shame of exposure can put a healthy fear in others.[12] Fear can be an excellent motivator to avoid the bad consequences of evil behaviour. Sexual addictions will not change because of fear but those who might become sex-offenders can, because of fear, either seek help or find thrills in less odious addictions. Not that this is healthy, but now I am speaking about the prevention of sexual abuse of our children, or the adults who are emotionally weak, struggling or in despair.

What hope is there for sex offenders?

It is not true that sex offences which involve other persons are 'just as bad as other sins'.[13] There is instant spiritual forgiveness for those who reach out to God and confess. There are also social effects of the loss of trust and the lingering doubts. The loss of a good name is a biblical disqualification for ministry.[14] Just like parents who commit suicide of parenthood through sexual abuse, a church leader also commits suicide of a calling. Even tearful repentance and years of waiting is not a promise that the calling of God will be given back again. I have met some of these tragic figures, once very much used by the Lord in public, still longing for public ministry as their calling, and yet they are not affirmed in their calling anymore. A parallel is possibly to be found in the story of Esau, who sold his first-born position for a plate of soup and could not get God to change his mind.[15]

Yet, there is hope. There is a vital ministry in the church. If that ministry had been there when they were in function, they might not have failed or looked for help so much sooner. They have a function in the church; as a stranded ship on a reef, they are a warning for others.[16] Most people involved in a spiritual ministry have sought prayer support by others for their work. Unable to function in a public ministry, there is still every freedom to have a private personal prayer life, supporting others in what they cannot do any more. I believe that such firm teaching needs to be stated from the start in order to prevent any falsely-motivated action to get back to a spiritual task.

Only time will tell if a person has proven to be trustworthy again. This means an open and broken heart, ready to receive firm, loving counsel. A willingness to show discipline and create a lasting change of abusive patterns might create a basis on which God will call again and his children will recognise this new calling. We cannot promise this at all. Some have to carry the consequences of their moral failure for a lifetime, just like many abuse survivors carry long-term results with them until they die.

Can it happen to my child?

The thought that sexual abuse could happen to their child is enough to make any parent cringe. I have seen 'lambs' of pastors get a murderous look in their eyes when they discovered what happened to their children! How does one deal with the fears, or what do you do with the anger, when you discover abuse? Is there anything which can be done by the family, in addition to what we discussed about 'church life'? More about this in the final chapter.

Notes

1. Bolton, Morris & MacEachron 1989
2. Alice Miller (1990)
3. David J. Hesselgrave (1984) Kleinman and Good (1985)
4. 1 Cor 6:11
5. 2 Tim 3:6
6. Gal 3:3
7. Since the 'discovery' of the Early Sexual Abuse Trauma, it becomes more and more evident that the whole abusive scene needs more attention (Briere 1993). This includes spiritual abuse, (Arterburn & Felton, 1991; Johnson & VanVonderen 1992). Spiritual abuse can especially occur among serious meaning Christians, who realise that there is a need for order and authority. As a

cultural backlash against a freewheeling society, such persons can, according to my own observation in pastoral care and painful personal experiences, have a fear of rebellious attitudes. Especially abuse survivors who grew up in an abusive atmosphere run the risk of either rejecting authority or of crumbling under it.

8. Reading the reviews and responses to Charlotte Davis Kasl's frank study on *Women, Sex and Addiction* (1989), it becomes clear that she has given much food for thought within the feminist movement about the abusive personality, rather than the typical male abuser.

9. David Finkelhor and Linda Meyer Williams 'Incest, A Chilling Report' by Heidi Vanderbilt, *Lear's*, Feb, 1992. A first-rate summary of what is currently understood in the field of sexual abuse, especially good as introductory material for educated readers. Reprints from: Lear's Dept. I, 665 Madison Avenue, New York, NY 10021 USA. It also reports on the work of psychologist Ruth Mathews of St. Paul, based on 100 female abusers, 65 adult and 35 adolescent girls.

10. Horton, Johnson, Roundy, Williams (1990), give clear evidence of the problems within the helping profession of treating abusers. An outstanding example of success is the programme developed by Dr. Henry Giarretto in California (1982). This programme provides not only individual and group therapy for the abused, but also for partners of the abusers, and abusers themselves. At some point in the programme these groups all meet together. The statistics for recidivism appears to be much lower than other programmes.

11. It is good to remember that also professionals differ in their opinion, as has been forcefully explained by Berliner and Loftus (1992). This is where we have to be very careful as pastoral counsellors. While a survivor is just in the process of recalling past abuse, the initial statements are often confused, like 'light cast through different filters stacked on top of each other'. Shocked parents or authorities can then easily 'jump the gun' and start questioning or accusing. In the process, the survivor is re-discovering 'what is what' and might have to revise earlier vague or confused memories. If by that time already a police statement has been taken, any corrections will bring the whole issue in doubt. In this highly-charged atmosphere it will be clear that those who stand next to the accused will respond as intensely as those who are supporting the victim-in-recovery. As many survivors are well aware of these fateful consequences and the struggle which will result, many choose just to be silent. The only problem is that if the accusation is true and an abuser is not stopped, then yet more victims will be made. Any pastoral coun-

sellor going through the above situations should therefore think twice before any public action is taken. In principle it seems best that another counsellor or Christian social worker should become involved in a possible confrontation. This will maintain the quietness and relaxedness in the helper/helpseeker relationship, which is so vital for the healing process.

12. 1 Tim 5:20
13. 1 Cor 6:18
14. 1 Tim 3:2
15. Heb 12:17
16. 1 Tim 5:20

CHAPTER FOURTEEN

'PLEASE GOD, NOT MY CHILD . . . '

I meet pastors who are worried, but what about parents? I am a grandfather. The idea that someone would hurt any of these children is enough to create intense feelings. Fears can paralyse us or make us overreact. Not just the abuse, but especially the response to abuse, is vital. Much damage can be prevented by appropriate responses, and much damage can be done if we do not realise the effect which our responses have on a child. The following principles can be a start for immediate action.[1]

1. Fear can block our vision or drive us to action

Fear can block rational thinking and often brings out our deepest instinctive defensive reactions. To learn to face fears realistically and act responsibly is one of the major aspects of growing up. Parents can learn to face these fears and find their own positive answers. This maturing of parents includes the development of a theology of suffering. If our attitude to potential danger is exclusively to pray for it not to happen, then we face serious questions when things go wrong. As Job and others discovered, life can at times be very tough and innocent people suffer. But it is possible to demonstrate to children how crises can be dealt with in a healthy way.

2. Maximise the offence, but minimise the fear

While we should not minimise the seriousness of sexual abuse, a fearful attitude about where they play and who they contact infects a child and hurts the development of their own safety systems. If they rebel, they might not see the danger when it is there. If they are gripped by fear, they easily show a fearful attitude which can affect their future. We need a firm attitude and an insistence on maximising the offence if an abuser is caught. 'Letting things go by just for this one time' only opens the door for other children to become victims at a later date.

Realism about the possibility of sexual abuse in our church can cause us to consider timely action. In the last chapter we saw how the church, as a community, can take steps to create a safe environment for children. In order to foster prevention we can give attention to the following points.

3. Children with a strong will can handle abuse better than those who have not learned to use their will constructively.

Andy was a little over three years old when the babysitter put him in her bed, and started to play with his sex organs. He did not want it and started to scream until his parents came home. He could not talk about it until a year later, but for a time refused to have a babysitter. His parents did not understand, but accepted his protestations. For a time, they would not leave him alone. Only a year later was he able to start talking about it and give a graphic description of what had happened.

Children will have to be encouraged to use their will early. Most parents do not realise how easy this is! Just get into a conflict of opposing wills, then ask yourself if this could be the occasion to choose to 'give in' and to bless a moment of persistence and stubbornness, and to affirm to your child that to have a mind and values of one's own is good! One father, who had asked me how to deal with a rather strong-willed child who did not respond well to punishment, took my advice on 'blessing the will'. We had just come out of his study and I was putting on my coat when a rather upset seven-year-old asked his father for permission to go out, even though dusk was settling. After finding out the reason and the timing, the father's initial response was 'No, not now!' As the argument increased in intensity and volume, he suddenly said, with a smile, 'O.K. son, I don't think that this is a very good idea. On the other hand, it's your choice. Go ahead, and let's talk about it when you come back.' I was most impressed by what he added. 'If it doesn't work out and you get into a mess, I won't blame you. Just come home and tell me. We'll work out what to do later.' The boy was so insistent about going because of a conflict he had with a friend which he wanted to settle at once. It was a good occasion to teach the boy about freedom and consequences. After some unsuccessful parental effort to change his mind, the boy was amazed at this sudden freedom. He then decided to stay at home and let things cool down first. It was hilarious to hear the father trying to convince the son that he should try, to find out what would happen, without fear of later punishment; and then the son arguing that he didn't want to go any more!

The will has to do with one's personal boundaries. Just as our body has a skin, our personality has borders as well. They give signals as to what we like and do not like. Abusers have an uncanny eye for people with weak boundaries. Child-rearing means also planning for the development of these private boundaries, the sense of privacy and propriety. In a western setting, this means for instance that when a child reaches a certain age, it becomes normal to knock on the door before entering their room!

4. The only secrets children should be encouraged to have are 'fun secrets'.

We all know about the delightful tension surrounding birthdays and Christmas. Secrecy can be fun. When secrets are no fun any more, children should be taught that no one, not even the parents, have the right to tell them not to talk about it. Children who have been brought up with unpleasant secrets can easily be manipulated by abusers not to tell their secrets either. Especially when abusers use threats, a child should know that they can always talk about secrets to their parents.

Parental support through positive teaching at appropriate times should include teaching of safe-touch. There are good books available to help in this.[2]

5. Give extra attention to appropriate sexual intimacy

Western society is flooded with overt or covert exploitation of sexuality. Children can learn the difference through good models of appropriate intimacy. There is a problem here, as many counsellors have shared with me their observation of the large number of sexually-dysfunctional marriages among evangelical Christians. Clearly there is a job for the church to do in teaching positive values and practising appropriate intimacy.

6. Maintain a 'godly suspicion'

The effect of humanism on Christianity seems to show up in an evolutionary idea of people becoming better and better as time goes on. The reality of sin, and the possibility of sexual deviance which is hurtful to children, needs to be more openly discussed. The apostle Paul was not reticent about it in his pastoral letters. If anything has been learned about people's behaviour in wartime or in concentration camps, it is the fact that, given enough pressure, many of us could commit actions we would not dream of at the present time. There are people who have not been exposed to good models of behaviour themselves, or they have sexually deviant 'cracks in their soul', for various reasons. For some, it shows up early and they become masters in hiding their need; others only discover later that there are hidden, insidious passions within themselves which radiate towards children.

7. Become active in the community to combat abuse and its consequences

Even when we protect our own children well, it does not stop abuse. We must become involved in school government, sports clubs, or other places where abuse can take place, to create a non-abusive environment.

Rather than wait until disaster strikes your family or neighbourhood (and thus instill fear into your child), you can take part in community-based action to discuss and seek together ways of prevention. School and mental-health authorities often have access to both materials and specialists to aid such a process. Community-based action needs to be rooted in common values, irrespective of religion. I find that talking about creation values, such as the need for the right timing in the sexualisation process, can be a helpful start. Legal aspects also have a place in a common platform.

Recent campaigns against child abuse in the Netherlands have had some startling results among committed Christians. While the government's foster-parent system has been declining in interest among the secular population, there is an upsurge of volunteers who do this out of Christian convictions.

If you *suspect* that a child has been abused

We do not have to re-invent the wheel. There are professionals who can help and suggest positive action.

Believe the child

Feedback from survivors at a later age often shows that the child believed he/she *did* share with an adult at the time about what was happening, but that the adult did not hear it or did not want to hear it. Whenever you pick up signals of sexual abuse, share your concern with a responsible church leader or social worker and ask for guidance. Be sure that you only share this with people who have both the understanding and the power to do something. Otherwise it could easily become the vilest slander!

One question will arise for sure: 'I want to believe the child, but can I trust the information given by a child? What they tell me is incredible; this cannot be true.' It might be the express purpose of some abusers to do some very ugly and incredible things, in order to ensure that noone will believe the child.

From a pastoral viewpoint, we do not need to be detectives. If a child presents a story, the first conclusion is easy; here is a real problem. Fantasy or truth, whatever the case, something is deeply wrong. Finkelhor's research, which I mentioned earlier, indicates that there is only a very small percentage of children who, for one reason or another, make up such a story. I personally witnessed how a boy of four startled his parents with accurate detail of the abuse by a neighbour a year before. Until then he never talked about it.

If we believe that when children, unprompted, tell different stories, they must be making things up or they are not trustworthy then we are putting adult thinking, from an adult-legal mind set, into the world of a child. Adult-accuracy is indeed a problem. I have experienced how children can tell stories which in themselves were contradicting. Then in time it all proved to be true, only there were three stories which the child had mixed up. The first time the child talked was as if there were three overhead projector slides put on top of each other. The initial positive response to their 'crazy story' encouraged the child to dare to give more details, to face the past realities more openly and to see the facts more clearly.

One approach I find helpful as a pastoral counsellor is to differentiate between subjective truth and objective truth. A trained counsellor should be able to discover whether the child believes that abuse has taken place. If so, it is—for him or her—a subjective truth. Whether their statement is legally correct or not is a different matter. Remember, a child is reporting on an experience for which it did not have words at the time. They were new feelings. The apostle John, in the book of Revelation, describes cosmic events which go beyond his capacity to describe. Thus he uses symbolism to tell a story which has captivated and been understood by people through the centuries, in many different cultures. A child also, might speak symbolically initially. At times, they may even test you, as the counsellor, to see whether you can handle the information they give!

It does not make any difference whether a child is telling an objective, subjective or parable truth, the healing principles are still the same. In due course, as we saw before, objective truth might come out. If not, we have still made a positive contribution to their healing process.

If we do not push for too many factual details, the child will also feel less pressured to check every statement for total accuracy. Often, when information is partially remembered or contains a considerable dose of subjective experience or parable truth, a child will come back to that later on, when the objective facts begin to surface. They will say 'You remember I told you that . . . well, that was not exactly the way but it was really like this . . . '. Often such stories will come out in layers like onion skins. It is better to help the child understand that it's not so important to get all the facts, but what they believe happened.

Once trust is established and the child knows you can handle factual information, a calm, factual 'debriefing' can be very helpful for a child, including specific details. Much care should be taken not to have suggestive questions. Also I would recommend that a 'third person' be in the room, if needed, to quietly follow what goes on and to be a witness, if this is ever needed later.

When you suspect abuse, you can immediately start with positive action. A non-abusive, non-manipulative family lifestyle is healing in itself. Give extra attention to the need to practice living in the opposite spirit to the atmosphere of abuse. Give the child a chance to be open emotionally about other issues. In time, he might dare to share the more difficult things. Watch out for an attitude of shame; give extra attention to an atmosphere of graciousness.

If the child accuses someone

Always believe the child. At the very worst, it could be a tragic misunderstanding by the child. But even then, the adult is better equipped to deal with the stress than the child. When it involves a trust relationship, such as a relative or a pastor, an outsider should come into the picture. Remember that it is the suffering in silence, the not-being-believed, which can be even more devastating than the actual abuse itself! If the accused abuser lives in the same house as the victim, one needs to find an answer to the following questions:

a) Does the accusation create such high tension in the accused person that this is taken out on the child or other family members?

b) What is the advice of child-care specialists on the situation? People who regularly face these questions can look more objectively than those who are involved in it emotionally.

c) What are the feelings of the victim? You should also understand that the victim can feel very guilty and have very ambiguous feelings of both disgust and affection towards the accused person.

d) What is, by adult standards, at this time the best for a child? It is my understanding that under all circumstances, the welfare of the child should take preference over the welfare of the adult, even if it means that an unjustly-accused adult has to be removed temporarily from family life.

e) Find out which persons the victim trusts. Include these in the decision-making process and in this way, through informal talks, find out what the child really feels, what the arguments are and what it wants. The final decision can then be taken with these trusted persons, who again can communicate and hopefully convince the younger victim that this was the best at the time.

If you *discover* that your child has been abused

Abuse is like emotional murder. You might even need some counselling for yourself in order to be a few steps ahead of your child in the recovery process! Where parents do this, it is less strange for chidren also to get special help.

The intense emotions of parents need to be taken seriously.

God warned Cain that anger was an open door for evil[3] and Paul
encourages us to be angry but to watch out that we do not trip
over it and sin[4]. You will need a very strong infusion of God's
peace to protect your heart and mind. This is very important for
your child,[5] as it will often blame itself for the obvious distress
that the disclosure has brought about. If possible, control your
own emotional expression in such a way that the child senses
your deep shock, but also your fortitude, your faith in life and
the reality that is a future.

Let your children know that they can always talk about it

When the child shows serious effects, as described in the culture
of the abused, a long-term relationship with a counsellor is to be
recommended. This should continue through developmental-
change periods when the child might need extra support, such
as entering puberty, falling in love, marriage, etc.

A seven year old boy might only as a young teenager realise
what the homosexual assault really meant. Questions about
one's own sexual preference or fear about homosexuality can
surface at that point. When he falls in love, another crisis could
arise. Similarly early sexual abuse in a woman's history might
call for some extra attention when she is preparing for marriage
or when her child reaches the age at which she herself was
abused.

*Children need to hear over and over again that they are not
guilty*

The deep sense of shame which we discussed before needs to be
monitored. They might not show shame about what happened,
due to denial, but respond with unreasonable shame in other
areas.

Be sensitive about forgiveness

The Lord's Prayer reminds us regularly of the need to forgive.
Children will need a good explanation of what forgiveness
means, or they will feel an inner resistance against prayer.

That in turn can cause new guilt and shame feelings and a sense of separation from God.

Do not forget the other family members

Serious crisis in the life of one family member affects every person of that family. Even children who have not been abused will, because of life in an abusive environment, experience directly or indirectly some of the effects of what happened to the other child. They become co-victims in the same way as children of alcoholics. Their borders have been violated, and a peaceful reinforcement of proper borders through gentle discipline will give the child a chance to listen to words of authority from an adult in a positive way. A child will learn to trust again. Abuse survivors are very easily upset by anger. It is tough for parents who have not been born with angels' wings to remember this. But just look at the pained eyes of a child and their automatic responses to your angry voice, and it might help you to think twice before you blow your top again!

Should we tell the police?

The strong emotions, which parents have when abuse is discovered, affirm the need for parents to be included in the process of decision-making on what happens after the abuse. Otherwise, they will feel helpless, the child will notice that, and as a consequence will suffer even more loneliness.

The social services should get involved. They can give advice how to handle the situation. Often they get signals from other sources as well, and a network of information about a particular abuser might emerge, so don't be silent!

Get good advice before you go into a court case

In some countries parents who want to do something about an abuser have no choice. Abuse will automatically turn into a court case whether they like it or not. The government needs citizens to make the legal system work. People are needed to state facts, to witness and, where necessary, to allow the often-traumatic ordeal of a court case to take its course. Going through a court case can be as abusive for a child as the event itself. Be sure to seek professional advice, and to support the child under these circumstances.

Believers in Jesus Christ live in two worlds, the kingdom of God and that of this world, with a government that has the responsibility to deal with wrongdoers.[6] Governments, too, can fail. Thus the assurance of God's justice is an additional help to believers. We can give our desire for revenge to the Lord, who can deal with wrongdoers in ways far beyond our power to do so. Rather than power fantasies, we have the reality of a just God who will take revenge, if we give our justified need for revenge to him.[7]

A local church fellowship is like a family. There are rules for the benefit of the whole. Just as the legal system has its reasons for removing the offender from the family, there can be a similar need to move an offender from a local fellowship to another one. The only question asked here should be 'What is right for the survivor?' If the offender wishes, help should be provided in seeking another congregation where tough grace can be shared. Grace, because God does accept sinners uncon-ditionally. Tough, because there must be an agreed code of behaviour (no involvement in Sunday School work, Boy Scouts, etc.) as well as a willingness to be honest and open, to bear the shame, with God's help and with the support of those around. While behavioural patterns take time to change, one can and should expect a humility and a willingness to do anything possible to make up for the damage done. Never should the abuser call a victim in order to apologise, or meet them alone. Whatever action is taken, it should always be in consultation with counsellors.

Which way to go? Flight into fancy or braving reality?

There was a time when we heard nothing at all about child abuse. I only recall one instance, in my youth, that a church member was apprehended for molesting boys. For those who have not suffered such ordeals themselves there is a danger of first overreacting and then quickly tiring of the subject. Remember, survivors face many lasting effects, and for them the issue is not resolved that quickly.

Even if one has worked through the pain of abuse oneself, it is still tough to hear it from others. The nightmare can easily start all over again. Would it not be easier if the great silence settled once again and talking about sexual abuse once more became taboo? How incest can quickly become old news is evidenced by the story of an aged mother, who told about her battle to break the silence and tell her children some of the reasons for her marital problems: an incestuous relationship with her father. When she finally told her adult children, they simply did not want to believe it and abused her emotionally by saying, 'Well, after everything else, we now have to get on the abuse bandwagon?'

The sheer amount of abuse seems impossible to deal with by the regular caring systems. Perhaps the church can make up for where it failed in the past, by continuing to give attention to this problem long after the abuse issue has become a non-issue again; a thing which one does not discuss.

The church can choose to look the other way, as it has done for a long time. If we do, we might run the danger of drowning in our troubles—the millstones of God's judgement on those who abuse children. The alternative might be that we receive even the help of angels in our battle for righteousness, joy and peace for everyone through the Holy Spirit.[8]

Into all the world

A good friend of mine wondered how my missionary and pastoral ministries could mix. He saw the pastoral task as taking care of the sheep, while the missionary task is to bring the sheep in. I pondered about that question until I realised that my missionary gift had become a tool to enter into the world of the abused.

It is that missionary gift which I urge the church to seek or renew. Not just to cross the borders of nations, but to cross cultural borders too. As the church as a whole becomes more aware of the need to let the gospel take root in every culture, not only sexual-abuse survivors but also other peripheral groups, who are equally powerless and live next to us in our western countries, will have a chance to hear the gospel in a way they can understand and make intelligent choices based on right information.

In my presentation in this book, I myself have often wondered how to place the focus more on the world. Yet this might have been exactly the problem, especially in churches where Christians are active in evangelism and missions. Have we 'looked at the tears far away, and not heard the cry close by?'

Yet, the suffering which we meet can help us focus at least somewhat to others in their need. There are great needs among children beyond our own direct sphere of influence.

In a special issue on street children, World Vision's Graeme Irvine paints a painful reality which has kept me pensive today.

> At least one hundred million children are living, working and often dying on the streets of the world's cities . . . In the United States it is estimated there are 300,000 child prostitutes, male and female, under the age of 16—the majority having sought escape from neglect or abuse by parents, only to be exploited by other adults . . . [9]

I ask myself the question that others have also posed; 'Teo, how much more hurt can you handle? Do you really want to read on? Don't you know yet how rotten it can all be? How many more calls can you accept from abused people?'

I agree with my inner discussion partner. So I say 'No,' and feel guilty. Graeme Irvine's hundred million children don't have the western luxury of trained specialists. How many do we need to train anyhow? There must be another answer. My restless mind refuses to be silenced. Again I discover how a dialogue can turn into a trialogue: Jesus the compassionate is there too, and beckons me to turn again to the main theme of my own book.

Yes, there is an answer for a broken world. Yes, there is a

channel of healing life. God gave Jesus to live in us today, to empower us for our calling, so that the church can step forward as a servant, sharing the message of grace and peace in order that survivors can also see *their* dialogue change into a trialogue.

There are things which people need to hear but for which we have no words. There is a language which surpasses the ability of any counsellor. It is the language of the Creator himself, which can reach the most broken person with words of hope. It is that confidence which helps us—when standing with survivors—to be silent where words are superfluous. Yet we are not helpless because there is Another who can help and whom we can introduce into that need.

A positive silence is at times the best medicine, but not so easy to create. It demands a sensitivity and an awareness of the presence of God and an awe of who he is, as well as a discipline which can be learned. Just recently, I was in such a situation. As I was pouring out my heart in prayer for the need of a particular person, he suddenly stopped me and said, 'Teo, could you shut up please, because I sense the Lord wants to say something himself and I can't hear him because of your prayer.' Helping abuse survivors needs above all an open relationship in which we learn that they can teach us how to help.

The fact that there is a God who reaches out to the broken-hearted and offers them the kingdom[10] balances the realistic question posed by secular and religious helpers; how can we reach the masses of victims? Our current methods are insufficient. Yet programmes can only work, if there are people who want to be with victims as they work through their grief, their shame and agony, for hours, days and weeks at a time. What if these people are not there? Those who have been helped by various publications, without personal assistance, had to rely on themselves. There are times that even believers realise that they are not understood by those close to them. Then, like Jesus did once in Gethsemane, they have to walk the road of recovery, with friends, at a distance.

The struggle with stigmatisation, loneliness and alienation can turn into a victory where silence becomes a temple, where the walls echo with God's love. That insight encourages me as a missionary as well. The message of Powerful Peace is not only for affluent westerners, with a verbal culture, with facilities to help you scream out your agony if necessary. No, it is also for those cultures where neither men nor women dare to speak about how they were violated, as speaking about it would be worse than the actual event. It could even cost them their lives.

Thus I dare to affirm, 'Yes, Lord, you are the light of the whole world. Your grace and peace is abundant enough.' Throughout the centuries, there have been men and women who did not study psychology, psychiatry or sociology, but who knew Jesus and were effective in introducing traumatised people to the healer *par excellence*, Jesus.

In the midst of the avalanche of sexual abuse traumas, there are signposts of hope. The church has a calling until our final Maranatha prayer, 'Come, Lord Jesus,' has been answered. Men and women of peace can share that Jesus in the world in which God has placed them, including the culture of the abused. On their way, they will probably dip into their pockets, pick up some more new books and take more courses. A sense of inadequacy can thus keep us on our toes, to give the best we have—for a child.

Notes

1. I recommend the writings of Jan Hindman as well as Beverly James (see the literature list) for further study.
2. *A Very Touching Book*, by Jan Hindman is one of those I like best.
3. Gen 4:7
4. Eph 4:26
5. Phil 4:7–8
6. Rom 13:3–4
7. Rom 12:19–21
8. Mt 18:10; Rom 14:17
9. Grame Irvine, 'Abandoned children' *Together, a Journal of World Vision International*, Oct-Dec 1991.
10. Mt 5:3

BIBLICAL REALISM

The harsh realities of sexual abuse, even among our own church members, might leave a lingering bad taste. Yet we need to be realistic; there are no signs that things are worse than in years past. What has changed is an increased openness to discuss this reality in a church setting. That is a reason for optimistic realism as well; the deeply ingrained patterns of denial are changing!

The church was silent; we neither saw nor heard, or if we did, we lacked the courage to act. If anyone wants proof that God is at work outside the church, it can be found in the fact that help for a major problem such as incest was initiated and developed in secular settings!

An open-minded reading of the Bible should at least have made us aware that there is nothing new under the sun and that evil, as it was found in humans from the very first pages of the Book, is still very much alive in us today. Evangelical believers, if anything, should have taken notice of the pervasiveness of sin, its prevalence and manifestations in the days when the New Testament was written, and also the answers given then.

Biblical realism affirms research findings that sexual abuse is not just an aberration, a quirk in otherwise-normal behaviour, but part of a larger syndrome. We know too much that such patterns have been transferred from generation to generation.

Dealing with sexual abuse is not just dealing with failing individuals and seeking help for their victims. We need to face these patterns and ask ourselves to what extent the customs and culture of a church support such patterns: through secret dealings with abuse rather than biblical openness, through religious manipulation, through insufficiently stressing the need of respect for the individual and normal patterns of human development. What about the place of women in church leadership? When women began to acquire not only a voice, but also power, as in the early missionary societies started by women two centuries ago, or in the feminist movement of recent decades, ugly issues were able to surface. When some lament about the lack of theological depth, the selective blindness to evil in our churches, I believe it is partly due to the absence of women's eyes in the corridors of church leadership.

That a church system can become an instrument of oppression, is voiced by Jesus himself. He pointed to this danger in one of his last talks with the disciples: when he comes back, will he find shepherds who lead his flock to peace, or slavedrivers who themselves suffer various addictions and abuse their authority?[1] If you want to hear the truth, ask an abuse survivor, who by nature is alert to power-abuse, what they think and feel about your church system!

Biblical realism also indicates how difficult it is to be consistently involved with the needs of others on a long-term basis. While denial and lack of insight in sexual abuse is being overcome, we face another danger, that of burn-out. The wave of incest awareness came at a time when the disciplines of both psychology and psychiatry were facing deep inner turmoil and a decline in direction. In some way, incest gave a new spark; therapists discovered a new growth field. In time, the question of the effectiveness of professional caring programmes will surface, simply because of the battle for organisational, financial and emotional resources in the mental health field. The general pattern in such battles seems to be a shift from specialists only to a greater involvement of volunteers. I expect the same to happen with incest. The rise of self-help groups and 'survivors for survivors' is a sign in that direction.

If anything, the church should be able to motivate volunteers and see to it that they receive adequate training and professional support. Victims of early sexual abuse have many deep wounds, and patient, loving, wise volunteers can give care of a quality that the mental health system can never achieve. After all, one cannot programme tender, loving care, but merely create a platform and an atmosphere in which miracles of unselfish dedication can take place. That, I believe, was and is the challenge of the church, provided she is willing to look at harsh realities with biblical realism and an awareness of divine grace. The Lord who calls also equips.

Notes

1. Mt 24:45–51

BIBLIOGRAPHY

Augsburger, David W., *Pastoral Counselling Across Cultures*, The Westminster Press, 1986.

Arterburn, Stephen and Felton, Jack, *Toxic Faith, Understanding and Overcoming Religious Addiction*, Thomas Nelson, Nashville, 1991.

Barret, David B., *World Christian Encyclopedia*, Oxford University Press, 1982.

Bass, Ellen and Davis, Laura, *The Courage to Heal*, Perennial Library, Harper and Row, New York, 1988.

Berger, Peter and Luckmann, Thomas, *The Social Construct of Reality, A Treatise in the Sociology of Knowledge*. Penguin Books, 1966.

Berger, Prof. W.J., *Zielszorger vandaag*, Voorhoeve, Den Haag, 1983.

Berliner, Lucy and Loftus, Elizabeth, 'Sexual Abuse Accusations', Desperately Seeking Reconcilliation, *Journal of Interpersonal Violence*, Vol. 7, No 4., December 1992, Sage Publications, 1992, pp 570–578.

Berne, Eric, *Games People Play*, Penguin, 1964.

Biehler, Robert F., *Psychology applied to teaching*, Houghton Mifflin Company, Boston, 1978.

Briere, John N., *Child Abuse Trauma, Theory and Treatment of the Lasting Effects*, Sage Publications, London, 1992.

Bolton, Morris and MacEachron, *Males At Risk: The Other Side of Child Sexual Abuse*, Sage Publications, London, 1989.

Briere John N., *Child Abuse Trauma*, Sage Publications, London, 1992.

Bright, John, *The Kingdom of God, The Biblical Concept and Its Meaning for the Church*, Abingdon, Nashville, 1953.

Capps, Donald, *Reframing, a new method in pastoral care*, Augsburg Fortress Press, Minneapolis, 1990.

Collins, Gary R., *The Christian psychology of Paul Tournier*, Baker Book House, Grand Rapids, 1973.

Cullmann, Oscar, *The Christology of the New Testament*, SCM Press, London, 1959.

Davis Kasl, C., *Women, Sex and Addiction*, Harper and Row, 1989.

Doyle, Celia, *Working With Abused Children*, Macmillan, London, 1990.

Eiser, Christine, *Chronic Childhood Diseases: an Introduction to Psychological Theory & Research'*, Cambridge University Press, 1990.

Encyclopedie van het Christendom, Katholiek deel, Elsevier, 1954.

Erickson, Joni with Joe Musser, '*Joni*' Zondervan, 1976.

Finkelhor, David, *A Sourcebook on Child Sexual Abuse*, Sage Publications, London, 1986.

Fortune, Marie M., *Sexual violence, The Unmentionable Sin; An Ethical and Pastoral Perspective*; The Pilgrim Press, New York, 1983.

Forward, S. and Buck, Craig, *Eindelijk Je Eigen Leven Leiden, loskomen van een beschadigde jeugd.* Kosmos, Utrecht et Antwerpen, 1991.

Fossum, Merle A. and Mason, Marilyn J., *Facing Shame, Families in Recovery*, Norton and Co., London, New York, 1986.

Fowke, Ruth, *Personality and Prayer*, Monograph, no date.

Frenken, J. and Van Stolk, B., *Hulpverleners en incestslachtoffers*, Van Loghum Slaterus, Deventer, 1987.

Frenken, J. and Van Stolk, B., *Behandeling van incestplegers.* Bohn Stafleu van Loghum, Houten/Antwerpen, 1990.

Frankl, Victor, De zin van het bestaan, '*Adam waar ben je?*' De betekenis van het mensbeeld in de Joodse traditie en in de *psychotherapie.* Ed. Tom de Bruin, Uitg. B. Folkertsma Stichting voor Talmudica, Hilversum, 1983.

Friedman, Edwin H., *Generation to Generation, Family Process in Church and Synagogue*, The Guildford Press, New York and London, 1985.

Giaretto, Henry, *Integrated Treatment of Child Sexual Abuse, A Treatment and Training Manual*, Science and Behavior Books Inc., Palo Alto, 1982.

Gillham, Bill, *The Facts about Child Sexual Abuse*, Cassel, London, 1991.

Glasser, William, *Reality Therapy*, Harper and Row, New York, 1965.

Green, Michael, *'To Corinth With Love'*, Hodder and Stoughton, 1982.

Hancock, Maxine and Burton Mains, Karen, *Child Sexual Abuse: A hope for healing*, Highland Books, Crowborough, East Sussex, 1987.

Heitritter, Lynn and Vought, Jeannette, *Helping Victims of Sexual abuse, a sensitive, Biblical Guide for Counselors, Victims and families*, Bethany House Publisher, Minneapolis, 1989.

Hesselgrave, David J., *Counseling Cross-Culturally*, Baker Book House, Grand Rapids, 1984.

Hiebert, Paul G., *Cultural Anthropology*, Baker Book House, Grand Rapids, 1986.

Hindman, Jan, *Just before dawn, From the Shadows of Tradition to New Reflections in Trauma Assessment and Treatment of Sexual Victimization*, (1989) and *The Mourning Breaks* (1991) AlexAndria Associates, Ontario, Oregon.

Horton, Johnson. Roundy, Williams ed., *The Incest Perpetrator; A family member no one wants to treat*, Sage Publications, London, 1990.

Howel, Signe and Willes, Roy, *Societies at peace, Anthropological perspectives*, Routledge, London and New York, 1989.

Hughes, Gerard W., *'God of Surprises'*, Darton, Longman and Todd, London, 1985.

Imbens, Annie and Jonker, Ineke, *Godsdienst en incest*, De Horstink, Amersfoort, 1991.

Irvine, Graeme, 'Abandoned children', *Together*, a Journal of World Vision International, Oct–Dec 1991.

James, Beverly, *Treating Traumatized Children, New insights and Creative Interventions*, Lexington Books, Lexington, 1989.

Johnson, David and VanVonderen, Jeff, *The Subtle Power of Spiritual Abuse, Recognising and Escaping Spiritual manipulation and False Spiritual Authority Within the Church*, Bethany House Publishers, Minneapolis, 1991.

Kleinman, Arthur and Good, Byron, *Culture and Depression: Studies in the Anthropology and Cross-Cultural Psychiatry of Affect and Disorder*, University of California Press, Los Angeles, 1985.

Kleinman, Arthur and Good, Byron, ed., *Anthropology and Cross-Cultural Psychiatry of Effect and Disorder*, University of California Press, 1985.

Ladd, George Eldon, *The Gospel of the Kingdom*, Eerdmans, Grand Rapids, 1981.

Laaser, Mark R., *The Secret Sin, Healing the Wounds of Sexual Addiction*, Zondervan, Grand Rapids, 1992.

Laidlaw, Toni Ann, Malmo, Cheryl and associates, *Healing Voices, feminist approaches to therapy with women*, Jossey-Bass Publishers, Oxford, 1990.

Lingefelter, Sherwood G. and Mayers, Marvin K., *Ministring Cross-Culturally*, Baker Book House, Grand Rapids, 1986.

Macaskill, Catherine, *Adopting or Fostering a Sexual Abused Child*, Batsford, London, 1991.

May, Gerald, MD, *Addiction and Grace, Love and Spirituality in the Healing of Addictions*, Harper Collins Publishers, New York, 1991.

Moir, Anne and Jessel, David, *Brain Sex, The Real Difference Between Men and Women*, Manadarin Paperbacks, London, 1989.

McClung, Floyd, *The Father-heart of God*, Kingsway, Eastbourne.

Miller, Alice, *Banished Knowledge, Facing Childhood Injuries*, Virago Press, London, 1990.

Nouwen, Henri J.M., *The Wounded Healer*, Image Books, Doubleday, New York, 1979.

O'Conner, Elizabeth, *Our Many Selves*, Harper and Row, New York, 1971.

Parson, Erwin Randolph, Ethnicity and Traumatic Stress: The Intersecting point in Psychotherapy. *Trauma and its Wake*, Vol. 1, *the Study and Treatment of Post-Traumatic Stress Disorder* edited by Charles R. Figley, Brubber/Mazzel New York, 1985.

Payne, Leanne, *Real Presence, The Christian Worldview of C.S. Lewis as Incarnational Reality*, Crossway Books, Westchester, Illinois, 1988.

Petursson, Hallgrimur, *Hymns of the Passion*, translated by Arthur Charles Gook, published by Hallgrims Church, Reykjavik, 1978.

Pride, Mary, *The Child Abuse Industry*, Crossway Books, Westchester, 1986.

Platvoet, Anna and Dubbink, Anneke *Incest, hun zorg, jouw zorg*, Orthovisies 30, Uitg. Wolters Noordhoff.

Poston, C. and Lison, K., *Incest Overleven; ervaringen van slachtoffers en therapeutische hulp*, Kosmos Utrecht et Antwerpen, 1990.

Prat, Fernand, S.J., *The Theology of Saint Paul*, Burns and Oates, London, 1959.

Putnam, Frank W., *Diagnosis and Treatment of Multiple Personality Disorder*, The Guilford Press, London, 1989.

Quinn, Phil, *Cry Out, inside the terrifying world of an abused child*, Kingsway Publications, Eastbourne, 1988.

Roth, Susan and Batson, Ronald, The Creative Balance: the Therapeutic Relationship and Thematic Issues in Trauma Resolution, *Journal of Traumatic Stress*, April 1993, Plenum Press.

Rutter, Peter, *Er Zijn Grenzen! Sex als machtmisbruik van hulpverleners met hun vrouwelijke cliënten*, Het Spectrum BV Utrecht, 1990.

Sanford, Paula, *Garlands for Ashes, Healing Victims of Sexual Abuse*, Victory House Publishers, Tulsa, 1988.

Schaumburg, Harry W., *False Intimacy, Understanding the Struggle of Sexual Addiction*, NavPress, Colorado, 1992.

Schmemann, Alexander, *For the Life of the World*, St. Vladimir's Seminary Press, 1973.

Schreiter, Robert J., *Constructing Local Theologies*, Maryknoll, New York, Orbis Books, 1985.

de Shazer, Steve, *Clues, Investigating Solutions in Brief Therapy*, Norton and Company, New York, London, 1988.

Snijders, Peter, *Incest, enkele aspekten en demensies*, unpublished doctoral thesis, University of Utrecht, 1992.

Tambiah, S.J., *Buddhism and the Spirit Cults in North-East Thailand*, Cambridge, 1970.

Thiessen, John C., *Pastoring the Asian Church*, Zondervan, 1962.

Tonna, Benjamin, *Gospel for the Cities*, Orbis Books, 1982.

Tournier, Paul, *The Violence Within*, Harper and Row, New York, 1978.

Tozer, A.W., *The Divine Conquest*, Kingway Publications, Eastbourne, 1988.

Utain, Marsha, with Barbara Oliver, monograph *Stepping out of Chaos*, no date, later in adapted form published in *The Healing Relationship*, Health Publications, 1991.

Vanderbilt, Heidi, INCEST, A Chilling Report, *Lear's* February 1992, 655 Madison Ave, New York.

de Waal, Esther, *Seeking God, the way of St. Benedict*, Collins/Fountpaperbacks, London, 1988.

van der Weele, T.J., *'De Kracht van Vrede', hulpverlening aan slachtoffers van sexueel geweld, een evangelisch/charismatische benadering*, Stichting Z.O.N., Harderwijk, 1990.

van der Weele, T.J., *Zegenend Helpen, een studie in het zegenen van hulpvragers, als onderdeel van de pastorale zorg*, Stichting Z.O.N., Harderwijk, 1992.

Wimber, John, *Power Evangelism*, Hodder and Stoughton, London, 1985.

Wimber, John, *Power Healing*, Hodder and Stoughton, London, 1986.

Wilson, Sandra D., *Released from Shame, Recovery for Adult*

Children of Dysfunctional Families, IVP Downers Grove, 1990.

Woelinga, van Staa en Eeland, *Hulpverlening aan sexueel misbruikte kinderen en hun gezin*, uitg. V.U. Amsterdam, 1989.

Gail, Elizabeth Wyatt, Johnson Powell, Gloria (eds.), *Lasting effects of child sexual abuse*, Sage Publications, London, 1988.

Yancey, Philip, *Where is God when it hurts?*, Zondervan, 1977.